FAITHFULNESS
AND
FORTITUDE

FAITHFULNESS AND FORTITUDE

In Conversation with the Theological Ethics of Stanley Hauerwas

Edited by

Mark Thiessen Nation
and
Samuel Wells

T&T CLARK
EDINBURGH

T&T CLARK LTD
59 GEORGE STREET
EDINBURGH EH2 2LQ
SCOTLAND
www.tandtclark.co.uk

First published 2000

ISBN 0 567 08738 7

British Library Cataloguing-in-Publication Data
A catalogue record for this book is available from the
British Library

Typeset by Fakenham Photosetting Ltd, Fakenham, Norfolk
Printed and bound in Great Britain by MPG Books, Bodmin

Contents

Contributors

Nigel Biggar is Professor of Theology at the University of Leeds, where he is also Director of the Institute for the Study of Theology, Ethics and Public Life.

Duncan B. Forrester is Professor of Christian Ethics and Practical Theology, University of Edinburgh.

Colin Gunton is Professor of Christian Doctrine at King's College, London, and Associate Minister of Brentwood United Reformed Church, Essex.

Stanley Hauerwas is Gilbert T. Rowe Professor of Theological Ethics at Duke University, North Carolina.

Ann Loades is Professor of Divinity, University of Durham.

Gerard Loughlin is Senior Lecturer and Head of the Department of Religious Studies, University of Newcastle upon Tyne.

Enda McDonagh is Professor Emeritus of Moral Theology at Maynooth University, and Chair of the Governing Body of University College, Cork.

John Milbank is the Frances Myers Ball Professor of Philosophical Theology at the University of Virginia.

Mark Thiessen Nation is Director of the London Mennonite Centre.

Stephen Sykes is Principal of St John's College, Durham.

Samuel Wells is Priest-in-Charge of St Elizabeth's, Earlham, Norwich.

Linda Woodhead is Lecturer in Christian Studies, Lancaster University.

INTRODUCING
HAUERWAS

1
Introduction to the Essays

Samuel Wells

One of the characteristic duties of the Church of England vicar is to conduct the funeral of any person in the parish whose family choose to say their last farewell the Anglican way. Not long ago I conducted the funeral of a 52-year-old road builder, of whose wide range of convivial friendships and colourful domestic history the family had given me a full account before the day. I explored with the huge congregation how God recreates us beyond death, shaping us in terms of the living pattern of the love we have offered and received in our earthly relationships. The family had asked if they could place a picture of Brian on the coffin, together with his favourite badge, which, they said, 'summed him up'. So it was that when the service was over, and I bowed to the altar with the coffin before it, my eyes rested on that badge, and its appropriate words: 'I'm Brian: who the f*** are you?'

I tell this story at the start of a book conversing with the theology of Stanley Hauerwas because I think Hauerwas would find the story funny. The effect the badge had on me was to deflate the balloon of my pastoral self-assurance, to confront me with the ordinary, sometimes confrontational, earthiness of human friendship, to remind me that there can be no final statement of a person's character, only a continuing conversation over worth and memory, and to bring me up short with my inability to answer the question satisfactorily. And to make me laugh. Stanley Hauerwas' work has had all these effects on me too. A collection of essays in his honour is not a premature literary draft of a funeral address: such a gift would probably elicit from him as uncongenial a response as the words of the badge. But, in that a funeral address considers character over time, the narrative of persons and communities within the greater story of God, the pattern of friendships and the place of faith in the world, the analogy is in some ways appropriate. We, the authors of these essays, have gathered not to bury Hauerwas, nor even specifically to praise him, but instead to give him what he has given us: serious questioning, combative engagement, robust conversation, and a constant call to the renewal of the traditions and practices and faithfulness of the Church.

The Reason for this Book

Three reasons came together to bring this book about. First, while the Christian world celebrates 2,000 years of the incarnation, the rather smaller world of theological ethics celebrates 60 years of Stanley Hauerwas. A birthday is a celebration of the gift of the person to the community. The gift of Stanley Hauerwas has been in 30 years of publishing, teaching and otherwise sharing the discourse of theology in the service of the Church. It is recorded that Samuel Taylor Coleridge said to Charles Lamb, 'Dear man, you've heard me preach, have you not?', to which Lamb replied, 'My dear fellow, I've scarcely heard you do anything else.' Hauerwas has indeed done scarcely anything else over thirty years other than wrestle over the integrity and embodiment of the gospel in a world of false stories.

Second, Stanley Hauerwas is the St Andrews Gifford Lecturer for 2000/01. While he has always resisted attempting a definitive statement of his theology, and maintained a fleetness of foot that has enabled him to elude the snares of quickly dated or discredited 'positions', his joining of the highly distinguished body of those who have delivered the Gifford Lectures offers a suitable moment to gauge the influence and dimensions of his contribution thus far. The essays of this collection offer a series of challenges and reflections on the nature and destiny of the theology of Stanley Hauerwas. They do so in an ad hoc style of engagement true to the manner of Hauerwas' own work.

Third, the collection arises out of the friendship of the two editors, authors who would not have come to know one another were it not for the influence Stanley Hauerwas has had on their lives, and his friendship with them. The two editors represent very different strands of the community created by his work. One is a North American resident in the United Kingdom, entering by conviction a minority and highly distinctive dimension of the Church, and seeking to understand that commitment in a British context. The other is a cradle member of the established Church of England (a church associated with many of the aberrations Hauerwas so ruthlessly exposes), who yet seeks to discover in that church's tradition the dynamic community for which Hauerwas is a prophet.

The Subject of this Book

The principal subject of this book is the theological ethics of Stanley Hauerwas. Hauerwas has redirected Christian ethics away from what is always right for everyone to what is currently faithful for the Church. He has exposed the inadequacy of the contemporary nostrums of health and welfare and family and citizenship, along with the mantras of love and justice. He has constantly embarrassed those who advocate or assume a liberal democracy which ignores the need for an underlying narrative to describe and prescribe the practices on which it has to rest. At the same time he offers a variety of descriptions of the Christian narrative and practices, and the reasons why they look so odd in contemporary Western society.

Hauerwas is a lively conversation partner – not content to let his readers draw their own conclusions and form their own characters, he longs for them to agree with him and shape their lives accordingly. He has no qualms about telling his students, 'I don't want you to think for yourselves: I want you to think like me.' He restlessly battles with the terms in which moral and political questions are conventionally set, frequently seizing the comfortable clothes of the issue, leaving it to limp away naked, awaiting derision from any small child who might happen to see it in its new light. He will not settle for a brisk formula which cannot be enfleshed in the banality of the Church; he will not consider an issue settled until a company of courageous people have shown by their faithfulness that they understand the sacrifices required by discipleship. He enters every argument knowing that Aristotle has already thought about it, Aquinas has reshaped the question, Barth has centred it on Christ and Wittgenstein has undermined any false security on the part of the opposition. Thus armed, he enters the fray of face-to-face debate, longing not to convict but to convert, leaving the secure citadel of temporal authority and rejoicing in the level field of truth and reason, story and tradition, vision and hope. He is never alone – he returns to the worshipping congregation, he looks for the communion of saints, and he is sustained by the good company of friends. Ethics is not about rare decisions, theology is not about distant truths: each is about daily practices, lifelong habits, ways of seeing, perceptions of difference, memories and stories and what is taken for granted. Mark Thiessen Nation describes in the essay that follows what it is to encounter Hauerwas' extraordinary theological conversation.

The subsidiary subject of this book is theology and the Church in the United Kingdom, a context as novel to one editor as it is familiar to the other. Hauerwas kindly wrote a foreword to the book *Transforming Fate Into Destiny*; and the form and location of this current book were inspired by the remarks he made there. He starts by saying, 'I like to think that theology is a communal activity'. Hence the communal character of this book, gathered in his honour. He goes on to ask,

> 'Why am I so much better understood in Europe than in America? American readers never seem to be able to get beyond the slogans that allegedly describe my work, for example, that I am a sectarian, and as a result they miss the details without which what I am trying to do is empty. ... I can only speculate why my work is better appreciated, or at least given a hearing, in

> Britain than in the United States. Surely part of the
> reason is the Church in Britain no longer has any
> pretensions of being 'in control'. As a result some of
> the things I say that seem 'outrageous' in America must
> seem rather commonplace in Britain and Europe.[1]

So much of what a theologian may take for granted in the
United States needs to be re-examined in a British context.

Understanding Stanley Hauerwas in a British context
thus requires an appreciation of the ways in which the
United Kingdom is not North America. The university
system is quite different, in its culture, in its engagement of
the population as a whole, and in its treatment of theology
in particular. The privatisation of ethics is profound in
Britain, but nothing like as all-pervasive as in some embodiments of the American dream. The churches in Britain are
much more focused on their perceived decline, and could
seldom be called complacent. With some exceptions, they
tend to consider themselves as institutions under numerical
and financial pressure, and constantly review a host of
alternative solutions to their perceived demise – from the
restoration of a supposed golden era of church attendance
and moral consensus in the near or distant past, to the
establishment of a new golden era of personal faith and
spiritual experience in the near or distant future. Though
the Church of England is tied to the state, the question of its
establishment is seldom regarded by either advocates or
opponents as a key issue in the mission or faithfulness of
the churches. Perhaps a more significant 'establishment'
lies in the field of health. The survival of the National
Health Service has directed the consideration of medical
matters more towards what can and should be provided for
all than towards what could be possible for some.

For all the significant differences, the compilation of this
book has suggested that the transition of Hauerwas' work
into a British context has been a relatively comfortable one.
He has become a name in every discussion, a required

---

[1] Samuel Wells, *Transforming Fate Into Destiny: The Theological Ethics of
Stanley Hauerwas* (Carlisle: Paternoster Press, 1998), x–xii.

footnote in every exploration, an acknowledged dimension in every effort at synthesis. The abiding issues, it seems, cross the Atlantic largely intact. Hauerwas' constructive contributions may grow and flourish in the United Kingdom, even when some of the objects of his fiercest attacks remain strangers to many of his British readers.

The Shape of this Book

Though the character of this book is highly appreciative of Hauerwas' contribution to theology, it is not uncritical. How then can a group of theologians best engage with Hauerwas' work? The essays in this collection ask three questions of Hauerwas' writings, questions which address the requirements of theology, past, present and future.

The first question relates to the past. Is Hauerwas' work faithful? Hauerwas has frequently pointed out that the task of the Church in general, and thus the particular task of theology in the service of the Church, is to be faithful. Hauerwas is ruthless in his criticism of those who will say whatever they need to say in order to preserve the Church's influence, or assure its relevance, or make it fashionable, or fill its pews. But is Hauerwas himself faithful to the tradition of the Church, and what does it mean to treat the tradition of the Church as one, holy, catholic and apostolic? Does this not leave people out? Does it not fail to tell the whole story? Does it not settle for the history that was written by the winners – winners who have often won because they sided with the contemporary 'powers'? Hauerwas loves Aristotle, but (after departing from his early interest in Iris Murdoch) talks little about Plato; he loves Aquinas, but seldom refers to Augustine; he loves Barth, but seldom refers to Luther and Calvin. Is his writing faithful to the whole tradition of theology and the entire history of the Church, losers included? For someone whose authority rests so much on tradition and the communion of saints, this remains a pressing question.

The second question relates to the present. To use his own language, is Hauerwas' work interesting? In other

words, does his work adequately describe the contemporary Church, the Christian life as lived in the West, the
character of faith as practised by contemporary believers?
Hauerwas likes to point out that although some criticisms
of his work may, strictly speaking, be true, they are not
interesting. In saying this he is making a claim that he has
correctly identified the character of the contemporary
Church, or the way theological work is tending, even if
some of his generalisations are inaccurate or his portraits
overdrawn. Answers to this question may well be largely a
matter of location and vocation. That is to say, the Church
may be half-full or half-empty, alive at the margins or
rotten at the core, depending on one's point of view; and
different parts of the Church will perceive the need to die
on different hills, seeing Hauerwas as too quiet on some
issues and too noisy on others, while still applauding his
theological method.

The third question is addressed to the future. It is the
question that arises from Paul's investigations in
theological ethics in 1 Corinthians, particularly his discussion of glossolalia in chapter 14. The question is, does
Hauerwas' work build up the Church? Regardless of
whether Hauerwas' Church really exists today, is it the
Church that God wants for the years to come? This is
perhaps the fairest question to ask of Hauerwas' work. For
he is not a historian: his version of the Christian story
cannot be expected to be free from occasional inaccuracies,
exaggerations, and absentees. He is not a journalist or
sociologist, and his descriptions of today's Church are, he
readily acknowledges, anecdotal and partial. But he is a
prophet, one who draws from the storehouse of memory
to challenge our present and redefine our hope. The way to
engage Hauerwas is not to ask where he is coming from
but to ask where he is going. If one can go there with him,
if one can discuss the means of his getting there, if one can
dare to go there ahead of him and anticipate a little, then
one is assessing his work in the most appropriate way. For
the test of Hauerwas' theology is the kind of Church that
issues from engagement with it.

In this spirit, this collection of essays seeks to assess

Hauerwas' work using three modes of enquiry, all of which are true to his own style of discourse. Hauerwas has frequently been baffled by those who have engaged his theological work in a form of debate whose terms misunderstand or disallow his method from the outset. We trust that this will not be true of this collection. The first form of engagement we are calling Embodiment. Frequently in his essays Hauerwas investigates what his theological claims might mean, or rather how they are performed, in the life of a university, hospital, disabled child, bereaved family, or local congregation. This first section develops this approach, discussing how Hauerwas' method has been, is and could be applied in a variety of contexts. The second group of essays form a more conventional style of assessment: the Test. Each takes a great issue that reflects not only on Hauerwas' work but on the full scope of Christian ethics and of theology in the service of the Church. Is Hauerwas mistaken in his notion of the Church, is he locked uncritically into an oppressive social system, can his portrayal of the Church stand up in the face of deep moral evil? The third group of essays develop a genre perhaps more associated with a volume of this kind: we are calling them Conversations. Given that Hauerwas' work takes its place in a venerable tradition, what kind of contribution might it make in continuing debate, contemporary moral deliberation, and aesthetic social criticism? It is time to introduce the essays themselves.

The Essays

Four essays embody Hauerwas' work by perceiving the world through his spectacles and discussing what it looks like. The differences are as much attributable to the authors' respective styles of engagement as they are to the different contexts they examine.

John Milbank addresses issues that arise in the contemporary university. He acknowledges that a widespread tendency is to assume that theology is 'fantasising about the void', and that justifying theology before a secular court is 'well-nigh impossible'. Undeterred, indeed spurred to confident riposte, Milbank responds that it is the other disciplines, rather than theology, that are, in fact, 'about nothing whatsoever', since they discuss objects outside any relation to God, and are thus atheistic, nihilistic – positive affirmations of the absoluteness of the void, 'and the capacity of that void to produce a solid something'. To explain why this fact remains largely unspoken, Milbank renarrates the historical emergence of theology, finding the key in Duns Scotus' (and later Descartes' and Kant's) identification of God and matter as separable objects worthy of study, and abandonment of the sense that the creature is nothing without God. Soon there appeared to be 'something more ontologically funda-mental than God', and God became a distant 'force'. Milbank criticises Barth and Hauerwas as being still guilty of this separation in studying the Church's practices as if they were facts that could be separated from revelation through creatures. But this criticism is a way of endorsing and grounding Hauerwas' opposition to the state's treatment of 'beliefs' as a matter for the private sphere.

Stephen Sykes takes the embodiment of Hauerwas' work into contemporary issues in mental health. His essay adopts not only the convictions but also the characteristic form of a Hauerwasian engagement. That is to say, he begins by an even-handed, yet nonetheless increasingly frustrated investigation of the notion of spirituality, with a particular eye on the way the term comes to be embodied in current health care legislation. He points out that the definitions of spirituality make little or no sense of how the Christian story might offer a profound dimension to the understanding of the case histories of at least some patients. The definitions in use follow the logic of what Hauerwas often loosely refers to as 'liberal democracy', and effectively write the Church out of the script of the mental hospital. In order to show how this understanding of spirituality is hopelessly thin, Sykes narrates the stories of two people, separated by two centuries and considerable differences in theological susceptibilities, to whose exp-erience of mental unrest the Christian story holds the key.

Sykes concludes, again in characteristic Hauerwasian style, by distinguishing between the moral status of the medical designation 'disease' and the social designation 'illness'.

Mark Thiessen Nation delves into what practices and implications derive from Hauerwas' writings about pacifism. Again this embodiment is done in a characteristically Hauerwasian way: it begins with an extended personal narrative, and grows into an exploration of how the Church practices peace. The personal narrative paints a stark picture of what it meant to become a Christian, a pacifist, and 18 years old in a context where the last of these meant one became liable to the Vietnam draft. Conscientious objection provoked opposition from father and pastor. But Nation describes how his pacifism, though surprising to his family and friends, was rooted in the practices of the Baptist church he was attending. It is the shape of Christian beliefs that makes Christians nonviolent, as the life of Dorothy Day and the practices such as giving humble testimony and washing feet make clear. If the Church as a whole is to be committed to peace, it must avoid the pitfalls of making 'peace' and 'justice' bigger notions than 'Lord' and 'Christ', it must ensure that lifetimes of commitment count for more than right positions on 'issues', and, like Bonhoeffer, it must recognise that in the archetypal 'What if?' scenario, the issue is not so much, 'What about Hitler?' but, 'What about the Church?'.

In the last essay in this section, Samuel Wells considers Hauerwas' work in the context of urban deprivation. Hauerwas' deep perception of tragedy and irony make him seem well suited to the bleaker aspects of parochial ministry. But Wells questions how the local church might respond to a much less characteristically Hauerwasian challenge: the invitation to join in a huge programme of locally-conceived and planned schemes of economic and social regeneration. If the local church is not to walk away, claiming a higher kingdom, in what ways should it engage and with what end in view? Wells reviews how the Christian story affirms and challenges the local story, how the local church needs to reconsider its status, and how the chief gifts the local church has to offer the process of regeneration are the practices through which it embodies its story week by week. The issue throughout is whether Hauerwas' portrayal of the distinctness of the Church makes the local church more or less able to engage in the practical processes of politics, the timeful habits of peace of which he frequently speaks. It is, just occasionally, a question, not just of what kind of *Church* Hauerwas supposes, but of what kind of *society* he would like to live in, if given the chance to have a considerable say.

The next three essays test Hauerwas' work in explicit terms against three of the most pressing standards of contemporary moral debate.

Nigel Biggar deals head-on with the issue of social withdrawal. He notes that if one wants to dismiss Hauerwas, the most common way of doing so is to call him a sectarian. Hauerwas' response to this charge is that the Church serves the world only if it knows and embodies what it has to say. Hauerwas' frustration is with Reinhold Niebuhr's 'realism', which gains a public voice by emptying itself of theological content. Apologetics, for Hauerwas, means 'making the modern world credible to the gospel'. Typical is his narration of freedom: he points out that the Kantian-Romantic ideal – to liberate the individual from tradition and historical community into creativity and universal fellowship – has led instead to disenchantment and alienation. Meanwhile tolerance – the readiness to entertain alien points of view in hope that the truth will out – has degenerated into a passivism towards all views which do not conflict with individual pursuit of private interests. Biggar concludes that Hauerwas is not a sectarian, but warns that Hauerwas' distinction between liberalism and Christianity is overdrawn and that Christians have a greater stake in the survival of the liberal project than Hauerwas acknowledges.

Linda Woodhead tackles the pressing question of whether women have a place in Hauerwas' peaceable kingdom. Woodhead is concerned to challenge Hauerwas in his own backyard – the specific contexts in which

Christianity is lived and practised. She sees a 'gendered perspective' as 'wholly congruent with Hauerwas' insights into the contextual nature of theology and faith', and in various ways pushes Hauerwas towards a fuller embodiment of these insights. Pointing out Hauerwas' awareness of his race, ethnicity and class, Woodhead considers why this reflexive awareness does not extend to gender. She observes that Hauerwas concentrates on the violence of war, rather than the less gendered notion of oppression; that he identifies feminism with the liberal Enlightenment project; that he is apparently comfortable with the 'totalising' metanarrative he calls '*the* Christian story', suggesting that there is only one definitive and valid Christian context; and that he generally ignores empirically-based studies from the social sciences, even when they concern congregational experience; all of which positions Woodhead questions for their descriptive accuracy and prescriptive desirability.

Duncan Forrester takes very seriously Hauerwas' intention of describing the Church as the alternative community in which the virtues are truly fostered, and whose worshipping life and moral formation constitute its chief service and witness to the world. When put to its sharpest test, this model, though deeply desirable, is found wanting. Forrester contrasts the sheer horror of the concentration camp at Dachau, the embodiment of moral evil, with the small but graceful church situated a hundred yards outside. Outside the camp, one would have thought, there would have been faithful worshippers practising the pursuits of holiness – yet those who did dreadful things across the fence no doubt came here on Sundays and were part of it all. Inside the camp, one thinks of unspeakable cruelty and grotesque savagery – yet there was astonishing goodness and care and love amongst those experiencing pitiless degradation. What did the prisoners think of the churchgoers? This is Forrester's poignant question. Both institutions had, in some ways, failed in their task. Each failure motivates the renewal of the calling of today's disciples once more to be the Church.

The next four essays converse with Hauerwas' theology in contrasting modes and styles.

Colin Gunton's essay is a thorough engagement with the trinitarian dimensions of Hauerwas' theological ethics. The Holy Spirit perfects the creation which the Father performs through the Son, not just at its beginning, but also at its eschatological destiny. Meanwhile it is the perfecting Spirit that maintains the incarnate Son's unblemished relation to the Father. God's 'character', his coincidence of being and act, is perfection. With this preliminary Gunton criticises Hauerwas' ethic of virtue as being insufficiently informed by a doctrine of redemption, and thus implicitly Pelagian – particularly if allied with an insistence on believers' baptism (an alliance Hauerwas does not himself make). If ethics is to concern perfections, rather than virtues, one needs a doctrine of sanctification as well as one of justification. The call to be a living sacrifice is a call to holiness – not just moral perfection, but the offering of the whole person to God. Virtues are the Holy Spirit's anticipations of this eschatological purpose. The virtues are provisional perfections, given for the sake of the world.

Ann Loades considers abortion, the archetypal ethical 'single issue', and one to which Hauerwas has returned on several occasions. A brief historical survey notes both the dangerous nature of childbirth, and the remarkable ignorance of the science of conception and gestation, in every century before the twentieth, observing also the relatively recent criminalisation of abortion. Loades examines a wide range of scriptural treatments of gestation, birth and nurture. Precedent is found for some subtleties of view, particularly in relation to cases where the mother's life is threatened. Feminist reflections yield three modes of grace: of consent to pregnancy, of openness to a variety of alternative nurturing patterns in the absence of a father, and of considered refusal. Loades then introduces some of the political and social choices made especially in the United States, and points out the way they and other developments such as assisted pregnancy tend towards 'commodifying' women's body 'products'. She concludes that Hauerwas' stress on the welcoming of children greatly improves the terms in which abortion is discussed – although a firm view against abortion makes no sense until the Church takes a parallel strong line on the affirmation of women.

Gerard Loughlin's essay returns to the crucial insight in Hauerwas' first book, *Vision and Virtue* – that one can learn how to see the world by reading the right kind of literature. Like Iris Murdoch, Hauerwas' early inspiration, Loughlin turns to Plato for his key theme: the cave, whose residents think it is the only world, and mistake the shadows on its wall for the realities of the universe. Loughlin sets side by side three 'caves': the pagan temple, place of demons; the cinema, most modern powerful creator of images; and the Church, with much to learn and reflect from the previous two. In the cinema and the Church, truth and reality are enlivened, not destroyed, by suspension. The 'demonic' power of film is expressed in the impact of Peter Blatty's *The Exorcist*: the anxiety concerns possession by the images on which one looks. The power of the modern 'cave of shadows' is represented by Stanley Kubrick's *A Clockwork Orange*, where the central character is deeply affected by an experience in the cinema. The power of the image to liberate is represented by Alex Proyas' *Dark City*, the story of a prisoner escaping from a 'cave'. The power of cinema as the Church's rival is exhibited in David Lodge's novel *The Picturegoers*. Loughlin concludes that the Church thrives on its own understanding of possession by images-transformation by projection. It sees itself as 'the cave in which life is made and formed'. And it worships a saviour born and reborn in a cave.

Enda McDonagh's essay concludes the collection with the same autobiographical approach that marked Nation and Wells' essays. He identifies with Hauerwas' efforts to describe the political reality of the Church's faithfulness. His journey is firmly set in the context of Ireland's turbulent history, and the intimate involvement of the churches in the politics of the island. He is keen to steer away from Constantinianism, seeing a humbler role for the Irish Church as servant of the people. He traces the significance of several themes close to Hauerwas' heart – the practice of penance, abortion, contraception, just war, and disestablishment. He explains how his experience of the Church in Africa, particularly in relation to the Zimbabwean military struggle and to Sub-Saharan HIV-Aids, is more promising than his experience nearer home. Again and again he perceives a tension between the wisdom tradition and the prophetic tradition in relation to the more conservative and more radical vocations of the Church. He believes that both traditions require the priestly dimension for their fulfilment.

Thus the essays cover all the great themes of Hauerwas' theological ethics: vision, virtue, narrative, community, peace, academy, suffering, liberalism, medicine, Church. It is not a systematic analysis, but Hauerwas is a firmly unsystematic theologian. The essays are a tribute, from a British Isles perspective, to the way the ordinariness of the Church has been enriched by a quite extraordinary man.

In response, Hauerwas provides a readers' guide, both to these essays, and to his work as a whole. He wrestles with the implications of his work – notably, that its intention is to 'mess with and mess up' lives such as those of the editors of this volume. He dwells on the irony that, while the theologians behind these essays take him very seriously, many theologians do not. He recognises the paradoxes of his own career – for example, that he wants to write 'close to the ground', yet he loves the university. He pleads for his readers to look beyond his epigrams, and understand why he calls them to rethink the way they do theology. He clarifies his stance on liberalism, on feminism, and on the sacrificial character of communal discipleship (or nonviolence). He concludes with a tribute to the people of character he longs for his work to encourage. It is to such people, and such communities, that these essays, and the whole of Hauerwas' work, are dedicated.

2
Stanley Hauerwas:
Where Would We Be Without Him?

Mark Thiessen Nation

How does one describe Stanley Hauerwas? The easiest way is the sort of factual description one finds on book jackets. He is the Gilbert T. Rowe Professor of Theological Ethics at Duke Divinity School, Durham, North Carolina. He is the author or co-author of twenty-one books, the co-editor of at least seven books, and the author of numerous other articles. He also serves as an editor for a number of book series and is on the editorial boards of several journals. He is slated to present the prestigious Gifford Lectures at St Andrews for the year 2000/01. And, finally, probably no one has more substantially changed the field of Christian ethics within the last twenty-five years than Stanley Hauerwas. All of this is true about Hauerwas; his academic accomplishments are quite substantial.

However, it seems appropriate, in an essay on Stanley Hauerwas, to begin a little differently, with the following two images. The first is drawn from the introduction to an interview with Stanley Hauerwas and William Willimon for the American Christian magazine, *The Door*.

> Stanley is a loud, blustery, locomotive of passion for the Gospel; his eyes deep, intense, penetrating, full of sparkle and fire; his discourses passion-filled, sputtering with expletives, crashing into everyone else's opinion in the room, his thoughts thundering into your consciousness – sometimes against your will, often making you angry at his lack of ... well ... sensitivity. And yet. And yet ... You realize this is a man who is so in love with the Gospel – so in its grip – that

he must say what he says or the rocks will say it for him. There is such clarity about Stanley Hauerwas. You have no doubts about what he thinks, about what he believes. And, there is no question in our minds that his clarity often leaves him alone, isolated from those whose ideas are of the mind and not of the heart. There are times when he spoke that a kind of holiness filled the room and you knew you were hearing the words of a prophet, and when the interview was over there were tears in the eyes of the interviewers.[1]

The second is drawn from Gail Godwin's novel, *The Finishing School*, and contains some telling remarks about congealing.

'There are two kinds of people,' she once decreed to me emphatically. 'One kind you can tell just by looking at them at what point they congealed into their final selves. It might be a very *nice* self, but you know you can expect no more surprises from it. Whereas the other kind keeps moving, changing. With these people, you can never say, "X stops here," or "Now I know all there is to know about Y." That doesn't mean they're unstable. Ah, no, far from it. They are *fluid*. They keep moving forward and making new trysts with life, and the motion of it keeps them young. In my opinion, they are the only people who are still alive. You must be constantly on your guard, Justin, against congealing.'[2]

Anyone who knows Stanley Hauerwas – and more than a few who have simply heard him speak once or twice – will recognise the Hauerwas captured in the characterisation of the first quotation. He is a man of deep conviction and unafraid to

[1] 'The Door Interview: Will Willimon and Stanley Hauerwas', *The Door* 129 (May/June 1993) 6. The interview, abbreviated and without this intro- duction, is reprinted in Stanley Hauerwas and William H. Willimon, *Where Resident Aliens Live* (Nashville, TN: Abingdon Press, 1996), 113–18.
[2] Quoted in Walter Brueggemann, *First and Second Samuel*, Interpretation: A Bible Commentary for Teaching and Preaching (Louisville, KY: John Knox Press, 1990), 7.

express his convictions even when – perhaps especially when – they might offend more than a few in a given audience. There are many dimensions left out of this description. I would certainly disagree with the claim that Stanley is lacking in sensitivity; at the same time, I know that he is sometimes experienced that way. However, it is quite simply not true that he is often 'isolated' or 'alone' in his thinking. I understand why someone might imagine that would be the case, because the image of him as a prophet is true enough. However, the funny thing is that this particular prophet has very many friends. He is also a prolific communicator. There is almost an endless flow of letters, phone calls, faxes, essays, books and lectures. Therefore, few of his ideas remain unshared for long. And they are tested, challenged, ingested, and reformulated by many others among his friends, colleagues, students and even foes. So, it is hardly accurate to say he is often 'alone' in his thinking, even if he may often be leading the way in thinking a certain way. But the second quotation is important because Hauerwas' 'clarity' may give some the wrong impression. It may lead some to conclude this is someone who is fixed, even congealed in his thoughts. Nothing could be further from the truth. Over twenty-five years ago the well-known American ethicist Paul Ramsey referred to Hauerwas as 'an omnivorous reader'. It is still true. Hauerwas' friends are often amazed that he reads *and* writes as much as he does. And, though one could hardly expect there would not be some repetition, these many writings reveal a mind ever open to new learning and steadfastly opposed to congealing. Stanley Hauerwas is still quite 'fluid'. And I am sure we can yet expect more than a few 'surprises' from him.

But how did this man come to be who he is? Of course, adequately to answer that question is beyond the scope of this present essay.[3] But perhaps a few signposts that have

---

[3] For surveys of Hauerwas' thought see Samuel Wells, *Transforming Fate Into Destiny: The Theological Ethics of Stanley Hauerwas* (Carlisle: Paternoster Press, 1998) and Arne Rasmusson, *The Church as 'Polis': From Political Theology to Theological Politics as Exemplified by Jürgen Moltmann and Stanley Hauerwas* (Lund: Lund University Press, 1994; Notre Dame, IN: University of Notre Dame Press, 1995). For further reading see the extensive bibliographies in each book.

marked the road down which Stanley Hauerwas has been may help illumine who this man named Stanley Hauerwas is.

Stanley Hauerwas was born on 24 July 1940 in Pleasant Grove, Texas (on the south-eastern side of Dallas), to Joanna and Coffee Hauerwas. His mother was 'from the dirt-poor backwoods of Mississippi'.[4] His grandfather Hauerwas had moved to Texas from Wisconsin via Alabama. Therefore, Stanley is only a second-generation Texan. But he is certainly a Texan, as anyone who has heard his famous accent can attest. As Hauerwas says: 'Texan is written in my voice, in my manners, and even more in my soul – I cannot be other than I am.'[5] For some who simply know Texans through stereotypes, Stanley does fit in some ways. He is loud and boisterous and he has cousins with names like 'Billy Dick'.[6]

But we need to understand why Hauerwas is proud of being a Texan. As he puts it: ' "Being a Texan" is for many of us one of our most valuable lessons, as it has taught us how to be different. Indeed, I sometimes think that without this I would have no idea what it might mean to be a Christian, as I would have no idea what it might mean to belong to a separate society.'[7]

But Texas for Stanley when he was growing up was mostly Pleasant Grove. It was Joanna, his mother, who taught Stanley 'never to quit'. And it was Coffee, his father, who taught Stanley that 'you get somewhere by laying one brick at a time'.[8] His father has clearly had a tremendous impact on Hauerwas. At his father's funeral in 1993, Hauerwas said his father was 'a good, kind, simple, gentle

---

[4] Stanley Hauerwas, 'A Tale of Two Stories: On Being a Christian and a Texan', in *Christian Existence Today: Essays on Church, World and Living in Between* (Durham, NC: Labyrinth Press, 1988; Reprinted: Grand Rapids, MI: Baker Books, 1995), 35.

[5] Hauerwas, 'A Tale of Two Stories', 29.

[6] Stanley Hauerwas, *Unleashing the Scripture: Freeing the Bible from Captivity to America* (Nashville, TN: Abingdon Press, 1993), 47.

[7] Hauerwas, 'A Tale of Two Stories', 36.

[8] Stanley Hauerwas, *Character and the Christian Life: A Study in Theological Ethics* (San Antonio, TX: Trinity University Press, 1985 [original 1975; 1985 edition has new introduction]), ix.

man'.[9] According to Hauerwas, his father was also a master bricklayer. 'For the simple gentleness of my father was that which comes to those honed by a craft that gives them a sense of the superior good. My father was incapable of laying brick rough just as he was incapable of being cruel.'[10]

Growing up for Stanley was also being a part of Pleasant Mound Methodist Church. It may be that this church caused the adult Stanley to be critical of 'pietism' and what causes him to say that 'by the time I was twelve I had enough [religious] experience to last me a lifetime'.[11] It may have been difficult to be reminded regularly in this evangelical Methodist church that sinners like Stanley needed to have the experience of being 'saved' – and then not to have that experience.[12] Nonetheless the church was central for the life of the Hauerwas family, as is indicated by the fact that one of the climactic moments in Coffee Hauerwas's life was 'when he was honored for supervising the building of Pleasant Mound Methodist Church'.[13] However much the adult Hauerwas may be critical of the preoccupation with the centrality of pietistic experience in this church, the importance the life of this worshipping community had for his own family may not be at all incidental to the centrality of the church community in his own mature theology and commitment.[14]

[9] Stanley Hauerwas, 'The Church's One Foundation Is Jesus Christ Her Lord', in *Theology Without Foundations: Religious Practice and the Future of Theological Truth*, eds. Stanley Hauerwas, Nancey Murphy and Mark Nation (Nashville, TN: Abingdon Press, 1994), 156. This essay is reprinted in Stanley Hauerwas, *In Good Company: The Church as Polis* (Notre Dame, IN: University of Notre Dame Press, 1995).

[10] Hauerwas, 'The Church's One Foundation', 158.

[11] Stanley Hauerwas, 'Gay Friendship', in *Sanctify Them in the Truth: Holiness Exemplified* (Edinburgh: T&T Clark, 1998), 108. Hauerwas recently said the following about pietism: 'Pietism confuses personal experience with ecclesial formation' (Rodney Clapp, 'What Would Pope Stanley Say?' *Books and Culture* [November/December 1998], 18).

[12] Hauerwas, 'A Tale of Two Stories', 39.

[13] Hauerwas, 'The Church's One Foundation', 158.

[14] It should also be said that despite Hauerwas' misgivings he says: 'I have no desire to rid myself of my particular background as an evangelical Methodist' (Stanley Hauerwas, *The Peaceable Kingdom: A Primer in Christian Ethics* [Notre Dame, IN: University of Notre Dame Press, 1983], xxi).

Yet, Hauerwas is also not naive about the failings of Texans. He knows them all too well: the hardness, the violence, and, especially, the racism. 'We Texans have little ability to know how to admit our failures, and cruelty, and our tragedies. We thus make a virtue out of some of our worst sins.'[15] And Hauerwas knows that these 'worst sins' deeply infect the souls of Texans and of southerners generally. 'I have no idea', says Hauerwas, 'how deeply the habits of racism are written into my life, but I know that they are not the kind of habits you simply "outgrow" or "get over". I have, therefore, refrained from pontificating on "race" because I feared that is what it would be – pontification.'[16]

Growing up in a relatively poor and uneducated home, Stanley did not assume he would go to university. After all, he had been learning the craft of bricklaying from his father since he was quite young. Perhaps he would follow in his father and grandfather's steps and be a bricklayer for the rest of his life. However, at age fifteen Stanley had dedicated his life to the ministry one Sunday night 'at the tenth singing of "I Surrender All"'. As he says, this may have been 'the only way I could think of to insure I was really among the blessed'.[17] Despite the fact that he never was ordained, his commitment to the ministry may have been what motivated him to go to university. Anyway, after graduation from secondary school, Stanley went to Southwestern University in Georgetown, Texas. Southwestern would be the beginning of Hauerwas' unquenchable thirst for learning. It was largely one teacher there who nurtured this thirst – philosophy professor John Score.

---

[15] Hauerwas, 'A Tale of Two Stories', 37.
[16] Stanley Hauerwas, 'Remembering Martin Luther King, Jr. Remembering: A Response to Christopher Beem', *Journal of Religious Ethics* 23 (Spring 1995): 136. This essay is reprinted in Stanley M. Hauerwas, *Wilderness Wanderings: Probing Twentieth-Century Theology and Philosophy* (Boulder, CO: Westview Press, 1997). See also Hauerwas' sensitive remarks about his father and racism: Hauerwas, 'The Church's One Foundation', 160.
[17] Hauerwas, 'A Tale of Two Stories', 39.

Though I was raised in a Christian home and grew up in the church, I never felt I knew well enough what Christianity involved to accept or reject it. I went through a time in college when I was sure Christianity could not be true. Then, through the study of philosophy, and under the gentle proddings of John Score, I came to realize I did not understand Christianity well enough to deserve an opinion. Indeed, I still often feel that is the case. I mention this only to point out that I have never felt the need to react against Christianity in the way many seem to do whose background provided more confidence that they knew in fact what Christianity involved both as belief and behavior. For me it has always been more a matter of trying to understand what we Christians should believe and do.[18]

After receiving a BA in philosophy from Southwestern, Hauerwas was off to Yale Divinity School. Over the next six years he was to receive a BD from Yale Divinity School, an MA and MPhil in philosophy from Yale University and a PhD in Christian ethics from Yale University. Hauerwas says two apparently contradictory things about being schooled at Yale. On the one hand he refers to how determinative it was. He remembers being on a faculty retreat after he had joined the faculty at the University of Notre Dame. They were discussing the reality of a theology department being located in a Catholic school. The various faculty were each sharing what it meant to bring their denominational tradition to their teaching. While wrestling with what he would say, Hauerwas thinks, " 'Hell, I'm not a Methodist. I went to Yale" '.[19] What he means by saying this is that 'for most of us theologians, where we went to graduate school informs our self-understanding more than our denominational identification does'.[20] Yet, on the other

[18] Hauerwas, *The Peaceable Kingdom*, xix.
[19] Stanley Hauerwas, 'The Testament of Friends', in *How My Mind Has Changed*, ed. James M. Wall and David Heim (Grand Rapids, MI: Wm B. Eerdmans, 1991), 5.
[20] Hauerwas, 'The Testament of Friends,' 5.

hand, he is quite bothered by the notion that there is such a thing as a 'Yale School' of thought. 'The current identification as well as criticism of the so-called Yale School cannot help but strike those of us who are allegedly members of that school as funny. Those of us who studied at Yale during the time in question had no idea that our teachers had any convictions, much less represented a "school".'[21]

But by the first comment, Hauerwas means to be making a normative claim: our Christian identities (which are always particular, traditioned) should be more decisive for our theology than paradigms within graduate schools. Whereas the second comment is intended to counter the over-simplifying, homogenising tendencies of labels. Hauerwas wants to keep alive the reality of the diversity of the views at Yale.

Of course the diversity was (and is) real. Hauerwas dedicated one of his recent books to all sixteen of his teachers at Yale Divinity School and Yale Graduate School.[22] One can see immediately from this list that there is, of course, significant diversity. While noting some exceptions, Hauerwas does claim, however, that '[m]y teachers during my years at Yale taught me that if Jesus had not really existed, if the Jews were not God's promised people, then it is all smoke and mirrors'.[23]

It is undoubtedly a mistake to think that we can easily know who among his teachers influenced Hauerwas in exactly what way. And we should be cautious about focusing only on those among his teachers who are quite well known. (After all, if he had not told us, we would not know that John Score had such an influence on his intellectual

---

[21] Hauerwas, *Wilderness Wanderings*, xiii. For a brief discussion of the 'Yale School', see Mark I. Wallace, *The Second Naiveté: Barth, Ricoeur, and the New Yale Theology*, Studies in American Biblical Hermeneutics 6 (Macon, GA: Mercer University Press, 1990), 87–110. Also see William C. Placher, 'Postliberal Theology', in *The Modern Theologians, Vol. II*, ed. David F. Ford (Oxford: Basil Blackwell, 1989), 115–28.
[22] Hauerwas, *Wilderness Wanderings*, vii: Julian Hartt, Robert Calhoun, George Lindbeck, James Gustafson, Hans Frei, Gene TeSelle, Paul Meyer, Jaroslav Pelikan, Brevard Childs, Rowan Greer, Liston Pope, Paul Holmer, David Little, Robert King, Wayne Meeks and Gay Noyce.
[23] Hauerwas, *Wilderness Wanderings*, xiii.

journey.) Nevertheless, we can name some of the influences without imagining that we are quite right about the relatives weight to ascribe to each. Without question, Julian Hartt, Paul Holmer, James Gustafson, Hans Frei and George Lindbeck have had a significant influence on Hauerwas.

Hauerwas went to Yale with the notion that 'the discipline best suited for allowing one to pursue the question of the truthfulness of Christianity was systematic theology'.[24] Under the influence of Julian Hartt and Paul Holmer he became sceptical of the notion of 'systematic' theology and decided to get a PhD in Christian ethics instead. 'At least such an activity was committed to trying to provide a means to suggest what difference Christian convictions make in how we live – and thus how they might be false or true.' Furthermore, says Hauerwas, '[m]y interest in ethics, I suspect, also came from the then unacknowledged but powerful and continuing influence of the emphasis on sanctification in my Methodist heritage'.[25] However, Hauerwas was never going to be totally comfortable studying Christian ethics either. For, after he heard that Hauerwas was pursuing a PhD in Christian ethics, Holmer made it clear to Hauerwas 'that there was no such subject and that to the extent that I was successful in pursuing such a subject, I was going to waste my life'.[26]

Hauerwas says that Holmer 'radically altered my life'.[27] There seem to be at least two ways in which that is the case. Holmer kept reminding Hauerwas that theology and Christian ethics should not be divorced from the life and practices of the Church (and nudged Hauerwas toward returning to the Church after some absence).[28] And he got Hauerwas to read Wittgenstein, resonances of whose thought can be detected in everything Hauerwas has written.[29] Hauerwas says that Wittgenstein 'slowly

[24] Hauerwas, *The Peaceable Kingdom*, xix–xx.
[25] Hauerwas, *The Peaceable Kingdom*, xx.
[26] Stanley Hauerwas, 'How to Go On When You Know You Are to Be Misunderstood, or How Paul Holmer Ruined My Life, or Making Sense of Paul Holmer', in *Wilderness Wanderings*, 147.
[27] Hauerwas, 'Making Sense of Paul Holmer', 144.
[28] Hauerwas, 'Making Sense of Paul Holmer', 143–52.
[29] So Hauerwas himself claims in *Wilderness Wanderings*, 11.

cured me of the notion that philosophy was primarily a matter of positions, ideas, and/or theories. From Wittgenstein, and later David Burrell, I learned to understand and also to do philosophy in a therapeutic mode.'[30]

James Gustafson was Hauerwas' doctoral advisor. Hauerwas was struck by Gustafson's suggestion that theological ethics might best focus on character and the virtues for displaying the nature of Christian moral existence. 'The issues underlying an account of character in moral psychology seemed to be precisely those that helped one to understand Jesus' life and its significance for us. It occurred to me that the correlation between our knowledge of God and of self, a correlation so well displayed by Calvin, might best be expressed in terms of character and the virtues'.[31]

Furthermore, says Hauerwas, '[u]nder the tutelage of Hans Frei, and continuing to read Barth, I came increasingly to appreciate how the more "orthodox" Christologies failed to do justice to the scriptural portrayal of Jesus. Indeed my first interest in narrative', says Hauerwas, 'was sparked by the realisation that the early church thought that narrative was the appropriate mode of expression for what they took to be the significance of Jesus.'[32] Such intuitions were also confirmed by his reading of H. Richard Niebuhr, Aristotle and Aquinas. They were to lead to his doctoral thesis, *Character and the Christian Life*, as well as to a significant dimension of his life's work.[33]

In this brief essay, what might one say about Hauerwas' intellectual trajectory since Yale? Anyone who hopes to track the intellectual influences on Hauerwas or the

---

[30] Hauerwas, *The Peaceable Kingdom*, xxi. See Brad Jeffrey Kallenberg, 'Changing the Subject in Postmodernity: Narrative Ethics and Philosophical Therapy in the Works of Stanley Hauerwas and Ludwig Wittgenstein' (PhD diss., Fuller Theological Seminary, 1998).

[31] Hauerwas, *The Peaceable Kingdom*, xxi–xxii.

[32] Hauerwas, *The Peaceable Kingdom*, xxi. A few pages later (xxv) Hauerwas says he really does not know where his emphasis on narrative originated. One can see in a recently published doctoral thesis, directed by Hauerwas, some of what Hauerwas learned from Frei. See Charles L. Campbell, *Preaching Jesus: New Directions for Homiletics in Hans Frei's Postliberal Theology* (Grand Rapids, MI: Wm B. Eerdmans, 1997), 1–114.

[33] See note 8, above.

intellectual development of Hauerwas needs to keep in mind at least five things.

First, somewhat against Hauerwas' own protestations, Yale has had a significant influence on him. There is no question that one can see the lasting imprint, however creatively reworked by Hauerwas, of a number of his teachers at Yale. Of course some of the influence is understandable and was, perhaps, hoped for and some of it veered in directions the teachers could never have anticipated. For instance, that Hans Frei helped instil both a love for Karl Barth and a way of reading Barth is not particularly surprising.

> As Hans Frei puts it, Barth was in the business of 'conceptual description: he took the classical themes of communal Christian language moulded by the Bible, tradition and constant usage in worship, practice, instruction and controversy, and he restated or redescribed them rather than evolving arguments on their behalf. It was of the utmost importance to him that this communal language, especially its biblical *fons et origo*, which he saw as indirectly one with the Word of God, has an integrity of its own: it was irreducible. But in that case its lengthy, even leisurely unfolding was equally indispensable.'[34]

That he would write very appreciatively of George Lindbeck's significant 1984 book, *The Nature of Doctrine*, is also not surprising.[35] On the other hand, it may have been James Gustafson who, indirectly, introduced Hauerwas to the writings of John Howard Yoder. However, Gustafson has not been pleased with the results of the influence of Yoder on Hauerwas.[36] Hauerwas says that his 'introduction to Yoder

[34] Stanley Hauerwas, 'On Honor: By Way of Comparison of Karl Barth and Trollope', in *Dispatches from the Front* (Durham, NC: Duke University Press, 1994), 59.

[35] Stanley Hauerwas, *Against the Nations: War and Survival in a Liberal Society* (Minneapolis, MN: Winston Press, 1985), 1–9. (This book was later reprinted by Harper & Row and now by University of Notre Dame Press.)

[36] See James M. Gustafson, 'The Sectarian Temptation: Reflections on Theology, the Church and the University', *The Catholic Theological Society of America: Proceedings* 40 (1985), 83–94. This essay is as much as anything a critique of Hauerwas. Gustafson several times mentions the Anabaptist influence on Hauerwas, without actually naming Yoder.

came in the bookstore at Yale Divinity School. Since Barth was playing a large part in my dissertation I bought a mimeographed 47-page pamphlet called *Karl Barth and Christian Pacifism* written by someone named J. H. Yoder ... I took it back to my carrel and began to read, and was absolutely stunned by Yoder's powerful analysis and critique of Barth.'[37]

At least as far as he remembered it in 1999, Hauerwas said that none of his teachers, including Gastafson, mentioned Yoder in any classes. And he does not have any knowledge that Gustafson was responsible for placing the mimeographed essay in the Yale Divinity School bookshop. However, it is quite possible that Gustafson was responsible for it being in the bookshop. I say this because this mimeographed essay was, understandably, relatively unknown. And, yet, Gustafson says in a footnote at about the time Hauerwas was studying with him: 'For a remarkable critical study of Barth on the point of pacifism, see John Howard Yoder, *Karl Barth and Christian Pacifism* (Basel; mimeographed, n. d.)'.[38] Furthermore, Gustafson was on the editorial committee that encouraged Yoder to expand this essay and publish it in the series, 'Studies in Christian Ethics'.[39] When Hauerwas began teaching at The University of Notre Dame, in 1970, knowing that Yoder taught at a school not far from Notre Dame, he searched for him, found him, and came away with a large stack of writings by Yoder. At the end of his reading he presented a paper and published two articles summarising Yoder's theological approach as it related to pacifism.[40] However, Hauerwas was not easily convinced by Yoder.

[37] Stanley Hauerwas, 'When the Politics of Jesus Makes a Difference', *Christian Century* 110 (13 October, 1993), 984.
[38] James M. Gustafson, *Christ and the Moral Life* (Chicago, IL: University of Chicago Press, 1968), 208 n. 38.
[39] See John H. Yoder, *Karl Barth and the Problem of War* (Nashville, TN: Abingdon Press, 1970).
[40] Stanley Hauerwas, 'The Nonresistant Church: The Theological Ethics of John Howard Yoder', in *Vision and Virtue* (Notre Dame, IN: University of Notre Dame Press, 1981) (original date of book: 1974) and Stanley Hauerwas, 'Messianic Pacifism', *Worldview* 16 (June 1973), 29–33. Also see Stanley Hauerwas and Chris K. Huebner, 'History, Theory, and Anabaptism: A Conversation on Theology after John Howard Yoder', in *The Wisdom of the Cross: Essays in Honor of John Howard Yoder*, eds. Stanley Hauerwas, Chris K. Huebner, Harry J. Huebner and Mark Thiessen Nation (Grand Rapids, MI: Wm B. Eerdmans, 1999).

Yoder was a pill I had no desire to swallow. His ecclesiology could not work apart from his understanding
of Jesus and the centrality of nonviolence as the
hallmark of the Christian life. The last thing I wanted
to be was a pacifist, mainly because I longed to do
ethics in a way that might be widely influential.
Moreover by disposition I am not much inclined to
nonviolence. But the more I read of Yoder the more I
was convinced that the main lines of his account of
Jesus and the correlative ethic of nonviolence were
correct. I was also slowly coming to see that there was
nothing very passive about Jesus' form of nonviolence,
rather his discipleship not only allowed but required
the Christian to be actively engaged in the creation of
conditions for justice and peace.

But Yoder did something else for me. His emphasis
on the significance of Jesus' whole life – that is, his
teachings as well as his death and resurrection –
provided me with the means to make my account of
character and virtue less formal. I was able to return to
my original project with fresh vision. I had perhaps
discovered a way, for example, to appreciate without
piously distorting Mark's powerful development of
discipleship, which takes Jesus' life to be a paradigm
for our own lives.[41]

However, Yoder was finally not only a pill that Hauerwas
swallowed, but one which has profoundly influenced the
rest of his life's work. No single writer has had as much
influence on Hauerwas as has Yoder.

Second, Hauerwas has been, since his days at
Southwestern University, an omnivorous reader. Any
simplistic reading of him that ignores this is, quite simply,
wrong. I myself have a very large personal library and
have been dubbed by friends a 'walking bibliography'.[42]

---

[41] Hauerwas, *The Peaceable Kingdom*, xxiv.
[42] This was said first in print by James E. Brenneman, *Canons in Conflict:
Negotiating Texts in True and False Prophecy* (Oxford: Oxford University
Press, 1997), x.

Yet I rarely have the experience of mentioning a book to Hauerwas that he is unfamiliar with; usually he has read it. From fiction to social science to philosophy to systematic theology to ethics to postmodern studies to . . . you name it. There are probably certain disciplines in which Hauerwas does not read much. But he reads more than anyone I have ever met and in conjunction with writing more than anyone I have ever met.[43] And for those who might imagine otherwise, it also needs to be said that he hardly reads only what he thinks he will agree with.

But, third, not all he reads is of equal importance to him. He is a discerning reader, with a strong central set of convictions. It would be somewhat difficult to compile a simple shortlist of essential reading for Hauerwas. Topping the list would perhaps be John Howard Yoder and Alasdair MacIntyre. Barth, Aquinas, and Aristotle would likely be on such a list. But then what?

Fourth, Hauerwas seeks to make the life of the Church – very much including, but not limited to, his own local church – central to what he writes. He has often written that theory threatens to overtake the role of the Church in his writings. I believe he is right to continue to wrestle with this tension. And wrestle he does. He also wrestles with his ecclesial commitments. He once said that his 'ecclesial preference is to be a high-church Mennonite'.[44] He has on numerous occasions expressed his deep appreciation for the Roman Catholic tradition.[45] He is most critical of his own denomination, the United Methodist Church. And though his loyalties, commitments, and criticisms are particular, nonetheless, he believes profoundly that '[n]o theologian should desire anything less than that his or her theology is catholic inasmuch as it is true to those

[43] It might be the case that John Yoder wrote as much; I have never carefully compared their output.

[44] Stanley Hauerwas, *A Community of Character: Toward a Constructive Christian Social Ethic* (Notre Dame, IN: University of Notre Dame Press, 1981), 6.

[45] See, e.g., Stanley Hauerwas, 'The Importance of Being Catholic: Unsolicited Advice from a Protestant Bystander', in *In Good Company*, 91–108.

Protestants and Roman Catholics who constitute the church catholic.'[46]

Fifth, Hauerwas is surrounded by very, very many friends. He has stated that 'I literally cannot write, and more importantly, cannot think without friends.'[47] I doubt that there is any theologian for whom that is more true than for Hauerwas. He deeply values and is committed to his friends. And some would be shocked to know the diversity of these friends. I have co-edited two books with Hauerwas. During the work on one of those his secretary told me that Hauerwas personally responds to between twenty and fifty pieces of correspondence every day.[48] Additionally, I often talk with Hauerwas by phone. He has call waiting. As often as not we are interrupted during our phone conversation by other incoming calls. Not all of these communications are with friends. But many are. The first time I met Hauerwas, in 1986, was at a dinner with some of his present and former graduate students. My initial impression has been reconfirmed many times: most of his doctoral students adore him and become life-long friends.[49]

It would be inappropriate to mention all of these friends and not also mention the other members of Hauerwas' family, however briefly. Hauerwas dedicated his first book to Anne and Adam, his wife and son. He described them as his 'most important friends'. 'They are gifts I cannot possess and are all the more valuable because of it', said Hauerwas.[50] Hauerwas was married to Anne for approximately twenty-five years. A few years after his first

---

[46] Hauerwas, *The Peaceable Kingdom*, xxvi.

[47] Hauerwas, *A Community of Character*, ix. See his extended reflections on friendship, written with his former student, Charles Pinches, in Stanley Hauerwas and Charles Pinches, *Christians Among the Virtues: Theological Conversations with Ancient and Modern Ethics* (Notre Dame, IN: University of Notre Dame Press, 1997), 31–51, 70–88.

[48] He does not use e-mail because he knows, quite rightly, that he would be overwhelmed by correspondence if he did so.

[49] I should also add that the two secretaries I have worked with at Duke also adore Stanley. This is also not unimportant in thinking about who Hauerwas is.

[50] Hauerwas, *Vision and Virtue*, viii.

marriage ended he married his present wife, Paula Gilbert, an ordained Methodist minister. 'That Paula has chosen me as the one with whom she is willing to share her solitude, her humour, and her love of God, all of which I suspect are closely connected, is an extraordinary gift', says Hauerwas.[51] It is obvious he is indeed grateful for the gift that Paula is to him. It is also obvious that he is very grateful for his close friendship with his son, Adam. As Hauerwas has put it, his friendship with his son 'is a gift I had no right to expect in this life but it is one for which I praise God daily'.[52] And he is quite pleased to have a daughter-in-law, Laura, that he enjoys, as well as a grandson, Joel Adam.[53] Anyone who has known Stanley Hauerwas very well knows how very much these relationships have meant and continue to mean to him.

It would also be inappropriate to end this essay without mentioning the schools at which Hauerwas has taught. Hauerwas' first teaching position, after leaving Yale, was at Augustana College, a Lutheran school in Rock Island, Illinois. He was there from the autumn of 1968 to the spring of 1970. From 1970 to 1984 he was at the University of Notre Dame in South Bend, Indiana. This Catholic school changed Hauerwas' life.[54] Undoubtedly that is partly because he often worshipped with the Catholics. It is also because of what he believes he learned from his Catholic colleagues at Notre Dame. He learned that 'the Catholics are stuck with claims of Christian continuity and unity across the centuries, with questions of what constitutes good order and authority within and between churches in widely different circumstances, and with moral commitments that are embarrassing in liberal cultures'.[55] (Of course, he tries to convince Catholics that

[51] Hauerwas, *In Good Company*, xv.
[52] Hauerwas, *Christian Existence Today*, ix.
[53] See the dedication in Stanley Hauerwas, *Prayers Plainly Spoken* (Downers Grove, IL: InterVarsity Press, 1999), 9 and London: Triangle 1999, ix.
[54] Stanley Hauerwas, 'A Homage to Mary and to the University Called Notre Dame', in *In Good Company*, 82.
[55] Stanley Hauerwas, 'Whose Church? Which Future?: Whither the Anabaptist Vision?', in *In Good Company*, 67.

these are all good things, properly understood.) And he formed some important and lasting friendships at Notre Dame. Finally, since the autumn of 1984 he has been at Duke Divinity School, at Duke University, in Durham, North Carolina. Here he is teaching in his own denomination's school, although teaching students from a wide variety of theological traditions. Here he has also developed numerous important friendships.

So, these are some of the particulars that make Stanley Hauerwas who he is. Stanley would never want us to forget these particulars (and others unnamed). And, yet, added together they do not totally explain this unique individual that is Stanley M. Hauerwas. Robert Bellah, co-author of *Habits of the Heart*, has said: 'Stanley Hauerwas's extraordinary intellectual energy constantly jolts one into reconsidering what one had previously taken for granted'.[56] Robert W. Jenson, systematic theologian, says about Hauerwas: 'Hauerwas is right about so much that nearly the whole American church and academy culpably have wrong, and he is so beneficial in his ability to say what others can or will not say, that he fully deserves his position as bellwether and *bête noire* of American theological ethics'.[57] Then there is Cornel West, an African American philosopher, cultural critic, and author of many books, who says: 'Stanley Hauerwas is one of the few prophetic voices of our time – idiosyncratic, cantankerous, and challenging'.[58] Michael Goldberg, rabbi and Jewish theologian, speaks for many when he says that Hauerwas 'may be the most consistently interesting – and provocative – religious thinker of our time'.[59] But, finally, it is not only that Hauerwas is interesting, but in our time of great cultural shifts his writings are very important, perhaps even vital. As Jean Bethke Elshtain, political philosopher,

---

[56] Blurb quoted on the back of Stanley Hauerwas, *Dispatches from the Front*.

[57] Robert W. Jenson, 'Hauerwas Examined', *First Things* 25 (August/ September 1992), 50.

[58] Blurb quoted on the back of Hauerwas, *Dispatches from the Front*.

[59] Michael Goldberg, *Theology and Narrative: A Critical Introduction*, second edition (Philadelphia, PA: Trinity Press International, 1991), 6.

social ethicist, and prolific author said to me in a letter, referring to Hauerwas: 'Where would we be without him?'[60] Indeed! Where would we be?

---

[60] Jean Bethke Elshtain to Mark Thiessen Nation, 10 June 1997, in possession of author.

EMBODYING HAUERWAS

3
The Conflict of the Faculties:
Theology and the Economy of the Sciences

John Milbank

The first thing which members of a modern theology or religious studies department must face up to is that a large percentage of their atheist or agnostic colleagues in the academic world probably consider theology or any other mode of religious reflection as none other than a fantasising about the void. As to the study of religion, they may very well consider it valid to ask just why it is that humanity has systematically pursued so many will o' the wisps, but they are far less likely to be convinced that one requires an entire separate department devoted to this task. If religion is a human phenomenon, they may be inclined to argue, then the human sciences – psychological, social and even biological – must take it within their purview for the sake of completeness. A separate department of religious studies, however purged of theology, still wafts behind it a trace of the odour of sanctity: for if the human sciences cannot deal comprehensively with religion, this still implies that there is something 'religious', something transcendentally in excess of the biological, historical, social and psychological.

In the face of such doubts there is, in the end, no convincing apologetic ground upon which theology and religious studies can stand. In secular terms, they should not exist. One might protest at this point that the question of God, or of other religious beliefs, remains something which can be given objective, rational consideration. And that may be fair enough, but such an issue is adequately dealt with in terms of the philosophy syllabus. Another, more valid, objection would be that there are other examples of subject areas organised by field of studies, rather than field plus angle of approach: urban studies for example, or environmental studies, which are unified only by an object of enquiry, to which several different disciplinary approaches may be taken. This is, of course, the case, but such subject areas are inherently vulnerable to collapse from within and takeover bids from without. They tend to exist at all only for temporary or expedient reasons. Moreover, in the case of religion, as we shall see, a third cause of strain is the question as to whether 'religion' defines with sufficient precision any discrete area of enquiry whatsoever.

Thus one is returned to the truth that self-justification of theology or religious studies before a secular court is well-nigh impossible, and that religious studies is in no better case here than theology. Nonetheless one should not despair, for one reason which is entirely cynical, and for another which is entirely theological. The cynical reason can be dealt with in a short paragraph; the theological one will occupy the rest of this essay. The cynical reason is that utter incoherence and lack of ability to withstand the critical trial of reason does not matter so long as one can come up with cash and customers; in our postmodern era the 'free, rational inquiry' of the Enlightenment which could reveal only formal truths as objectively real, thus handing over the whole realm of the substantive to the play of agnostic forces, has itself been inevitably invaded by such forces, since form feeds only on the substantive, and never perfectly inhabits its own purity. Enlightenment, therefore, is bound to evolve into the postmodern mixture of the purest, most unbounded and therefore most rigorous logic, plus the most untrammelled sway of vanity and fashion. In many ways a 'religious studies department' is well adapted to our era. But we should be warned: the point of fashion is to change, and religious constituencies may well yet further wither away, or more probably mutate and take their custom elsewhere, far away from universities (or what in the future will remain of them).

The cynical reason for not despairing, as outlined above,

may be entertained by religious studies, and even by theology, so long as it remains aware that it is, indeed, cynicism. However the second, and alone substantive, or genuinely hopeful reason for not despairing, is not available to religious studies. It is a theological reason alone. This is the possibility that the secular atheist, or agnostic, consensus might be challenged. And the grounds for this challenge would be simply that they have got everything the wrong way round. They claim that theology, alone amongst purported academic disciplines, is really 'about nothing'. But theological reason, if it is true to itself, replies to this with a counter-claim – all other disciplines, which claim to be about objects regardless of whether or not these objects are related to God, are, just for this reason about nothing whatsoever. This claim holds true for theology, however much these disciplines may assist us, in both good and evil fashion, in practical negotiations with the objective appearances of things, for, if we take an appearance as a mere 'object', that is to say if we take it in abstraction from the question whether or not it discloses in some degree God – as being his creature – we treat it effectively in an atheistic manner, whether or not we remain agnostic as to the answer to the question. And atheism is but a polite English name for what on the Continent has more often been called what it is: nihilism. It is not, in any sense, as its own apologetic insinuates, the negative doubting of God: on the contrary, it is the positive affirmation of the absoluteness of the void, and the capacity of that void to generate the appearance of a solid something – for all that this appearance, if it arises from nothing, must be without ontological remainder, and must at every instant vanish, not just from our sight but in itself. The object, concerning whose participation in infinite actuality – God – we maintain a gnoseological suspense, is an object construed as indeed a will o' the wisp. For if it is taken apart from God, as something in itself, then this must mean a something arising from nothing: therefore the object – the very objectivity of the object as that which appears to the evidence of sight without reference to its origins, or its inevitably hidden aspects – is constituted by its disguise of the real, a real which is really nothing. By contrast, the only 'something' for this secular outlook is the appearance of the object which is *mere* appearance or illusion, since there can be no disclosive relation between something and nothing: of nothing there is nothing to disclose. It seems that atheism turns out to be much more difficult and indeed mystical than theology, as serious atheists, unlike smug, thoughtless ones, have always known.

Thus for theology, other disciplines, even if they can show us how, amorally, to seek more and more to possess a realm of illusion (though such possession will finally defeat us) and although they can refine more and more the increasingly bizarre and nihilistic paradoxes of logic and mathematics, as well as physics divorced from metaphysics and biology divorced from teleology, are, precisely as secular disciplines (although they will nearly always possess also an implicit and redeeming super-natural orientation), through and through nihilistic. By contrast, theology understands itself as alone studying things as ineliminably real, in that they are taken as having their source in an original indefeasible actuality. A conse-quence of this view is that theology also understands itself as alone able to remain with the question of truth, without running into inevitable aporias. For theology, indeed, truth is an adequation or correspondence of knowledge with the real, since the one entirely real reality, God, is itself both infinitely actual and infinitely knowing. As real, he is also manifest and self-aware, or truthful. For us to express a truth means that to a degree we correspond in our being to God via an awareness of aspects of the creation to whose lesser reality we also correspond, since the creation is rooted in God, and its being is entirely from God. From this theological perspective alone it makes sense to say that knowing corresponds to being, even though we have no other access to being, other than via knowing, and thus a claim that our knowledge 'corresponds' can never be checked up upon. We cannot compare what is known with the knowledge of it, since what is known is not available other than through knowledge. Hence a claim to know truly, a claim to know at all, as Plato argued, only makes sense within the framework of *meathexis* (participation), for it amounts to a faith that what one shows or expresses in knowledge radiates mysteriously, and in a limited measure yet not deceptively, from a plenitudinous origin that is both the source of all things and the genuine depth of all things.

Outside this theological framework, the redundancy theorists of truth are right: 'truth' is an eliminable term since it only means that what is 'is', and 'is' in this context can only mean that which appears to us (in terms of both nature and culture) to be – the world as we either pragmatically or conventionally reckon with it.[1] However, there is no secure phenomenalist resting point here, no safe version of transcendental 'limits of human reason' within which there may persist a certain sort of certainty concerning the real. For behind the complacency of so-called redundancy or disquotational theory lurks the more fearful spectre of 'diagonalisation'. With the diagonalising perspective, to say that true statements pertain to the world as we pragmatically or conventionally handle it raises the reflexive problem of how that statement itself is legitimated, since it cannot itself be pragmatically or conventionally grounded or disquotationally reduced.[2] It seems that in one instance we cannot substitute for the word true – that is the instance when we say 'it is true that all uses of the word true can be translated into other terms'. For even if we say instead 'all uses of the word true can be translated into other terms', the fact that we need to make this assertion shows that to affirm the redundancy theory

[1] See Arthur Fine, *The Shaky Game* (Chicago: University of Chicago Press, 1986), 112–71; Hilary Putnam, *Pragmatism: An Open Question* (Oxford: Blackwell, 1995); Donald Davidson, 'The Structure and Content of Truth', in the *Journal of Philosophy* 87 (June 1990), 279–326; Richard Rorty 'Pragmatism, Davidson and Truth', in *Truth and Interpretation* ed. Ernest LePore (Oxford: Blackwell, 1986), 333–55; Bruce D. Marshall. 'We Shall Bear the Image of the Man of Heaven'; 'Theology and the Concept of Truth', in *Rethinking Metaphysics*, eds. G. L. Jones and S. E. Rowl (Oxford: Blackwell, 1995), 93–117.

[2] On 'diagonalisation', see Graham Priest, *Beyond the Limits of Thought* (Cambridge: Cambridge University Press, 1995).

is to assert that the redundancy of use of the word 'truth' corresponds to the way things are, such that after all we encounter here an unavoidable speculative gap between knowledge and being where use of the word 'true' or equivalent phrasing still has an irreducible function. In a corresponding fashion, if we elect to think that it is true that 'true' indicates only what appears to us to be the case, then (as Plato pointed out in the *Theaetetus*)[3] we still have to say 'it appears to me that truth reduces to whatever appears to anyone to be'. And here again truth is not disquotable, nor reducible to appearance, since an 'appearance' which establishes that truth resides only in appearings-to-be cannot itself be within the normal plane of appearances, but is rather a meta-appearing which establishes the absoluteness of this plane. Yet at the same time a meta-appearing must after all be regarded as also just another contingent and subjective appearing and so as contradictorily belonging on the same first-order plane after all. In this way it is, in principle, open to challenge by another appearance which could disclose the non-ultimateness of mere appearing-to-be itself. So here once again, there arises an unavoidable – if undecidable – issue about correspondence and thus about truth.

It has now been seen, both from the way in which 'truth' is not redundant in asserting its redundancy, and the way in which the theory of truth as appearance both is not and yet is itself an appearance, that these theories are beset by deconstructive paradox. Thus to uphold the limits of pragmatic or conventional reason, and a disquotational theory of truth with its accompanying phenomenalism, one must also transgress those limits or 'diagonalise' out of them, to use the jargon, and risk the notion that one's decision to regard the world only pragmatically or else conventionally does after all correspond – beyond mere pragmatism or conventionalism – to the way things are. This 'way things are', this implicit ontology, would be that the world is through and through phenomenal without disclosure of anything deeper, that is to say that for

[3] Plato, *Theaetetus* 161C–162A.

working purposes it is a meaningless and partially manip-
ulable flux floating above a void (an implied 'centre' of lack
of reasons and non-origination). So after all, phenomena
without truth, that is to say, phenomena containing no
inner impetus to self-disclosure (as in a theological theory
which accepts an ontological dimension to truth) do
nonetheless disclose the truth of the void. But as we have
seen, this is a self-cancelling form of self-disclosure, which
announces the equal untruth as much as truth of what is
disclosed, since the void discloses nothing, and in consequence the truth entertained here is a truth crossed out, a
contradictory untruth, just as the result, as Hegel realised,
of any transcendental limitation of possible knowledge is a
constitutive contradiction. For if, as we have seen, in the
theory under consideration, all truth relates only to
appearances, then according to the logic of set-theory this
statement itself both must and yet cannot be merely
phenomenal: it is simultaneously groundless, floating in a
void, and yet grounded within the phenomenal horizon.
Hence, just as for secular knowledge all appearances
equally are and are not, so also reality is disclosed truly
and yet as entirely untrue. Plato, followed by Augustine,
Dionysius and the whole Christian tradition up to Aquinas
and Eckhart (and in his wake Nicholas of Cusa), was right:
in the mere finite flux taken in itself there resides no truth,
and the principle of non-contradiction of logic itself cannot
be upheld or grounded logically, but only through assent
to the realm of eternal unchanging forms, or of the ideas in
the mind of God, where what is actual abides, and as
infinite or 'outside itself' escapes all set-theoretical contra-
dictions.

The above reasonings suggest that theology, in the face
of secular attack, is only on secure ground if it adopts the
most extreme mode of counterattack: namely that unless
other disciplines are (at least implicitly) ordered to
theology (assuming that this means participation in God's
self-knowledge – as in the Augustinian tradition) they are
objectively and demonstrably null and void, altogether
lacking in truth, which to have any meaning must involve
some sort of adequation (for mere 'coherence' can only

concern the coherence of conventions or appearances). But one might well protest, how does this picture relate to the real situation in today's universities where it is simply not the case that with 100 per cent consistency secular academics say to students of theology or religion, 'You speak of nothing' and even less true that those students solemnly intone in reply, 'No, it is rather you who speak of nothing.' However, to understand why what I believe is the real situation rarely emerges to the surface, one needs to consider briefly the historical emergence of modern theology and religious studies, and in particular the often hidden role of the state in this emergence.

There are four significant dimensions here which I want now to enumerate.

First, around 1300 or so, theology itself perversely invented the possibility of an entirely non-theological mode of knowledge. Duns Scotus and his successors through Suarez and Descartes to Kant, elaborated the notion that is was possible adequately to think of Being as such, apart from its instantiation as the infinite actuality of God. In consequence it became legitimate to think of the being of a creature apart from its creaturehood. But this alters altogether the meaning of contingency. No longer is the apparent being of a thing taken as God's willed partial disclosure of himself; instead it is taken as raw possibility. For if God has been bracketed out, the being of a creature is exhaustively that which appears to our knowledge, and that which appears to our knowledge, that which we can clearly and distinctly grasp, is simply that which is thinkably coherent and so possible. Thus a being taken in abstraction from God is immediately reduced to its enablement by possible being, rather than prior actuality. But if possibility is prior, then a 'might not be' or 'nothing' is on the same level with being, and meontology as funda-mental as ontology. As J-F. Courtine puts it, the contention of Eckhart (but also of Augustine and Aquinas) which was the inner kernel of orthodoxy tragically rejected as heterodox by the Catholic Church itself before and around 1300 – namely that in its most actual self the creature in some sense is God, and of itself is nothing, is negatively demonstrated to be correct by all subsequent deviant scholasticism. In this later, and decadent, development, the inner essence of a finite being becomes nothing as much as something, so that in Suarez and then in Wolff, and even in Kant's first critique, the real subject of ontology is not *ens*, but *aliquid* (something) or *objectum*, the 'transcendental' reality that might equally be or not be. I have already indicated how this, the substructure of most modern pragmatism, most phenomenology, and most analytic philosophy – is implicitly nihilist – rendering the question of 'postmodernism' a trivial irrelevance.[4]

The second dimension is closely related to the first. Once the fundamental Augustinian-Dionysian-Thomist structure of analogy of being and participation in being had been destroyed by the Scotist view that finite and infinite being 'are' in the same univocal sense, theology gradually changed its character. For Aquinas, to talk adequately of anything, one had to speak of it as a creature, to refer its being to God as alone truly being in himself. In consequence, metaphysics, understood by Aquinas primarily as ontology, diagonalised out of itself in dealing with one topic – namely the first cause, God – that fell within its purview. Paradoxically this one topic, God, is for the Thomist view of metaphysics (as not for Aristotle who remained with a strange aporetic tension) bigger, of greater scope than its supposed all comprehensive subject matter of *ens commune* – 'being in common'.[5] There is, however, no real paradox here, only because this subject matter of metaphysics, *ens commune*, is itself provided by a higher cause, which is the subject of a higher science. But here, uniquely, the cause and the science are at one – they are the first cause and its own self-knowledge: God himself and

---

[4] See Jean-François Courtine, *Suarez et le problème de la métaphysique* (Paris: Presses Universitaires de France, 1990); Eric Alliez, *Capital Times* trans. George van den Abbeele (Minneapolis: Minnesota University Press, 1996), 141–241.

[5] See Courtine, *Suarez et le problème de la métaphysique*; Alain de Libera, *Le problème de l'etre chez Maître Eckhart: Logique et métaphysique de l'analogie* (Geneva: *Cahiers de la Revue de Théologie at de Philosophie* 4, 1980); Edward Booth, *Aristotelian Aporetic Ontology in Islamic and Christian Thinkers* (Cambridge: Cambridge University Press, 1983).

his *scientia Dei* which is theology, utterly ineffable and beyond our grasp. The basic conclusions of metaphysics, that there is a cause of being, and that this cause of being is itself a plenitudinous being, are for Aquinas flickering and uncertain, just because we only ever weakly participate in being and truth, and are, besides, fallen creatures. They are only truly confirmed, established from their ground, by God's imparting to us his own self-knowledge, through his entry gradually into human time (the typology of the Old Testament) and finally with Christ at the incarnation. This entry not only confirms God as first cause and *esse ipsum* to our wavering reason, but also discloses the inner reality of God as Trinitarian, namely as an infinite will to give being, to be known and loved through self-manifestation which pre-grounds the creative act.

But after Aquinas and Eckhart, this sense of theology as participation in the science of God and the blessed gradually evaporated, and indeed was subject already to a kind of secularisation such that theology as such was really already abandoned. How? Because instead of the most fundamental determination of being as theological, one now has a theologically-neutral determination of being, and theology is forced to work within this framework as if, idolatrously, there was something more ontologically fundamental than God. For the figure of participation is substituted the figure of distance: as if God were a very remote, infinitely-large object. And where in-finite was traditionally a negative description of God, it now, in the late Middle Ages, became a positive definition of his essence. And of course a God whose defining nature is to be unbounded, and a God of which nothing finite necessarily discloses anything, since its finite essence is simply a logical or grammatical 'might not be', is a God who quickly becomes hypostasised will or force. The late mediaeval imagining of a reality divided between infinite arbitrariness on the one hand and finite contingent possibilities on the other already projected in advance a nihilistic imagining of a blind flux undergirding meaningless and delusory appearances. Increasingly the

Scotist 'proofs of God' in terms of the necessary priority of infinite Being, did not seem like proofs of God, as opposed to proofs of some sort of immanent absolute or even immanent absolute void: a conclusion eventually arrived at by Spinoza. As a result, theology was thrown more and more back on a new sort of foundation in positive revelation. But in this case also, it was just as true that theology took for granted a philosophical pre-establishment of what an object or a fact was: something clear and evident, without depth, unambiguous and provable according to 'evidence'. God was now seen as disclosing himself in facts which, increasingly, to distinguish themselves as divine facts, had to be miraculous facts, or else their recognition depended upon an entirely separate, internal – and only accidentally related to the revealed object – movement of our understanding by the Holy Spirit.[6] The traditional integrity of theology was thereby lost: for previously theology was not a secondary reflection upon data, whether of Scripture or tradition; on the contrary, theology was the event of divine disclosure, a happening in which inner inspiration and outward expression in signs were seamlessly and intrinsically united. Instead of this sophisticated and believable notion that theology concerns the gradually renewed disclosure of God himself through creatures which makes use of the ceaseless becoming of creation in time, an entirely superstitious and contemptible notion of an arbitrary and blind faith in certain supposedly revealed facts was substituted. Yet this strange fideistic superstition is itself captive to the emerging secularity of a God reduced to the status of an object, and so able to disclose himself according to his arbitrary will, through lesser objective possibilities. Thus, although this circumstance was for a long time hidden, the mainstream of learned theology effectively ceased to be theology long ago. Above all, it ceased to be about God, because it ceased to be itself the existential event of divine illumination, and

---

[6] See Avery Dulles, *The Assurance of Things Hoped For: A Theology of Christian Faith* (Oxford; Oxford University Press, 1994); René Latourelle, *Theology of Revelation* (Staten Island, NY: Alba House, 1967).

became instead a second-order reflection on facts or practices of some sort. (When, for example, Barth says that theology is primarily about the Church and its conformity to Scripture it seems to me that he has not escaped this post-1300 decadence).[7]

The third dimension concerns the state. Ockhamist distance from an absolute voluntarist God, from the outset meshed nicely with, and was used to support, a new conception of earthly authority as legitimate according to the exercise of power by a single sovereign centre if constituted by and exercised in the right formal terms, quite apart from the question of the inherent justice of its acts. This meant that public life, as fallen entirely under such sovereign sway, was subject to a paradoxically theological secularisation, in that its ordering, though divinely legitimate, no longer in any way reflected divine order or cosmic hierarchy. Partly as a result, 'religion' ceased to betoken specific patterns of individual participation in public practice, ceased, in short to be a 'virtue', and became instead a private attitude; not even any longer a disposition to virtue, but rather an act of assent to certain emotionally neutral 'beliefs' in certain revealed facts and propositions. Moreover, in the early modern period, while the state was unable altogether to escape the assumption that the practice of religion alone held society together, it quickly came to suppose that the state simply required general assent to some set of beliefs for the sake of disciplined and uniform public worship, plus the supernatural sanctioning of morality and its own positive laws. In that moment the notion of 'a religion', and of a plurality of 'religions' was born, and later inappropriately used to classify the practices and inherited wisdoms of other cultures.[8] Even today, the state retains some vestigial interest in the usefulness of a

[7] Karl Barth, *Dogmatics in Outline*, trans. G. T. Thomson (London: SCM Press, 1996), 9–14.
[8] See Peter Harrison, *Religion and the Religious Enlightenment* (Cambridge: Cambridge University Press, 1990); Talal Asad, *Genealogies of Religion* (Baltimore: Johns Hopkins University Press, 1993); W. T. Cavanaugh, ' "A fire strong enough to consume the house": The Wars of Religion and the Rise of the State', *Modern Theology* 11 (1995), 397–420).

private sphere of piety, and therefore tends to encourage the notion that there is a 'religious' dimension of life, which assists the state's own ends without trespassing on its sovereignty.

Concomitantly, it still prefers the public dimension of religion – mystical attachment to corporate bodies and organisations of social practice – to be alienated to its own domain: hence the occasionally re-emerging phenomenon of 'civil religion'.

The fourth dimension, after those of modern ontology without God, modern debased theology, and the modern theopolitical co-determination of the state and religion, concern the emergence of a notion of 'ritual' activity. In the Middle Ages, and in most traditional societies, all proper action is ritual in the sense that it reflects a cosmic order: as Talal Asad has stressed, the monk's writing in the scriptorium or labouring in the field was as much liturgical as his saying of the offices in chapel.[9] And all these ritual acts were no mysterious symbolic language for some sort of psychological secret attitude; on the contrary they were simply plain, ordinary, transparent acts, whose structure nonetheless pointed to an inexhaustable depth of divine mystery. But later, with the reduction of religion to mean primarily a set of beliefs, actions related to those beliefs started to be thought of as strange, as hovering between real, normal actions, and certain psychological dispositions: in this way a realm of 'ritual' or 'symbolic actions' was born, which helped to strengthen the illusion that these are religious phenomena, available for study and inquiry. Whereas, in fact, this is a modern Western projection: traditional Hinduism, for example, was not a religion, not an aspect of the Indian way of life, it simply was that life or rather plural lives in their specific totality, their specific structuring and specific visions.

Taken altogether these four dimensions have helped to shape the modern disciplines of theology and religious studies. Theology has been regarded, unlike philosophy, as a 'positive science' concerned with a certain delimited

---

[9] Asad, *Genealogies of Religion*, 125–71.

field, rather than as the very consummation and transfigu-
ration of philosophy or the science of being as such. It has
also been frequently regarded by the state as primarily
functional and practical in character. In Kant's strange last
published work, *The Conflict of the Faculties*, he argued that
the higher university faculties, theology, law and medicine,
can be allowed only limited freedom, since they serve the
practical and legal purposes of the state, whereas
philosophy, a lower faculty, as being without public
responsibilities or direct public consequences, is free to
pursue pure truth without hindrance.[10] But this, we can
now see, is the perfect political equivalence of nihilism:
philosophy which can only after all for Kant attain the
truth of appearances can think what it likes (is a kind of
adventure playground, without upshot), and yet beyond
philosophy, and beyond appearances in the noumenal
void, a strict formalism for the safeguarding and sacralising
of an empty freedom as the essence of subjectivity,
pertains. And it is finally theology justified by practical
truth which upholds this politically amoral realm of strict
and empty formalism. It is no longer, by Kant, allowed,
beyond the formal exigencies of the state legal practice, to
think the ratio between the unknown and manifest appearances (thanks to Kant's strict duality of the sublime and the
beautiful), despite the fact that this is the only true site
for Christian theology.[11] Within the bounds laid down by
the state, theology is instead confined to upholding a
supposedly universal morality and to better scholarly
establishment of the facts which are now taken to ground
belief. Thus theology in the course of the nineteenth
century acquired wholly questionable sub-disciplines
which were no longer expected to participate in God's self-
knowledge, but were instead expected simply to establish
the foundational facts with pure historical neutrality (on

[10]   Immanuel Kant, 'The Conflict of the Faculties', in *Religion and Rational Theology*, trans. A. W. Wood and G. di Giovanni (Cambridge: Cambridge University Press, 1996) 233–329.
[11]   See John Milbank, 'Sublimity, the Modern Transcendent', in *Religion, Modernity and Postmodernity*, ed. P. Heelas and P. Morris (Oxford: Blackwell, 1998).

which the Church as department of state depends): Biblical criticism, church history (as no longer a reflection on divine providence), historical theology and so forth. Even after the decline of public belief, theology has hoped that this self-desiccation of its unity into non-theological components will win it general respectability. But it is a short-term strategy, and in the end theology is here only preparing its own auctioning-off to other faculties: to history, Oriental studies, classics, and the like. So the task now for theology is not, of course, to abandon historical scholarship, but to reinvent Biblical studies, church history and so forth as also attempts, beyond scholarship, to participate in the mind of God.

Alongside theology, religious studies has emerged as the study of a questionably (for reasons we have seen) discrete area of human existence. To that extent, it is not a readily defensible discipline, even if history of religions at its best has attempted an interesting sort of historical ethnography and *histoire totale* of human culture. But what alone really drives the study of religion as a distinct discipline is either a vacuous and impossible pluralist theology (whose impossibility I have discussed elsewhere),[12] or else the atheist or agnostic attempt to explain whatever in human culture falls outside the norms of Western, post-Scotist reason. It is perfectly all right to admit such attempts within a theology and religious studies department, as long as one insists that the department is still – as a whole and primarily – committed to theology. For otherwise, if one adopts a neutral stance, one is really giving free rein to one inevitable ambition of such inquiries, namely to get rid of theology as an academic venture. By all means, we should include in our endeavours, for example, the psychology of religion: but never should we be under any illusion that this is partially in order to encourage a dialogue between theology and psychology. Why not? Because while theology is perfectly open and always has been to discourses about physical

---

[12] John Milbank, 'The End of Dialogue', in *Christian Uniqueness Reconsidered*, ed. Gavin d'Costa (New York: Orbis 1990), 174–92.

influences on the soul (the traditional theory of melancholy and so forth), it regards itself, in one central aspect, as the discourse about the soul's psychic reality. Hence psychology, outside of physical and behavioural science, is a rival of theology: indeed it is easy to show genealogically that it is itself but the faint trace of religious belief in the soul, an absurd attempt to talk about the soul without God, despite the fact that the soul as 'spiritual' has only been historically constituted in terms of our point of contact with transcendence.[13] Such an attempt is strictly analogous to all post-Scotist attempts to talk about actuality apart from God, and with the same result: finite actuality, here spiritual actuality, must fade away. And, furthermore, the attempt also inherits a theological privatisation of religion whereby, instead of the 'humanly psychic' simply being taken as coterminous with all specifically human outward activity as the spring of 'life' and principle of order in such activity (as the psychic is also the principle of life and the measure of all other, non-human, realities) it is seen as denoting some elusive, mysterious, supposedly 'internal' aspect of our existence, such that the 'psychic' is supposed to be more manifest to laboratory investigation of an isolated individual under artificial experimental con-ditions, than in ordinary interpersonal everyday life.

Thus in relation to secular inquiries into religion, theology should never surrender its hegemony. But ironi-cally, nor should the practitioners of such enquiries want it to, at least if they wish to remain focused upon religion or, *a fortiori*, to remain located within a religious studies department. For without theology's unique assertion of a *raison d'être*, namely maintenance of at least the possibility of an alternative to secular nihilism, the long-term threat of an 'auctioning off' of such secular studies of religion remains.

And rather similar considerations apply to the study of other religions (though that is the wrong term). One should say here, first of all, that theology itself should of course

---

[13] The point is well made from a stance hostile to religion by Richard Webster in his *Why Freud Was Wrong* (London: HarperCollins, 1996), esp. 457–77.

include a reflection on the theological meaning of the history of religions. Alongside this, a religious studies department will validly include 'neutral' studies of such history, besides, where possible, encouragement of interior intellectual developments of other traditions by practitioners of such traditions themselves – although I think we need to be aware of the degree to which the tradition of such reflection in the case of Hinduism, Buddhism, and Islam has been historically ruptured: we must not be taken in by inauthentic modern simulacra of such reflection. The facts of history and simple pressure of numbers dictates that such reflection will continue to be more carried out by Christians and by Jews. But there are also two further points. The first is that the very rationale for allowing a pluralist encouragement of different traditions of reasoned enquiry, also demands continuing Christian theological hegemony. Why? Because this rationale denies that reason can ever be divorced first from a more than rational commitment, and second from the specificity of time and place. Thus, this rationale itself requires that as Christian theologians we sustain our tradition of reflection as a matter of more than rational commitment, which means in turn that we have to insist that a faculty of religion is, whatever else it is, at least a faculty of theology, meaning, of course, Christian theology, as well as that more simply 'metaphysical' theology inherited from the Greeks and common to the three monotheistic faiths. But in addition, the realities of time and place to which a theory of 'traditioned' reason is committed, still in Europe and America for the moment require the culturally-prior role of Christian reflection. And since the notion of traditioned reason alone can withstand the sway of a supposedly neutral reason, and since this notion demands for the above reasons that we sustain the distinction of Christian commitment and assert its priority for theology and religious studies, then it is paradoxically this priority alone which shelters other modes of traditional or religious reflection. By contrast, a strictly secular, neutral regard would simply sweep them away in the wake of Christian theology itself.

It is inconceivable and simply idolatrous to suppose that theology could ever be a component of some supposedly more inclusive and hybrid discipline of religion and theology in general (even though, of course, it is possible to imagine that a Christian theology 'track' within a department of religion and theology could readily share in common courses on say the Old Testament, Greek Philosophy and Mediaeval Philosophy with Islamic, Jewish and History of Religions tracks). And yet, I can hear a Muslim or a Jew protest, is there not something very strange about what you say? How can Christian theology shelter other religious visions, if it is within this tradition alone that secular nihilism was pre-invented. There is no answer I can give here which they will find acceptable, and yet there is an answer which is highly relevant for Christians. This is that despite the fact that Christian learned theology abandoned the framework of analogy and participation for a kind of proto-nihilism, it was nonetheless Christian thinkers alone in the Middle Ages who fully succeeded in elaborating such a framework. Without the encouragement of the Trinitarian sense that God is in himself the God who expresses himself creatively, and the Christological sense that God only speaks from within history and can only restore a broken history by kenotically entering personally within it, the Arabic and Jewish scholastics (*as well as* the Jewish Kabbalists) tended not to be able to reconcile God's simplicity and supremacy of will with his eminent possession of the excellencies of goodness, truth and beauty manifest in the creation (despite their intense will to do so). With the abandonment of participation by Christian theologians, such an inability invaded Christendom also, with the inverse consequence that the trinitarian and christological doctrines started to lose their centrality and inherent logic, becoming the subjects of mere authorised belief.[14] For this reason it can

[14] See John Milbank, 'History of the One God', in *Heythrop Journal* 38 (1997), 371–400, and David B. Burrell, *Knowing the Unknowable God* (Notre Dame: University of Notre Dame Press, 1986), *Freedom and Creation in Three Traditions* (Notre Dame: University of Notre Dame Press, 1993).

validly be asserted (and should be accepted by Christians), that the call to recover analogy and participation, which is equivalent to a call to reinstate the hegemony of theology as an alternative to nihilism, will tend to be also (if by no means exclusively since one has no warrant to rule out the possibility of future more successful Jewish and Islamic neoplatonisms), a call to recover specifically Christian theology.

4
Spirituality and Mental Sickness

Stephen Sykes

I

In this contribution it is my intention to treat the question of the relationship between spirituality and mental sickness.[1] In his important and provocative essay, 'Salvation and Health: Why Medicine Needs the Church',[2] Stanley Hauerwas observes the existence of two equally unsatisfactory proposals for the terms on which religion and medicine should be related, either by a sharpening of the boundary between the bodily and the spiritual or by the 'resacralising' of medical care. He writes:

> If the theologian attempts to underwrite the medical ethos drawing on the particular convictions of Christians, just to the extent those convictions are particular will serve only to emphasise society's lack of common morality. Thus theologians, in the interest of cultural consensus, often try to down-play the distinctiveness of their theological convictions in the interest of societal harmony.[3]

---

[1] As will become clear the terms used to speak of this matter are used deliberately. I am avoiding both 'disease' and 'illness', though in ordinary speech these are frequently used synonymously with 'sickness'. Nor am I treating the issue of mental health, a broader issue altogether, except insofar as the recovery from mental sickness is an aspect of health, or at least of healing.

[2] First published in Earl Shelp (ed.), *Theology and Bioethics* (Dordrecht: D. Reidel, 1985) and reprinted in Stanley Hauerwas, *Suffering Presence* (Notre Dame, IN: University of Notre Dame Press, 1986; Edinburgh: T&T Clark, 1988).

[3] Hauerwas, 'Salvation and Health', *Suffering Presence*, 74.

To consider spirituality and mental sickness is, of course, to treat a special subset of the general question of religion and medicine. But it proves to be an especially enlightening case. My argument will be that only particularity will do for those in the grip of mental sickness.[4] This is to make both a general philosophical or methodological point, and also to undergird an aspect of Hauerwas' main argument in an area which he has not, so far, treated explicitly.[5]

II

In Britain the term 'spirituality' has arrived in public discourse. To such a degree has its presence been felt that it makes some sense to ask whether you can 'get it' on the National Health along with false teeth, spectacles and sex change operations.

Outside the context of the United Kingdom (England, Scotland, Wales and Northern Ireland), the question 'Can you get X on the National Health?' needs interpretation. Now in its fiftieth year, the National Health Service was introduced by the Labour government after the Second World War as a way of delivering health care free at the point of need to every citizen, a service paid for out of taxation.[6] Despite the objections of a handful of resolute ideologues, it has established itself to an astonishing degree in the affections of the population. It used to cover not merely medical interventions and medicines, but also dentistry and the services of opticians. There always were

---

[4] There is a specifically Christian argument for this attention to particularity, which Hauerwas develops in his essay, 'Salvation and Health'. He writes, 'medicine needs the church ... as a resource of the habits and practices necessary to sustain the care of those in pain over the long haul. For it is no easy matter to be with the ill, especially when we cannot do much for them other than simply be present' (81). I have heard precisely this view from experienced staff working with the chronically mentally sick. But there is a Christian task of being present with a patient of another religion.

[5] It goes without saying that the helpful and moving treatment of people with learning difficulties (so-called 'mental handicap') does not bear directly on the issue surrounding mental sickness.

[6] See G. Rivett, *From Cradle to Grave: Fifty Years of the NHS* (London: King's Fund Publishing, 1998).

cosmetic exclusions, but, on the whole, if someone said they needed something urgently enough it was likely to be provided. Hence the saying, 'You can get it on the National Health.'

In the 1980s the twin developments of increasingly expensive, technologically sophisticated, diagnostics and interventions, and an inexorably rising tide of health expectations, drew the NHS into a state of permanent and irresolvable crisis. For the first time the public was brought face to face with the finitude of health care budgets, and the word 'rationing' was mentioned. Contributions and means' testing became ways of generating revenue. Private health care provision grew rapidly as a way of meeting the demand for certain forms of elective surgery and other non-urgent services. To a large degree dentistry and optometry were privatised. Hence the need to ask whether a service is currently available 'on the National Health'.

At the point at which hospitals entered the National Health Service, there were of course some very searching questions to ask whether or not chaplaincy provision did or did not belong to the service. In the event, following discussion between the Secretary of State for Health and the Archbishop of Canterbury, chaplaincy was written into the 1946 NHS Act. In practice the question had nothing to do with the issue of establishment. England and Scotland had (different) established churches; Wales and Northern Ireland had not. The issue was resolved locally and pragmatically. It was only in the later 1980s that the question arose in a more systematic way, as a consequence of two related developments introduced by the Conservative government: the internal separation of health purchasers and health providers, and the intervention of a consumer-type charter (the Patient's Charter) as a further means of raising standards of provision. It was in this charter that we find reference to 'respect for privacy, dignity and religious beliefs', followed by a Health Service Guideline (HSG(92)2) exhorting, 'where necessary, ... every effort to provide for the spiritual needs of patients and staff'. Hence the question whether you can now 'get' spirituality on the NHS.

It is ironic enough that the question of spirituality should arise in the context of the widespread commodification of health care, the imposition of an internal market, with the ethos of value for money. It was widely, but in the event inaccurately, predicted, that hospital chaplaincy could not survive economic scrutiny. Again the outcomes are local and pragmatic, but the cumulative evidence is that chaplaincy, far from shrinking, has flourished. A hospital chaplain may well regard the reference to spiritual needs in the Patient's Charter as his or her foot in the door.

It is doubly ironic, however, both that British public rhetoric should have travelled a considerable distance into multiculturalism since 1948, and that the word 'spirituality' should itself have broadened out from its origins in Christian vocabulary. We are, it is repeated endlessly, no longer a Christian but a multi-religious, multi-cultural and multi-ethnic society. This proposition is most often found on the lips of secularised white liberals, who have little or no idea of the real size of the respective religious communities in the United Kingdom, who constantly confuse cultural and religious questions, but who are quite sure that the influence of Christianity in public life is too great and ought to be diminished. For such people it would be entirely desirable that the word 'spirituality' should be defined in such a way as to embrace, in the first place, all religions, and in the second place, if at all possible, all philosophies of life. Only under such circumstances would it be tolerable that 'spirituality' should be available on the NHS.

I have outlined this point of view in a somewhat sharp manner, though it is rare for it to be held openly in that form. My experience of this position is that it is usually held presuppositionally and implicitly, in ignorance of its roots in philosophical liberalism. Even those who are somewhat inclined to this belief system are open to local compromises of a pragmatic kind, provided that outcomes move in what they deem to be a suitably progressive direction.

But there are substantial problems, which it is the intention of this contribution to analyse. The first derives from the history of the word 'spirituality' and what is involved in its definition. The second is disclosed from a closer examination of the implication of spirituality for mental sickness. The argument from both enquiries will lead to the conclusion that there is no viable alternative, if the spiritual needs of a patient are to be taken seriously, to attention to particulars. It will be argued that there is no thoroughfare between the generalising drift of the under-standing of spirituality which I have depicted, and what is required if a person in mental distress is to be spiritually sustained.

One further introductory matter must be made clear, especially in the light of my earlier comments, and in view of the fact that as a diocesan bishop of the Church of England I participated briefly and in a modest way in the government of the United Kingdom through member-ship of its second chamber.[7] My instinct would be to be fiercely defensive of the interests and commitments of wholehearted participants of other religious traditions. Knowledge of such through personal acquaintance both alerts me to the danger of majoritarian presumptuousness and of the unconscious marginalisation of minorities, and also convinces me that their concerns and interests are not advanced by the abolition of any form of religious particu-larism. The Christian establishments of England and Scotland do not, in my experience, work to the disad-vantage of other religious traditions. On the other hand, the disestablishment of the Church in Wales has not resulted in the collapse of Christianity in that nation, nor (so far as I am aware) in any notable advancement of the civil liberties of minority religious groups. As my argument will make clear, the paying of attention to partic-ulars, not least in the mental health field, is supportive of

---

[7] I am aware that so thorough an identification with the 'establishment' puts me at odds with the author of *After Christendom?* (Nashville, TN: Abingdon Press, 1991). My intention to correspond with Stanley during that period of involvement with 'the powers that be' came, alas, to nothing. It was a modest reassurance to know that, in his view, there is no great virtue in being 'out of power' and that 'the question for Christians is not whether we rule, but how' (*After Christendom?*, 166).

the needs and interests of each religious group, indeed of sub-groups within each general tradition.

III

The etymological derivation of 'spirituality' is directly from a Latin word *spirit(u)alitas*, an abstract noun formed, of course, on the basis of *spiritus* (spirit) and *spirit(u)alis* (spiritual). *Spiritus* was frequently used in the Latin versions of the New Testament to translate the Greek *pneuma*, which itself was deployed in a wide variety of meanings including 'wind', 'breath', 'life' and 'soul'. The Hebrew Bible spoke of the Spirit of God, and the New Testament of the Holy Spirit. *Spiritus* was the Latin translation for both these terms. There is notorious difficulty in the translation of certain passages from the letters of St Paul, where there is an opposition between *pneuma* (Latin, *spiritus*) and *sarx* (Latin, *caro*), or between *pneumatikos* (Latin, *spiritalis*) (often rendered as 'spiritual') or *sarkinos* (Latin, *carnalis*) and *sarkikos* (often rendered as 'carnal').[8]

In the immensely influential King James (Authorised) translation of the Scriptures one such passage read as follows:

> (1) There is therefore now no condemnation to them which are in Christ Jesus, who walk not after the flesh, but after the Spirit ... (6) For to be carnally minded is death; but to be spiritually minded is life and peace ... (13) For if ye live after the flesh, ye shall die: but if ye through the Spirit do mortify the deeds of the body, ye shall live. (from Romans 8.1–13)

Modern commentators point out that the key word in this passage is *pneuma*. Some take the view that on each

---

[8] See the article 'Pneuma, pneumatikos' in *The Theological Dictionary of the New Testament*, Vol. VI (Grand Rapids, MI: Wm B. Eerdmans, 1968), 332–455.

occasion the reference is to the Holy Spirit of God; others that it is sometimes to a created spiritual capacity in humankind. Thus to be 'spiritually minded' could be either to share the mind of the Holy Spirit (as distinct from the values, desires and purposes of fallen human nature or 'the flesh'); or to focus on the higher capacities of the human.[9]

A similar uncertainty attends the translation of 'the deeds of the body'. It could mean literally the body's activities, such as sleeping, working and so forth; or alternatively the activities and schemings of fallen human nature. The 'flesh', the 'carnal mind', the 'deeds of the body' are, however interpreted, undoubtedly set in opposition to the 'law of the Spirit of life'. The implication that what is bodily is, *ipso facto*, sinful, is ready to hand. And though the doctrine of the incarnation of the Son of God ('of the seed of David according to the flesh', Romans 1.3; but compare 'in the likeness of sinful flesh', Romans 8.3) argues against the idea that the flesh is inherently corrupt and corrupting, nonetheless Christian thought has always struggled with negativism about the body (not least in relation to sexuality). And the corollary of that pessimism is a corresponding deformation in the category of the 'spiritual'.

Modern translators demonstrate their keenness to avoid attaching negative connotations to the 'flesh' by translating the Greek term as 'lower nature', 'human nature', 'sinful nature', 'unspiritual nature' or 'old nature'. But the use of these terms is itself evidence of a modern sensitivity. The history of Christian thought provides evidence of two distinct trends. The first is to assimilate spirituality to the specific action of the Holy Spirit of God. In this sense a fifth-century author writes, 'So act as to advance in spirituality'.[10] The second, however, built upon and sharpened the ambiguous distinction noted above in the writings of Paul, to provide a 'spiritual' contrast with corporality or

---

[9] C. E. B. Cranfield, *The Epistle to the Romans*, Vol. 2, (Edinburgh: T&T Clark, 1975), 370–403.

[10] Pseudo-Jerome, Epist. 7. *PL* 30:114D–115A, cited in art. 'Spirituality, Christian' in *The New Dictionary of Catholic Spirituality* (Collegeville, MN: Liturgical Press, 1993), 932.

materiality. The seeds of disdain for the body and for matter were already being sown. It did not help that ecclesiastical matters or persons, as distinct from lay or 'worldly' existences, came to be spoken of as the 'spiritual estate', or 'lords spiritual' and their property, revenue or rights as the 'spiritualities'. All these uses were taken into English, and indeed continue in the Church of England to this day.

The editors of the *Oxford English Dictionary* note that the use of 'spirituality' to mean the quality or condition of being spiritual in the moral or religious sense, developed quite rapidly in the seventeenth century. In French *spiritualité* was a word used to denote the devout life; a German equivalent was *Frommigkeit*. In English there is an eighteenth-century example of this precise usage in William Cowper's works where, in a letter, the poet refers to 'that spirituality which once enlivened all our intercourse'.[11]

All these European uses are, naturally enough, Christian. They are polyvalent, trading upon the complexity of the biblical background and terminology for the divine Spirit and human spirit. When used by a devout evangelical like William Cowper, 'spirituality' would imply both enjoyment of fellowship in the Holy Spirit and the realisation of the human capacity for deep friendship. In other contexts it might well lose some of the Christian theological overtones of the former kind.

This brief review would be incomplete without mention of the major advance of the term in the twentieth century, largely as a result of two influential French Roman Catholic works, Auguste Sandreau's *Manuel de spiritualité* (1917), and the four volume *La spiritualité catholique* by the Abbé Pierre Pourra, and the massive *Dictionnaire de spiritualité ascétique et mystique,* begun in 1932 and only completed in sixteen volumes in 1994.[12] In the latter, the article on

---

[11] Cited in the *Oxford English Dictionary* from the 1837 edition of his works, Vol. XV, 194.
[12] See L. Tinsley, *The French Expressions for Spirituality and Devotion* (New York: Catholic University of America Press, 1953).

Spiritualité by Aimé Solignac distinguishes helpfully
between three meanings of the word: the first contains a
specifically religious application to the spiritual life, and is
frequently opposed to carnal or animal experience; the
second is a philosophical usage to denote a specifically
non-corporeal mode of being or of knowing; and the third,
as we already noted, is the juridical idea of the functions,
possessions and rights of the clergy as distinct from those
which are merely temporal.[13] What happens in the
twentieth century, at an accelerating rate after the 1950s, is
a twofold development: the application of the term 'spirituality' to the religious life of religions other than
Christianity, and the deployment of the term philosophi-
cally in such examples as 'the spirituality of feminism',
'spirituality of Marxism' and so forth.[14] The latter are by no
means misuses of the term, though they are analogical, as
we shall see. But their currency greatly increases the
likelihood of ambiguity and misunderstanding. One may
propose a rule for the contemporary use of 'spirituality':
no-one should use this term unadvisedly, lightly or
wantonly, but discretely and soberly, conscious of its
historical roots, complexity and ambivalence.

The natural assumption we make, when confronted
with a complex term, is that clarity can only be achieved by
careful definition. There is, however, quite a large class of
general terms which we use with deliberate and
unavoidable ambiguity to indicate a field of phenomena.
Consider, for example, the case of 'art'. We know enough
about the term to use it in ordinary conversation, and for
the titles of books and courses; we can readily distinguish
between what is undoubted art, such as the Mona Lisa, and
what is not art, such as a plate of food or a pile of chicken
droppings. On the other hand such is the ambiguity of the
term, that we can take in our stride the possibility that

[13] Art. 'Spiritualité, le mot et l'histoire', in *Dictionnaire de spiritualité
ascétique et mystique* (Beauchesne, Paris, 1990), 1141–60.
[14] Art. 'Spirituality', in *A Dictionary of Christian Spirituality* (London: SCM
Press, 1986), 361–3.

some plates of food may be works of art, and the fact that art galleries have given space to unusual substances.

In relation to terms like 'art', 'power' or 'religion' it is generally a mistake to attempt to proceed to clarity by means of the kind of definition which would finally determine whether or not a given phenomenon was an instance of the general term. Or if very precise definition is attempted, then the implicit theory (necessarily a debatable theory) begins to obtrude into the terms of the definition, with the result that the universality or normativity of the definition is sacrificed to the partiality of the preferred theory. What happens then, of course, is that only protagonists of that theory find the definition clear and helpful; others are forced to invent a rival.

How then are the terms to be understood, if there are no precise definitions of them? It is always possible, as Wittgenstein suggested, to indicate the kind of thing one means by pointing to an example. 'That', one may say, indicating a framed masterpiece, 'is art'; likewise, 'that', indicating the current state of my desk, 'is not art'. A good number of examples increase clarity, but it does not finally help in establishing the boundaries beyond dispute. Based on examples a very broad definition may be constructed. Clarity emerges by thinking through the examples, not by refining the terms of definition. It is a theory, not the act of definition, which eventually may determine boundaries between 'art' and 'not art'. But theory wrapped up as definition can be seriously misleading.

A recent work which deals with the issue of spirituality in relation to health care rather clearly illustrates the difficulties. A number of authors offer definitions of 'spirituality' or 'the spiritual'. It is defined, for example, as: 'A search for existential meaning within a life experience, with reference to a power other than the self, which may not necessarily be called "God" '.[15]

The author offers a Venn diagram of interrelationships:

[15] Peter Speck, in M. Cobb and V. Robshaw (eds), *The Spiritual Challenge of Health Care* (Edinburgh: Churchill Livingstone, 1998), 21ff.

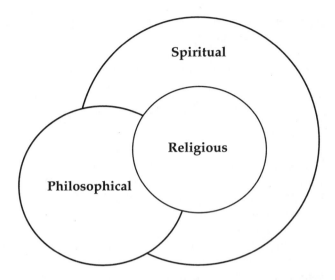

Or another contributor in similar vein proposes a definition as follows:

> The human propensity to find meaning in life through self-transcendence ... evident in perspectives and behaviours that express a sense of relatedness to a transcendent dimension or to something greater than the self, and may or may not include religious participation.[16]

In both cases one notes the concern to ensure that the definition of 'spirituality' is broader than that of religion. This feature has been noted by a third contributor who offers to compare what counts as 'spirituality' in five of the world religions. He comes to the following bleak, but not unjustified conclusion:

> The health care understanding of 'spirituality' is a secularised version of the Christian understanding of spirituality ... For those from other religious

---

[16] Pamela Reed in *Family Community Health* 14 (1991), 15.

traditions, such an account seems strange and, often deeply irreligious.[17]

It is at this point that it becomes irresistible to introduce the comment of the ever-surprising Scottish *Encyclopaedia of Religion and Ethics* (13 vols, T&T Clark, 1908–26), still being reprinted after 70 years. Its brief article on Spirituality opens with the following quotable sentences:

> The term 'spirituality' has been used in a great variety of ways. The French have appropriated it as the name for the finer perceptions of life; by the American transcendentalists it is used as a special mark of superior intellects; it is often applied to those mediums through which departed spirits are said to reach common earth; Evangelical Christianity reserves the term to describe the warmer religious emotions; and it has its proper and peculiar application as the distinguishing quality of NT believers.[18]

My conclusions at this stage are:

> (i) that 'spirituality' is an instance of a general term which is characterised by unavoidable ambiguity;
> (ii) that it is not clarified by attempting to offer the kind of definition which purports to resolve the boundary disputes;
> (iii) that all such definitions are theory-laden, and that the theories themselves need careful elucidation and discussion; and
> (iv) that it is preferable to elucidate the term by pointing out instances of what is indubitably spirituality.

To proceed somewhat slowly and carefully at this point, it is necessary to ask what follows from the fact that, as we

---

[17] Ian Markham, in Cobb and Robshaw, *The Spiritual Challenge of Health Care*, 74.
[18] Art. 'Spirituality', *Encyclopaedia of Religion and Ethics*, Vol. XI (1920), 808.

have seen, the term 'spirituality' grew within the Latin Christian tradition and was based on an opposition between what is 'spiritual' and what is 'carnal' contained in the Letters of St Paul and therefore common to all Christian traditions. It does not follow that Christians have acquired, as it were, patent rights over the way in which the term is used in all subsequent discourse. The body–soul dichotomy is a commonplace of Greek philosophy before Christ, and there is in Hebrew religion an understanding of personhood involving the animation of flesh by the breath of God (in Greek the term is translated by *pneuma*). The relationship became complex because, with the intro- duction of Hellenism into the ancient Near East, a somewhat similar though never identical distinction between soul and body began to figure in Israelite thought. For example, for Philo, a first-century eclectic Jewish philosopher of Alexandria, the flesh of humankind is the cause and seat of ignorance and the soul is the vehicle for the higher life. But this constitutes only one strand in the Jewish traditions of the day; other authorities stick more closely and literally to the biblical text. In relation to all of them it would make sense to use the term 'spirituality', provided one did not import either philosophical or Christian assumptions into its use. In other words the discipline of attending to differences in the practices and conceptualities of particular traditions and sub-traditions facilitates the use of a general term to signify something in Hebrew and Jewish thought analogous to its established use in Christianity. But it is the particularities which inform the content of the general term 'spirituality'. By itself it signifies not much more than the consequences of living wholeheartedly within the religion (or sub-section of the religion) known as X.

Applied to the Christian faith in general it would entail understanding that a Christian sees his or her life as involving fellowship (*koinonia*) with God, through the power of the atoning death of Jesus Christ, God's only Son. To define 'spirituality' as 'the human propensity to find meaning in life' is not merely to retreat from the concrete specificity of Christian spirituality. It is a transformation from a God-centred account to one focused on humanity, which, if offered as a substitute for a Christian under-standing, would be simply in massive contradiction to the main strands of the Christian tradition.

One would expect that similar claims would emanate from Jewish, Muslim, Hindu and Buddhist authorities. If the word were acceptable to them (which could be presup-posed), their understandings of 'spirituality' would be related to their own specific practices and conceptualities and to those of sub-traditions within the broadly denomi-nated group. To understand 'spirituality' as a general term requires disciplined attention to particularities, not the imposition of a general theory under the guise of a definition.

Can, then, the term function successfully outside the context of religion, for example in the phrase 'the spiritu-ality of feminism'? If so, it would be vital to acknowledge that the use could only be enlightening if it were recog-nised to be analogical. There may be enough similarity to make the usage not positively misleading, though one might wonder why another term like 'ethos' should not be preferred. But even if it were the case that there were grounds for using 'spirituality' outside the context of religion, it would not follow that one definition would capture all that is common to the various usages. A may be like B in virtue of feature p; and A may be like C in virtue of feature q. But there is no reason to think that, as a consequence, A, B and C share anything in common.

This conclusion is undoubtedly inconvenient to legis-lators. But we should notice that there are other general terms in wide use also enshrined in UK legislation, such as 'religion' and 'worship'. These raise similar difficulties. But it cannot be required by Parliament that every kindly soul giving thought to the meaning of life has something in common, named 'spirituality', with Christians, Jews, Muslims, Buddhists and Hindus. If the word is to be used at all we proceed to some clarity, not by definitions, but by attending to particular traditions. But this, it turns out, is precisely what is needed for those suffering from sickness of the mind.

IV

At this point I want to refer to two vivid accounts from Christians, separated in time by more than two hundred years, of the spiritual crises which accompanied their mental sickness. The first is William Cowper (1731–1800), the unforgettable narrative of whose attempts at suicide, committal to a mental hospital, conversion and subsequent recovery is contained in his autobiographical work *Adelphi*.[19] Though the whole narrative is cast in the classic form of an evangelical conversion, with its account of early indifference, preliminary stirrings of interest, culminating in a wholehearted transformation provoked by the text of Scripture and followed by an indescribable experience of joy and peace, nonetheless this is woven together with a searing account of an acute psychotic state followed by substantial recovery of health.

Cowper had been struck down with fear at the prospect of public examination of his credentials to hold secretarial office in the House of Lords. He describes his inability to sleep, his paranoia and his unsuccessful attempts to commit suicide. Friends finally realised the seriousness of his sickness, and conveyed him to Dr Cotton's *Collegium Insanorum* in St Albans. Cowper gives a vivid account of his arrival and first encounters. It was, we are perhaps surprised to learn, a benign institution – at least in Cowper's experience – though it has not so far proved possible to discover either the theory or the practice which characterised its regime.

Cowper tells us that he was deeply convinced that God would shortly take vengeance upon him for his sins, and that he would be cast into hell. Becoming accustomed to this gloomy prospect he remarks somewhat wryly, he eventually rather wished he had seized greater opportunities for wickedness in earlier days. His movement

---

[19] The first printed edition of *Adelphi* appeared posthumously in 1802. It was evidently written in 1770, the year of his brother's death; J. King and C. Ryskamp (eds.), *The Letters and Prose Writings of William Cowper*, Vol. 1 (Oxford: Oxford University Press, 1979).

towards conversion was accompanied by better sleep and happier dreams, and also by renewed contact with the Bible. It was eight months after his arrival that he read (in Romans 3.25) that Jesus was the propitiation for our sin; 'immediately I received strength to believe it'. Indeed his euphoria was such as to alarm his doctor. 'Too happy to sleep much, yet I rose refreshed as after long rest ... Oh that this ardour of my first love had continued'.[20] He continued in the college for a further twelve months enjoying daily conversation with Dr Cotton, leaving in June 1765 for the town of Huntingdon.

There is, of course, an economic background to this eighteen-month stay in a hospital. Cowper had access to just sufficient private income, and also had important London friends. But he was fortunate indeed to find so sympathetic a regime; the more purely medical prescriptions by the same doctor in a later acute episode had no obvious efficacy. Looking back on the sickness Cowper writes, 'A vein of self-loathing and abhorrence ran through all my misery'.[21] Tempting though it might be to relate this to a failed love-relationship, or to a mysterious deformity much spoken of by Cowper's biographers, as he tells his own narrative his recovery derived from the personal appropriation of the Christian doctrine of the atoning sacrifice of Christ. Moreover the doctor responsible for his care was a man ready and able to sustain religiously edifying discourse with his patient; 'the Gospel was always the delightful theme for our conversation'.[22]

My second example is from a contemporary, the noted Anglican priest and spiritual writer, Jim Cotter.[23] Writing of the background to his severe reactive depression, he speaks of never having been 'comfortably at home in my flesh-body', of his homosexual orientation and difficulties of sustaining intimacy in a relationship, of two bereavements incompletely grieved over and of an unexpressed

---

[20] Cowper, *Adelphi*, 40.
[21] Cowper, *Adelphi*, 34.
[22] Cowper, *Adelphi*, 40.
[23] J. Cotter, *Brainsquall: Soundings from a Deep Depression* (Sheffield and Cambridge: Carins/Arthur James, 1997), 20.

deep anger 'focused from time to time on parents and churches'.[24]

In a central part of his reflections, Cotter offers a series of meditations on the theme of power and powerlessness.

> There is a terrifying aspect of love: the love that is insistent, consistent, that will not let go, that will take you through breakdown, breakup, heartbreak, that is with you and in you as you journey. I dare not say that God *caused* my crisis, but I can claim that God keeps faith, keeps contact, keeps loving, bearing with me all the consequences of the misuses of our human freedom.[25]

He makes it clear that it was precisely a conviction of God's love, manifested in Jesus' touching untouchables by word and deed, which enabled him to come to terms with the stigma of being gay and having been sectioned.

> For me, it was a new conversion, a penny-dropping moment of disclosure, a historian's considered opinion about what was at the heart of Jesus' mission meeting a profound personal need at a moment when I could receive it.[26]

There are, of course, certain parallels with Cowper's account. Both experience at one and the same time a sickness of the mind and a religious crisis. For both there is a deliverance from deeply laid feelings of worthlessness, amounting to a conversion or new conversion. Both draw upon biblical tradition as interpreted within the Church for their liberation. But at the same time no one can miss the differences, and it is the differences which make the difference. For Cowper, Christ's propitiatory sacrificial death was the content of the deliverance from the conviction of God's vengeful wrath. There is not a hint of

---

[24] Cotter, *Brainsquall*, 13.
[25] Cotter, *Brainsquall*, 42–3.
[26] Cotter, *Brainsquall*, 71.

that in Cotter's account, two hundred years later. For him it is Christ's breaking of the religious taboos of his day which was crucial, especially to self-acceptance of his sexual orientation.

But at the same time, different though the content of the two liberations are, they are both clearly the product of interpretative traditions of a given period. It is obvious to the modern reader that Cowper has constructed his account in the form of an evangelical conversion narrative, whose doctrinal basis is the penal satisfaction theory of the atonement popularised by late Calvinism. It is no less obvious – indeed Cotter's explicit reference to a late twentieth century New Testament historian makes it plain – that he has also constructed an account. In his case it has taken the form of a narrative of self-acceptance whose warrant lies in a hypothetical reconstruction of Jesus' ministry. It is not incidental to Cotter's purpose that the author in question, a Roman Catholic, is reported to have been in trouble with ecclesiastical authority, and that two other scholars who disagreed with his conclusion are said to be 'more acceptable ... to religious establishments; and themselves nearer to their centre'.[27]

What both these narratives teach us is the vital importance of attentiveness to particularity. It would not have been of much help to Cotter to have wondered whether he had yet come to believe and to accept for himself Jesus' propitiatory sacrifice; nor, on the other hand, to Cowper, to have been invited to accept his 'flesh-body'. Both accounts are at the same time real and constructed; neither could be subjected to external reconstruction without significant loss to the sufferer. In particular it would not seem to be helpful to propose that their 'real' content was some human search for existential meaning. An observer viewpoint on the narratives is simply that – another construction. Nor indeed is the medical interpretation of the person's sickness free from the constraints of

[27] Cotter, *Brainsquall*, 73. The reference is to John Dominic Crossan, *Jesus: A Revolutionary Biography* (HarperSanFrancisco: San Francisco, 1994).

time and culture. In my next section, I propose to deal with the relationship between differing constructions and their impact upon healing.

V

The medical anthropologist Arthur Kleinman, in his important work *Patients and Healers in the Context of Culture*, claims as a 'key axiom in medical anthropology' a dichotomy between 'disease' and 'illness'.

> *Disease* refers to the malfunctioning of biological and/or psychological processes, while the term *illness* refers to the psychosocial experience and meaning of perceived disease ... Constructing illness from disease is a central function of health care systems (a coping function) and the first stage of healing.[28]

It would be tempting, perhaps particularly from a strictly medical point of view, to equate the distinction with a simple fact–value dichotomy. On this interpretation the 'disease' would be the bio-medical facts of the matter, while the 'illness' would be what any given culture might make of the condition, its (not infrequently mistaken) interpretative overlay. But that is not Kleinman's point. Both disease and illness are, according to him, 'constructs in particular configurations of social reality ..., explanatory models anchored in the different explanatory systems and social structural arrangements comprising the separate sectors (and subsectors) of local health care systems'.[29]

Against this supposed dichotomy it could be objected that no such distinction exists in ordinary language, where 'disease' and 'illness' are frequently interchangeable terms. But such would be by no means a decisive consideration, even if one concedes (as I believe one must) that the

---

[28] A. Kleinman, *Patients and Healers in the Context of Culture* (Berkeley, CA: University of California Press, 1980), 72.
[29] Kleinman, *Patients and Healers*, 73.

'dichotomy' is highly prescriptive in the manner in which it is expressed. Kleinman's principal point is a contention of great force, namely that the way in which both medical personnel and lay people interpret sickness is in terms of explanatory models which do not have any simple status as 'fact'. Some of these models are oriented towards the individual's bio-medical condition, as perceived by a particular tradition of medical intervention, others are oriented towards his or her behaviour and relationships in the social world. As Kleinman observes, 'at times we can talk securely about disease *qua* disease, but illness cannot be understood in that way: it can only be understood in a specific context of norms, symbolic meanings, and social interaction'.[30]

One way in which the dichotomy can be put to work is in relation to the stories in the New Testament Gospels of Jesus' curing people suffering from 'evil spirits and diseases' (see, for example, Luke 7.21; 8.2, 26–39; 9.1, 37–43; 10.14–20). Lacking at this distance any precise knowledge of what would count as 'disease' and what as 'evil spirits', it is helpful to say of both that they are constructs within a specific context of norms and symbolic meanings. These meanings would include, of course, the theological significance of the Messiah making war upon evil, as a sign of the arrival of the last days. It is simply impossible to say whether the naked, demon-possessed man who lived among the tombs on the far shore of Galilee (Luke 11.26–39) was suffering from what a modern psychiatrist would identify as a specific disease of the mind. The recognition has the useful consequence of both discouraging modern psychiatric science from treating the Christian traditions of exorcism as primitive practices which we have outgrown, and also of denying to over-enthusiastic contemporary Christian would-be exorcists the warrant of biblical authority.

A recent Muslim writer makes use of Kleinman's dichotomy in helpfully disputing the apparent implication that 'cultures' are identifiable, separate and self-contained

---

[30] Kleinman, *Patients and Healers*, 77.

entities. Such an assumption, he notes, would lead one to expect to be able to describe an 'Islamic view', of mental health (as distinct from a 'Western view') which could then be useful in interpreting the experience of Muslim clients or patients.[31] He rightly points out that these alleged points of view are themselves constructs, which are anything but simple, known, uniform and contrasting essences. To a Christian writer this is an important observation, because of the suspicions with which Christian points of view frequently disappear behind 'Western' constructs, despite the fact that the latter may originate in models of rationality or human nature which are in no way distinctively Christian in source or form, though they may have been assimilated to certain Christian themes or elements.

Where then does the root of the distinction between a religiously inspired view of humankind, and that of a religiously neutral or secular understanding, lie? Aziz Esmail identifies the site of the contrast in attitudes towards individual autonomy. Whereas the Jewish, Christian and Muslim religions place human beings in a symbol system which makes them members of communities and thus essentially relational beings, disenchanted Western science has adopted a Hobbesian view of humanity, according to which each individual is engaged in a struggle for self-fulfilment and autonomy; communities are only made with difficulty. The purpose of this observation is not, however, to destroy the claims of modern psychiatry. Rather, it is to propose that understanding both 'disease' and 'illness' contain evaluative elements.

> It is not by rejecting the insights of modern medicine and science that the science of the mind will move forward. It is not by a return to pre-scientific or pre-modern systems that our knowledge of human nature will advance. It is by a joint engagement between various cultural communities, in re-assessing

[31] Aziz Esmail, 'Islamic Communities and Mental Health', in Dinesh Bhugra (ed.), *Psychiatry and Religion* (London: Routledge, 1996), 138–54.

the philosophical ground beneath modern medicine (and by extension other professions) that the next advance will come.[32]

This 'intercultural creativity' demands of psychiatrists that they recognise the importance of philosophical reflection. Models of disease are not simple scientific facts, but symbolic constructs with a history and philosophical implications. As Bill Fulford puts it:

> Philosophy can contribute to good practice in this area by helping us to retain an imaginative, flexible and adaptive approach to clinical work, sensitive to the values, wishes and experiences of the users of psychiatric services, and open to the diverse paradigms of the multidisciplinary team.[33]

VI

To return to the issue of the definition of 'spirituality' which was our starting point, it should now be apparent that the proper function of the term is to point not to one thing, but to a collection of disparate phenomena. The word is an arrow and an exclamation mark. Look here and be attentive! We have considered the narratives of two different and highly articulate Christian writers. But exactly the same point can and should be made of the religiously inarticulate, for whom a mental sickness may also be a crisis of identity and direction. In Kleinman's terms, for everyone there is the experience of illness as well as disease. By inviting a physician to attend to a patient's spiritual needs and concerns, which is entirely right and proper, one is not asking him or her for a definition of 'spirituality'. It is rather to propose alertness to a highly specific way in which the patient is set within a

---

[32] Esmail, 'Islamic Communities and Mental Health', 152.
[33] Bill Fulford, in Cobb and Robshaw, *The Spiritual Challenge of Health Care*, 18.

faith-tradition. A mental sickness presents itself both as a disease and as an illness. That faith-tradition may well be the key to a patient's illness, in the precise sense that the construct 'illness' is the first stage in healing.

Implicit in the same approach is the request to those engaged in psychiatric interventions that they have the humility to see their own understanding of disease in an historical and philosophical context, as an organically focused construct. In neither construct are we engaged in evading the issue of truth. The psychiatrist is bound to be open to the reformulation of models of disease in the light of further enquiry and evidence. Issues of truth also arise in religious discourse, though it is not (usually) within the competence or training of a psychiatrist to offer judgements between rival claims. And truth is also involved, of course, in the distinction between delusion and belief, though that discussion is well beyond the brief of this essay.

5

The First Word Christians Have to Say About Violence Is 'Church': On Bonhoeffer, Baptists, and Becoming a Peace Church

Mark Thiessen Nation

Introduction: Pacifist and Enemy of the State

In March of 1936 Bishop Theodor Heckel, the official in charge of church foreign affairs for Germany, referred to Dietrich Bonhoeffer as 'a pacifist and an enemy of the state'.[1] These epithets were intended to discredit Bonhoeffer both theologically and politically. For who, in Nazi Germany, would give any credence to the thoughts of a pacifist or an enemy of the state? It is almost impossible for us imaginatively to place ourselves back in that time and place – and to imagine how offensive much of what Bonhoeffer said and did was. That is because now most of us believe Bonhoeffer had the right positions on political issues. And most have come to believe that if Bonhoeffer was ever committed to pacifism it was something he outgrew. But his mature commitment to peace and justice is something we admire; he was prophetic.

Today Stanley Hauerwas is a pacifist and is often referred to as a sectarian or a tribalist, not quite the same as 'enemy of the state', but perhaps intended to connote an enemy of the good of the state. The aim is to label him dismissively as someone who doesn't care about the world, who doesn't

---

[1] The reference for this statement is given in an earlier essay I wrote on Bonhoeffer. See Mark Nation, ' "Pacifist and Enemy of the State": Bonhoeffer's "Straight and Unbroken Course" from Costly Discipleship to Conspiracy', *Journal of Theology for Southern Africa* 77 (1991), 61–77, specific reference 61.

care about the big issues of peace and justice beyond the walls of the church, and someone who can safely be ignored by anyone not wishing to be sectarian.[2] Now I am not in this essay going to engage in a substantial comparison of Bonhoeffer and Hauerwas. But I think it might be instructive to consider the possibility that the central theological concerns informing Bonhoeffer's approach to peace and justice are in some important ways similar to Hauerwas'.[3] (I will return briefly to Bonhoeffer at the end of this essay.)

Most readers of this essay would probably still agree with the sentiments with which Hauerwas first approached the writings of John Howard Yoder, who convinced him to be a pacifist: 'the last thing I wanted to be was a pacifist'.[4] However, if theologians, ethicists, and peace and justice activists are to understand Hauerwas' writings on peace it is vital for them to understand that he could only have been convinced to be a pacifist by compelling theological arguments.[5] Hauerwas is first and always a Christian theologian. For him peace is centrally a theological issue. This

[2] These claims are quite preposterous. Some of the quotations from Hauerwas in this essay should make that clear. His own many writings on many different subjects should also make this clear. But also see the books on Hauerwas by Wells and Rasmusson, mentioned in footnotes in the biographical sketch of Hauerwas, above, as well as the essay by Nigel Biggar in this book.
[3] For ways of construing Bonhoeffer that make this claim clearer, see Mark Thiessen Nation, 'Discipleship in a World Full of Nazis: Dietrich Bonhoeffer's Polyphonic Pacifism as Social Ethics', in *The Wisdom of the Cross: Essays in Honor of John Howard Yoder*, eds. Stanley Hauerwas, Chris K. Huebner, Harry J. Huebner and Mark Thiessen Nation (Grand Rapids, MI: Wm B. Eerdmans, 1999), 249–77; and L. Gregory Jones, 'The Cost of Forgiveness: Dietrich Bonhoeffer and the Reclamation of a Christian Vision and Practice', in *Embodying Forgiveness: A Theological Analysis* (Grand Rapids, MI: Wm B. Eerdmans, 1995), 3–33.
[4] Stanley Hauerwas, *The Peaceable Kingdom* (Notre Dame, IN: University of Notre Dame Press, 1983), xxiv.
[5] For Hauerwas' accounts of Yoder's compelling theology, see Stanley Hauerwas, 'Messianic Pacifism', *Worldview* 16 (1973), 29–33; Stanley Hauerwas, 'The Nonresistant Church: The Theological Ethics of John Howard Yoder', in *Vision and Virtue* (Notre Dame, IN: Fides/Claretian, 1974 [reprinted University of Notre Dame Press, 1981], 197–221; Stanley Hauerwas, 'When the Politics of Jesus Makes a Difference', *Christian Century* 110 (13 October 1993), 982–7; and Stanley Hauerwas and Chris K. Huebner, 'History, Theology, and Anabaptism: A Conversation on Theology after John Howard Yoder', in *The Wisdom of the Cross*, 391–408.

can be seen in some of his comments on the use of the word pacifism: 'Christians are non-violent not because certain implications may follow from their beliefs, but because the very shape of their beliefs form them to be non-violent'.[6] In another place he says that pacifism, as he understands it, is not intelligible apart from the cross and resurrection of Jesus.[7] Or again, 'pacifism ... is not some "teaching" about nonviolence but rather is a way of talking about a community that has learned to deal with conflicts through truth rather than violence – and that truth is no general or universal teaching about agape but the concrete presence of a life'.[8] Which is to say that for Hauerwas, as for Bonhoeffer, convictions about peace are integrally related to theology and the life of the Church. Another way Hauerwas has put the same concern, speaking specifically about war, is to say: 'The first word we as Christians have to say to the world about war is 'church.'' '.[9]

Since Church and its convictions and practices are fundamental to Hauerwas' own understanding of pacifism, it seems appropriate for me to provide an account of my own conversion to pacifism within the context of the life of a church. I am an American living in London. I grew up in a small, poor, rural community in southern Illinois. When I was a child my parents were not Christians; thus I did not grow up in church. But at age 17, in 1970, I became a Christian.[10] I entered a new world that set me in a new direction and began the process of making me a new person. Now for this story.

---

[6] Stanley Hauerwas, 'Pacifism: Some Philosophical Considerations', *Faith and Philosophy* 2 (1985), 100.

[7] Stanley Hauerwas, 'The Testament of Friends', in *How My Mind Has Changed*, eds. James M. Wall and David Heim (Grand Rapids, MI: Wm B. Eerdmans, 1991), 4.

[8] Stanley Hauerwas, 'Epilogue: A Pacifist Response to the Bishops', in Paul Ramsey *Speak Up for Just War or Pacifism: A Critique of the United Methodist Bishops' Pastoral Letter 'In Defense of Creation'*, (University Park, PA: University of Pennsylvania Press, 1988), 162–3.

[9] Hauerwas, 'Epilogue', in *Speak Up for Just War or Pacifism*, 152.

[10] My entry into the Christian faith and the Church was a dramatic event. My life assumed a new direction beginning one particular evening. However, I am well aware that others begin their Christian life very differently. And I am aware that becoming Christian is a lifelong process.

Becoming Christian and Pacifist During the Vietnam Era

During 1970 many American universities were closed down temporarily because of student protests. Four university students fell dead after National Guardsmen opened fire on 1,000 student protesters at Kent State University in Ohio. On 9 May of that year over 75,000 demonstrators gathered in Washington, DC. These domestic demonstrations, and the violence attendant upon them, were related to significant disagreements over military involvement in Vietnam.

I knew about the conflict in Vietnam. It was hard not to: visual images of killing and dying in Vietnam were a regular feature of television newscasts and the front pages of newspapers. But I didn't know much. Though a-political is a term I long ago grew suspicious of as self-description, nonetheless in 1970 I was as close to being a-political as one could be. At age 17 I cared very little about news beyond the local. I almost never read newspapers. But because I watched the evening news, even I was made aware of the war in Vietnam.

There was one thing that related to this war of which I was quite conscious. Becoming 18. For at the age of 18 all males had to register with the military service. And at least it appeared, in 1970, that the odds were good that someone like myself would be going to Vietnam to fight. Like most young men I had no yearning to be killed in a war I knew nearly nothing about. However, it never occurred to me at age 16 to question whether I should be willing to kill others in war if my country asked me to. But my way of looking at all of this was about to change drastically.[11]

In October 1971 I became 18. However, one year earlier

---

[11] I believed then and still believe that a commitment to nonviolence is implied by the Gospel and its embodiment through the Church. However, I also believe that even for those Christians not so convinced there should still be a serious wrestling with the justifiability of any given call from the government to kill other human beings created in the image of God. Those Christians (including theologians) who reject pacifism need to ask what guidance is given to Christians in churches to reflect critically upon any specific military actions engaged in by the governments, including those where military service is demanded. (For references see note 69, below.)

I had become a Christian. Between the time I became a Christian and October 1971 some might say I did a good deal of soul searching. And that would be one way to put it. It did involve a great deal of inner turmoil and wrestling. But 'soul searching' is too subjective a term. For what was really happening is more remarkable than that. I was learning what it was to be Christian by being determinatively shaped by the life of the church in which I became a Christian, the First General Baptist Church of McLeansboro, Illinois.

In October 1971 I registered as a conscientious objector to war. I became a conscientious objector in a small, generally conservative town. I only know of one other person from my home county who also registered as a conscientious objector during the Vietnam War. I became a c.o. in the face of objections from my father who, as a World War II veteran and a non-Christian, could not understand my decision as anything other than cowardice. I became a c.o. in the face of the objections of my pastor, who was also a World War II veteran. However my pastor and I had a good relationship. And, at least my memory is, that, in the end, he gave me his blessing, even though he thought I was wrong. I also became a c.o., a pacifist, in a Baptist church that never would have imagined giving birth to a pacifist. And, yet, in retrospect, I can see that it was the life of this General Baptist church that helped me to hear the powerful and life-changing words of Jesus during that year:

> You have heard that it was said, 'You shall love your neighbour and hate your enemy.' But I say to you, Love your enemies and pray for those who persecute you, so that you may be children of your Father in heaven; for he makes his sun rise on the evil and on the good, and sends rain on the righteous and on the unrighteous. (Matthew 5.43–45, NRSV)

This passage, as I recall many years later, was the basis for the paper I wrote for the military service agency that granted me conscientious objector status. I am sure that my paper was full of naïveté and poorly-considered arguments. However, my convictions were genuine; my sincerity may have shone through my poorly-written paper.

I mention the context within which I first wrestled with the question of violence for several reasons. Chief among them is that the context within which we first wrestle with violence often becomes rather determinative for how we continue to think about violence. I have noticed this in conversations with many pacifists and peace activists (as well as with veterans of wars).[12] Whether it was World War II or Vietnam or the Falklands War or the 1980s' focus on the nuclear arms race or the Gulf War or Bosnia or elsewhere: the contexts within which peacemakers first came to their convictions often have a powerful hold on their future understanding of related issues. There are important lessons to learn from these and other contexts, lessons that make us sensitive to the horror and terrible realities of violence and gross injustice. However, there is also a caution to be issued. When these lessons become our central focus it is distorting. I used to like the statement by the radical Catholic Ammon Hennacy: 'Being a pacifist between wars is like being a vegetarian between meals'.[13] On first reflection this is a clever statement.[14] On second

[12] Of course, in the case of military veterans, the experiences are even more enduring, because they are, often, repeated traumatic experiences on the edge of death.
[13] I have not been able to track down this quotation. I first heard it or read it in the mid-1970s. Hennacy was involved for many years with the Catholic Worker movement.
[14] This statement is a threefold reminder for pacifists. First, it is a reminder that many men and women have paid greatly through doing military service for their countries during wars. Second, it is a reminder that pacifists should not take lightly the reality, within countries that provide for exemptions for conscientious objectors, that they are excused from such extraordinarily costly service. Third, and related, pacifists always need to remember that pacifism is not simply a conviction evoked during wartime. It is rather connected to a set of convictions and moral practices that relate to everyday living, with or without wars. (On the first point see the interesting comments by Stanley Hauerwas in 'Pacifism: A Form of Politics', in *Peace Betrayed? Essays on Pacifism and Politics*, ed. Michael Cromartie [Washington, DC: Ethics and Public Policy Center, 1990], 140–1 and 'Whose "Just" War? Which Peace?', in *Dispatches from the Front: Engagements with the Secular* [Durham, NC: Duke University Press, 1994], 152.)

reflection it is too clever by half. Pacifism, as a Christian conviction, is not primarily about war, nor for Christians is it even primarily about realities in the larger society. It is, rather, integrally related to a set of convictions and a way of living that only has certain manifestations during a time of war. Stanley Hauerwas puts the matter just right:

> to say one is a pacifist gives the impression that pacifism is a position that is intelligible apart from the theological convictions that form it. But that is exactly what I wish to deny. Christians are non-violent not because certain implications may follow from their beliefs, but because the very shape of their beliefs form them to be non-violent.[15]

The theological convictions that form us to be nonviolent always come in a specific shape. Mine were first formed in the context of a Baptist church.

Becoming a Baptist Pacifist

At the end of 1997 I was asked to preach at the church in which I became a Christian, for the first time in almost twenty-five years. For my sermon I decided to make a play on the title of the book by Robert Fulghum: my sermon was 'All I Really Need to Know About the Christian Faith I Learned Here'.[16] As I reflected on it, I realised that the substance of my Christian faith was, in fact, derived from the teachings and practices of this church. My under-standing of pacifism and concern about justice began there, however much that might have surprised them.

It was from them that I first learned the call to serious

---

[15] Stanley Hauerwas, 'Pacifism: Some Philosophical Considerations', 100.
[16] Fulghum's book is *All I Really Need to Know I Learned in Kindergarten* (New York: Fawcett Books, 1993). I certainly also agree with the senti-ments expressed by Catherine Wallace: 'We may be taught everything we need to know in kindergarten, but it is a life's work to learn those lessons thoroughly' (Catherine M. Wallace, *For Fidelity: How Intimacy and Commitment Enrich Our Lives* [New York: Vintage Books, 1998], 88).

discipleship. From sermons, but also from musical solos that were sung and testimonies that were offered, I got the clear message that the faith we proclaimed on Sunday related to the life we lived throughout the week. I have been convinced for a while now that this is a major separating point between churches: do they or do they not emphasise that worship is integrally related to daily living? Although probably all denominational traditions have teachings that suggest this, some churches emphasise it more than others. Now, of course, some of the specifics they named were different from the specifics I would come to name. But the emphasis on discipleship was prominent. I got the message from this church that my life in Christ was to relate to everyday living.

Sermons. It is interesting to me that I learned pacifism partly from the sermons preached in this church in the early 1970s. And, yet, not totally surprising. My memory is that my pastor, Bill Duncan, preached only evangelistic sermons. (Certainly we had an altar call for sinners to come forward at every service.) But I remember what was preached in these evangelistic sermons, some variation of John 3.16: 'For God so loved the world that he gave His only begotten Son. . . .' Yes, the message I heard at least twice per week was God loves the world; Jesus died for everyone. When you connect this to the first emphasis – that our convictions were to relate to everyday life – then it makes sense. Why was I going to go several thousand miles away and kill people that God loves and for whom Jesus died?

This came home to me a few years ago when I was teaching a Christian ethics class at Fuller Theological Seminary in Pasadena, California. I had just given a lecture on why nonviolence is implied by the heart of the Christian Gospel. A number of students in the class were uncomfortable. Some appreciated what I said. One of them was an African named James. He was an evangelist working mostly among Muslims in Africa. His life had been threatened more than once. However, it never occurred to him to consider killing these people he was working among. Why? Centrally, it was because he was well aware that killing would not only kill the people with whom he was to share the Gospel, it also would kill the effectiveness of the Gospel. He knew that killing was inconsistent with the content of what he wanted to share. It struck me that the same was true for the inner-city mission organisation my wife had worked with for more than twenty years in Los Angeles. It was not that they had a position called pacifism. But, quite intentionally, in order to share the Gospel of Christ, they lived in the most dangerous area of Los Angeles. I can just hear the arguments from typical middle-class white Americans on why you have to be armed with weapons in order to defend yourself against the sort of people that live in south-central Los Angeles. However, such thinking would not have occurred to my wife and her fellow missionaries. Why? You can't witness to Christ while killing the very people (or their relatives) with whom you are called to share the Gospel. Practically it develops mistrust. But more fundamentally the actions are incongruous with the message. God loves everyone. Jesus died for everyone. Jesus can redeem anyone. This message should be combined with patience, long-suffering, acts of sacrifice and service, not killing. These missionaries know and live this, even though the organisation does not have a developed position called pacifism.

The General Baptist church of which I was a part was a holiness church. It was also an expressive church, with hand raising, 'Amens', occasional shouts and testimonies. Testimonies were a regular part of the church services. I believe a very important part.[17] It was one of the most vivid ways in which I learned that our worship had to be connected to our everyday lives. Two men who regularly testified were brothers named Bob and Carlton Brockett. They often sat close to each other and were very different. Bob was a big man with a deep voice. He looked like someone who did hard physical labour much of his life, as

---

[17] Some of what was accomplished through these times of testimony was similar to what is accomplished through small groups in current churches. See, e.g., Robert Wuthnow, ed., 'I Come Away Stronger': How Small Groups Are Shaping American Religion (Grand Rapids, MI: Wm B. Eerdmans, 1994).

he did: he worked on the railroad. I remember that he had very rough hands. However, he was very different from the average man I knew who did such work. Many of them were gruff with a facade that communicated toughness and pride. Bob, however, would almost always cry during his testimony. Of course he would share about various things. But often, with a deep humility that seemed totally genuine, he would thank God for his life, his family, his church, and the many gifts he had received in his life, which he knew he didn't really deserve. I remember on more than one occasion he would give thanks that God had called us young ministers to preach. And I would cry, knowing he meant it and that his prayers (and the prayers of others) were undergirding my developing ministry. Carlton was a smaller man. He too was emotional, but in a different way. In his testimony he would get to 'preachin', as people would say. By the end of his testimony Carlton would also always be expressing his gratitude and unworthiness. But before he got there he would be encouraging all of us to live faithfully to the Gospel, just as he knew he needed to do the same. Carlton: bold convictions. Bob: obvious humility. They were brothers who loved each other, loved the church and its Lord, and who communicated a complementary message.[18]

Footwashing was also at this time one of the practices of this General Baptist church. I am grateful for that. I shall always remember the image of Bob Brockett getting down on his hands and knees, washing my feet, crying tears of joy and thanksgiving, and letting me wash his. I was 17 or 18. He was almost forty years my senior. I was new to the Christian faith; he had been raised in it. He was a man I looked up to and knew I had much to learn from – and he was washing my feet. It was humbling. I also remember Bill Duncan ('Brother Bill'), our pastor, washing my feet

---

[18] I also remember that Bob smoked cigarettes. In retrospect, in some ways, I am grateful for that. He was a deacon. A man I respected as much as any man in the church. And yet he engaged in a practice that was (unofficially) a sin in our church. I am sure this reality lodged as a footnote in my soul about what it means to be holy in the midst of imperfections.

and letting me wash his. Again, I had a great deal of respect for Bill Duncan. He knew infinitely more than I knew about the Christian faith and was a fine Christian man. And here he was washing my feet. It was a powerful image of Christ's servanthood and our call to be servants in following Jesus. It was a vivid lesson in our need to be humble in our love for one another. I needed to respect my leaders and elders, as I did. They needed to know that each of us, finally, in the presence of God, was one foot washer among other foot washers in the body of Christ.

I was told when I was back home in 1997 that the Ku Klux Klan was active in my home county, because one black minister had begun a ministry at the edge of that county. When I was a kid, to my knowledge, there was no KKK presence because there was no black presence; the county was all-white. To this day I remember a conversation I had with several other boys when we were about aged ten. In this small town one of the events children looked forward to when I was a child was the Autumn Festival. On this particular day several of us boys were standing around sharing our excitement about the upcoming annual Autumn Festival – a time filled with festival rides, games, friends, and other fun. However, for the moment there was a damper on our excitement. For we had just noticed some African Americans walking around the town square. Almost with one voice we expressed our fear: 'These niggers had better get out of town soon, for any nigger remaining in this town beyond sundown will be hanged.'[19] I am not certain where we had heard these precise thoughts expressed. But demeaning references to blacks were hardly uncommon.

Having grown up in this racist environment, there is another memory that will always stay with me. Ralph Ferguson, a wonderful African American man, was a member of the congregation I pastored in Los Angeles, California in the early 1990s. He was very active in this church, a Church of

[19] I was told during my last visit home that there had been road signs until sometime in the 1950s on all the highways entering my hometown that said the same thing.

the Brethren, a church that also practised foot washing, once a year on Maundy Thursday.[20] Ralph participated in the foot washing. To have this man, this black brother in Christ, wash my feet and let me wash his was a very moving experience.[21] The image of Ralph, a black man from the south – a man who knows quite personally the meaning of racism – washing my feet is but a powerful reminder that the word 'nigger' can only cross these lips to remind me and others of the far too frequent sin of white individuals and white communities against African Americans and this peculiar sin all of us white Americans must continually battle.[22]

Now, to be clear, the Baptist church in which I became a Christian did not directly challenge racism. But the practice of foot washing combined with testimonies and sermons about the cross and the salvation God offers to *everyone* were potentially subversive.[23] Even if these practices were not, in this church's teachings, directly connected to matters like racism or love of enemies at the time, they embodied a set of convictions that were explosive.[24]

[20]   For British readers, The Church of the Brethren named here should not be confused with the Brethren Church in Britain. This denomination began in the early eighteenth century within German pietism. Within the first generation two things happened. First, this movement was deeply influenced by the Anabaptist/Mennonite tradition. Second, virtually everyone within this movement emigrated to the USA. For various reasons this denomination has had close ties over the centuries with Mennonites. For the definitive history of the Brethren movement within which this church stands, see Donald Durnbaugh, *Fruit of the Vine: A History of the Brethren 1708–1995* (Elgin, IL: Brethren Press, 1997).
[21]   I have also had numerous moving conversations with my good friend, African American Pentecostal pastor, Alton Trimble. His ministry in Los Angeles is inspiring. The many candid conversations we have had have deeply enriched me and deepened my commitment to fighting racism whenever I see it.
[22]   I am conscious of the differences in history in this regard between Britain and America. However, at least one black British Christian has told me that racism is a significant reality here as well.
[23]   Alan Kreider tells me that once when David Martin, a sociologist of religion, visited the London Mennonite Centre he commented on the foot washing. He said that he knows there is something radical going on when foot washing is being practised.
[24]   Of course, this account is much too simple. Between 1970 and the early 1990s I had read books by Martin Luther King, Jr, John Perkins, and a variety of articles and had had a few wonderful friendships with African American Christians.

Many other elements of this church's life could also be mentioned. The prayers reminded me of the need we had for God and one another. The music, led and often sung by Fred Brockett, reminded me of the multi-dimensional reality of our life with God. The love exhibited by church members for one another and the sense I had of the depth of commitment of people's lives to the God they worshipped and the people they journeyed with reminded me of the call to daily faithfulness. And as a vital backdrop behind all of this was a powerful sense of the presence of a wondrous and gracious God who made our lives possible. The various facets of this church's life transformed mine.

Through sermons, testimonies, foot washings, and the call to daily discipleship I was taught the centrality of Jesus Christ for our lives. Jesus Christ was to be praised not only during the times of gathered worship, but also in the ways we lived our lives. Occasionally there were (what I would come to think of as) corruptions, that is to say there were those times – especially on the Sunday closest to the Fourth of July – when nationalism was brought into the worship service.[25] These times were rare. Nonetheless, apparently, these rare services expressed the conviction of most men within the church of how their faith related to military service. I could not do that. As I was coming to see it, Jesus was indeed Lord during worship, during my daily walk with God, *and* when I came to consider the question of serving in the military. The church's life and teachings the year round provided the prism through which I interpreted such issues. It did not occur to me to make a major decision about going into the military to kill human beings created in the image of God without considering how it related to discipleship, to following Jesus. Nor did it make sense to me to interpret the Bible in relation to violence primarily in light of one worship service connected to Independence Day. No, out of my regular reading of the

[25] The Fourth of July is also known as 'Independence Day'. It is a day when America celebrates its independence from Britain. It is probably the most patriotic (and, often, nationalistic) day of the year. The Sunday closest to 11 November ('Veterans' Day') can also be similar. However, in my experience, it is usually less dramatic than 'Independence Day'.

New Testament, encouraged by the church, it seemed that Jesus' call to love our enemies was consistent with much else in the New Testament as well as what I heard regularly within the church services.[26]

Why is it that I have focused on this Baptist church and my early Christian life within it? Partly it is simply because this is a story I know in some detail; it is my story. But I hope it is more than that. I could have written about someone like Dietrich Bonhoeffer. But Bonhoeffer was an extraordinary person. And the times in which he lived were extraordinary. I am much more ordinary, average. The early 1970s in the USA were tense, but closer to average than Nazi Germany. And in some ways this church was average. Or, if anything, this church, if one were predicting, would seem less likely than the average church to produce a pacifist or someone who would go on to get a master's degree in peace studies, found an ecumenical peace and justice organisation, and become the programme director for a Mennonite Centre in London, England. In fact, this church is probably not drastically unlike the church in which Stanley Hauerwas was raised.[27]

One way to read my story is to say that I as an individual stood against my church. However, as I see it, I followed the logic of the central teachings and practices of my church. I refused to say that these Christian convictions were only private or removed from demands of the nation-state. That others in this and many other churches usually do not see this is what led Hauerwas to say: 'No task is

[26] It would be many years before I would have any understanding of how the Old Testament related to my convictions. In fact, it was several years before I would read any books that confirmed the convictions I had come to on my own. One of the first was John Howard Yoder, *The Politics of Jesus*, second edition (Grand Rapids, MI: Wm B. Eerdmans, 1994 [first edition 1972]).

[27] Despite his criticisms of his own church, Hauerwas suggests that it may be his church that helped make him open to the writings of John H. Yoder. See Stanley Hauerwas and Chris K. Huebner, 'History, Theory, and Anabaptism', in *The Wisdom of the Cross*, 394.

more important than for the Church to take the Bible out of the hands of individual Christians.'[28] Hauerwas continues:

> [Individual] Christians are trained to believe that they are capable of reading the Bible without spiritual and moral transformation. They read the Bible not as Christians, not as a people set apart, but as democratic citizens who think their 'common sense' is sufficient for 'understanding' the Scripture. They feel no need to stand under the authority of a truthful community to be told how to read. Instead they assume that they have all the 'religious experience' necessary to know what the Bible is about. As a result the Bible inherently becomes the ideology for a politics quite different from the politics of the Church.[29]

In saying this Hauerwas is emphasising that we cannot allow the Bible to be read primarily in light of the claims of our nation-state. Sometimes, such as the Sunday nearest Independence Day in the USA or Remembrance Day in the UK, these claims are imported into the midst of the worship service. But Christians always need to remember that central theological claims – such as the claim that Jesus is Lord – have political implications that should shape our lives.[30]

One thing that should not be imagined is that this essay is intended only to be for Baptists. Quite the contrary. The point is precisely the opposite. The central point is that concerns about peace and justice, on the part of Christians, should be integrally related to the life and teachings of the

---

[28] Stanley Hauerwas, *Unleashing the Scripture: Freeing the Bible from Captivity to America* (Nashville, TN: Abingdon Press, 1993), 15. The original sentence ends with 'in North America'. I am not sure I agree with this statement, taken literally. Had the Scriptures been taken out of my hands, for instance, a significant component of what I heard would have been lost. However, I agree with the basic, important, points being made.
[29] Hauerwas, *Unleashing the Scripture*, 15. Again, the term at the beginning of this sentence is 'North American'.
[30] On this see John Howard Yoder, *The Christian Witness to the State* (Eugene, OR: Wipf & Stock, 1997 [original edition 1964] and Hauerwas, 'Epilogue'.

Church. I have attempted to display some of the ways in which, even within the context of a church that was not itself focusing on peace and justice, one can see how connections were made, because of the very nature of the Gospel. This is not to encourage churches like this one to continue to divorce the worship life of the Church from issues like racism or killing. Not at all. But it is intended to help us appreciate the richness inherent in the ordinariness of the life of churches, in this case a particular kind of Baptist church. And it is to suggest that it is not necessary to move to a liberal theology removed from the typical practices and teachings of the Church in order to arrive at a commitment to peace and justice, as some denominational peace fellowships seem to imply. Again, this is not a peculiarly Baptist or Mennonite contention. Anglo-Catholic Kenneth Leech has in his own way made a similar claim in his little book *Subversive Orthodoxy*.[31] Moreover, this is what Stanley Hauerwas has been about in his many writings.[32]

Dorothy Day is an almost perfect illustration of this. Dorothy Day was the remarkable founder of the Catholic Worker movement.[33] She was a pacifist, social activist, writer, and servant of the poor for most of her adult life. Her church, the Roman Catholic Church, especially in the days before Vatican II, might also appear an unlikely source of inspiration for a commitment to peace and justice.[34] But for the radical named Dorothy Day this church was absolutely central in her life. She said that the

[31] Kenneth Leech, *Subversive Orthodoxy: Traditional Faith & Radical Commitment* (Toronto, Ontario: Anglican Book Centre, 1992).
[32] For an interesting discussion of some of the ways in which this redefines political alliances, see Scott H. Moore, 'The End of Stereotypes: How the *First Things* and Baxter Controversies Inaugurate Extraordinary Politics', *Pro Ecclesia* 7 (1998), 17–47.
[33] This was an American movement. But there are also, now, Catholic Worker hospitality houses in England.
[34] I am well aware that Dorothy Day had a commitment to justice before she became Catholic. However, she is a wonderful example of Hauerwas' claim that Christian pacifism is unintelligible apart from a set of Christian convictions and practices. Day's commitments regarding peace and justice were radically redefined by the Catholic Church. And she continually drew inspiration for her 'politics' from the Church.

Roman mass 'is the heart of our life, brings us into the
closest of all contacts with our Lord Jesus Christ, enabling
us literally to "put on Christ" and to begin to say "Now,
not I live, but Jesus Christ in me" '.[35] She was impatient
with priests who did not take the mass seriously. 'I am
begging them,' she said, 'to speak as if the words were holy
and inspired with power in themselves to produce in us
the understanding – the participation that could change
our lives.'[36] She attended mass and read psalms almost
daily and clearly knew the Scriptures quite well. As she
said: 'The Word was in Scripture and the Bread on the altar
and I was to live by both, I had to live by both or wither
away'.[37] It was partly because her life was lived so
profoundly in the presence of God that she was deeply
troubled by some Catholic radicals in the 1960s who,
though political radicals, were being unfaithful Catholics
as Dorothy Day saw it.[38] It was also why she could not
imagine living her life as a Catholic any other way than as
a peacemaker who served the poor.

Dorothy Day was an embodiment of Hauerwas' claim
that 'Christians are non-violent not because certain implications may follow from their beliefs, but because the very
shape of their beliefs form them to be non-violent'.[39] Her
life is also a reminder that 'the kind of claims Christians
make for nonviolence require living representatives if they
are to be convincing. The rational power of nonviolence as
a morality for anyone depends on the existence of
examples, that is, people who have learned to live nonviolently.'[40]

It is not only that the life of Dorothy Day and the more
average lives of many others I have known in various

[35] Quoted in 'Dorothy Day', ch. 4 of William O. Paulsell, *Tough Minds,
Tender Hearts: Six Prophets of Justice* (Mahweh, NJ: Paulist Press, 1990), 101.
[36] Quoted in 'Dorothy Day', 102.
[37] Quoted in William D. Miller, 'Dorothy Day and the Bible', in Ernest R.
Sandeen, ed., *The Bible and Social Reform*. (Philadelphia, PA: Fortress
Press/Chico, CA: Scholars Press, 1982), 174.
[38] See William D. Miller, *Dorothy Day: A Biography* (San Francisco, CA:
Harper & Row, 1982), 460–92.
[39] Hauerwas, 'Pacifism: Some Philosophical Considerations', 100.
[40] Hauerwas, 'Pacifism: Some Philosophical Considerations', 103.

churches have made a set of convictions related to pacifism intelligible. But it is also that Dorothy Day and many other saints have helped me to see that the convictions that shape me to be nonviolent also shape me to care about the poor, care about injustice, work against capital punishment, work for human rights, care about violence the USA was inflicting on other nations, and, in short, care about how my life lived in the context of other Christians related to the culture and world around me.[41] They have sometimes taught me these things by teaching or writing, sometimes by example, sometimes quite unintentionally.

All of this is a reminder of the importance of attending to the ways in which Christian virtues are formed within the context of our lives and churches. As John Yoder reminds us, there are several advantages to a focus on virtue.

> Virtue is narrative; it has length. The present is embedded in a past which has made me who I am and reaches toward a hope which is already present to faith. Virtue as well has breadth; it is communal. My decision has neighbours, persons who count on me, persons far and near, and groups, with whom I am bound by reciprocal promises and role expectations. Virtue also has depth; it implies and celebrates understandings about the nature of persons, the nature of God, the goodness and fallenness of creation, the inwardness and the transparency of self, the miracles of redemptive transformation. . . .[42]

---

[41] Stanley Hauerwas would want me to remember that many of the terms I have used in this sentence are 'dangerous' terms; that is to say, they are terms – realities – that take on a life of their own divorced from our life lived among saints. I agree. I have used shorthand terms for quick communication. But those of us Christians who are called to work actively in the world of politics/the public, we need to be vigilant to remember that the language (and concomitant convictions and practices) of the world are different from ours, however much we may be able to interface with the larger world on specific issues.
[42] John Howard Yoder, *Nevertheless: The Varieties and Shortcomings of Religious Pacifism*, revised and expanded edition (Scottdale, PA: Herald Press, 1992), 130.

Stanley Hauerwas is right when he says that '[a]n emphasis on the significance of the virtues does not conceptually require a pacifist position'. However, he is also right that 'such an emphasis might at least make one more receptive to some accounts of pacifism'.[43]

Through Thick and Thin

Thus far in this essay I have spoken mostly about the Church. Perhaps I should say more about those larger issues of peace and justice in the world beyond the walls of the Church? Okay, let us assume that we accept that the Church motivates us to be concerned about peace and justice. Let's get on with it. Let's do what we have been motivated to do. But you see it is not that simple. It is much more than motivation. The question remains: How will we do what we do? How will we approach taking positions on issues? What shape will our social and political involvement take? The problem is, as social theorist Michael Walzer has argued, there are no general concepts called peace and justice. To believe that is to be in the grip of a myth, albeit a widely believed myth in the developed world. We believe, says Walzer, that 'it is everyone's morality because it is no one's in particular ... And if we succeed in understanding this morality, we should be able to construct a complete objective ... code – a kind of moral Esperanto.'[44] 'But our intuition is wrong here', says Walzer. 'Morality is thick from the beginning, culturally integrated, fully resonant, and it reveals itself thinly only on special occasions, when moral language is turned to specific purposes.'[45] Which is to say, the world – the language – of Washington or of Parliament or of some international peace organisation is not universal or inherently superior to the specific language of a church, it is simply a language

---

[43] Hauerwas, 'Pacifism: Some Philosophical Considerations', 102.
[44] Michael Walzer, *Thick and Thin: Moral Argument at Home and Abroad* (Notre Dame, IN: University of Notre Dame Press, 1994), 7.
[45] Walzer, *Thick and Thin*, 4.

102 FAITHFULNESS AND FORTITUDE

with a different narrative and 'thick description' claiming different definitions of reality.[46]

I don't know how many Christian peace and justice activists I've met over the years who, because their lives are so engaged with political issues, come to define their concerns about peace and justice centrally by whatever liberal or radical subculture they happen to be connected with politically. But as Hauerwas and William Willimon put it:

> Big words like 'peace' and 'justice,' slogans the church adopts under the presumption that, even if people do not know what 'Jesus Christ is Lord' means, they will know what peace and justice means, are words awaiting content. The church really does not know what these words mean apart from the life and death of Jesus of Nazareth. ... It is Jesus' story that gives content to our faith, and teaches us to be suspicious of any political slogan that does not need God to make itself credible.[47]

Another way to put this is to say that we must be conscious of our first language as we also learn more than one first language. It is from the Church – even if with some struggle – that our first language regarding peace and justice is derived. This quite naturally follows from the confessions of faith we make when we are in church, the very language of our faith itself. We worship God. This God is defined centrally by the One whom we proclaim as Lord, Jesus the Messiah. And this worship is to be connected to the whole of our lives.

Walter Brueggemann gives an instance of how the

---

[46] On the matter of particularity and claims to truth, see John Howard Yoder, ' "But We Do See Jesus": The Particularity of Incarnation and the Universality of Truth', in *The Priestly Kingdom: Social Ethics as Gospel* (Notre Dame, IN: University of Notre Dame Press, 1984), 46–62 and John Howard Yoder, 'On Not Being Ashamed of the Gospel: Particularity, Pluralism, and Validation', *Faith and Philosophy* 9 (1992), 285–300.
[47] Stanley Hauerwas and William Willimon, *Resident Aliens* (Nashville, TN: Abingdon Press, 1989), 38.

community of faith provides our mother tongue by looking
at an incident from the Old Testament.[48] In 701 BCE there is
an encounter between the Assyrians and Judah. Jerusalem
is under siege. The Assyrian army is ready to negotiate, i.e.,
really to receive a surrender on the part of Judah. The
negotiation happens at the wall of the city. Aramaic is the
language common to the Assyrians and the Judeans who
would do the negotiations at the wall on behalf of Judah.
However, it is not the language of most Judeans 'behind
the wall'. That language is Hebrew, the language they
would normally use in everyday commerce, within
families, in worship, etc. In that language – their mother
tongue – they are also confident that their God is a real and
faithful God. In fact, their life together is shaped in various
and sundry ways in light of their trust in this God.
However, when the Judean negotiators meet the Assyrians
at the wall, the Judeans not only must speak in a second
language – Aramaic – they also must be conscious of the
fact that the Assyrians believe the Judeans' God is a false
one – with all that flows from that. The Assyrians live a
different way, believing in different gods.

Brueggemann draws a number of lessons from this
encounter, among them the following:

> Christians should be nurtured to be bilingual, to know
> how to speak the language on the wall in the presence
> of the imperial negotiators, but also how to speak the
> language behind the wall in the community of faith,
> where a different set of assumptions, a different
> perception of the world, a different epistemology are at
> work. The conversation on the wall is crucial, because
> the Assyrians are real dialogue partners who must be
> taken seriously. They will not go away. But unless there
> is another conversation behind the wall in another
> language about another agenda, Judah on the wall will

[48] The story is from 2 Kings 18–19. Brueggemann's discussion of it, from
which the following is borrowed, is Walter Brueggemann, 'The
Legitimacy of a Sectarian Hermeneutic', in *Interpretation and Obedience:
From Faithful Reading to Faithful Living* (Minneapolis, MN: Fortress Press,
1991), 41–69.

only submit to and echo imperial perceptions of reality. When imperial perceptions of reality prevail, everything is already conceded. If the conversation with the empire at the wall is either the only conversation or the decisive one, Israel will decide that Yahweh is indeed like all the other impotent gods and consequently will endorse imperial policies as nonnegotiable realities. The ground for any alternative will have been forfeited.[49]

All of this is to say, that while we will engage in conversations, negotiations, and lobbying 'at the wall' it is crucial to remember that 'the primal conversation in the Old Testament is behind the wall, and this does not change in the New Testament'.[50]

Wayne Meeks provides complementary insights in his book, *The Origins of Christian Morality*. In the early church, says Meeks, becoming a Christian meant something like the experience of an immigrant who leaves his or her native land and then assimilates to the culture of a new, adopted homeland. Such a transfer of allegiances and transformation of mores requires a re-socialisation. That is, something like the primary socialisation that occurs normally in the interactions between child and family, the process in which the self receives those components of its structure and those basic values that are contributed by its environment, is re-enacted in a new context.[51]

Put differently, '[m]orality is an integral part of a community's culture'.[52] So much so that 'making morals

---

[49] Brueggemann, 'The Legitimacy of a Sectarian Hermeneutic', 44.

[50] Brueggemann, 'The Legitimacy of a Sectarian Hermeneutic', 60. Brueggemann's analysis is wonderful. My only criticism is with his use of the phrase 'imperial perception'. It is not simply a matter of two options: behind-the-wall language and imperial language or perceptions. A variety of 'languages' are spoken outside the wall. Though we may have higher opinions of some languages and perceptions outside the wall than of others, nonetheless our framework for making such discriminations is our language (and concomitant convictions and behaviours) spoken behind the wall. (See John Howard Yoder, 'On Not Being Ashamed of the Gospel', 285–300.)

[51] Wayne Meeks, *The Origins of Christian Morality: The First Two Centuries* (New Haven, CT: Yale University Press, 1993), 12.

[52] Meeks, *The Origins of Christian Morality*, 10.

means making community'.[53] Borrowing from anthropologist Clifford Geertz, Meeks says that 'religion supports proper conduct by picturing a world in which such conduct is only common sense'.[54]

Becoming a Peace Church

What I am suggesting is that we as Christians and as Christian theologians should want Christian language, including Christian language about peace and justice, to become simply 'common sense' for those who are a part of the Church. One way to put this is that we want the Church, our church, to be a peace church. That is why I became Mennonite some years ago. I wanted to be a part of a church that realised that peacemaking was integral to its life. I wanted to be a part of a peace church. I am grateful that the Mennonites have as a part of their 'Confession of faith' the following:

> We believe that peace is the will of God. God created the world in peace, and God's peace is most fully revealed in Jesus Christ, who is our peace and the peace of the whole world. Led by the Holy Spirit, we follow Christ in the way of peace, doing justice, bringing reconciliation, and practising nonresistance even in the face of violence and warfare.[55]

I have no illusions that the Mennonites provide the only model for being a peace church. Nor that other churches couldn't be better at being peace churches. However, at their best, Mennonites have realised two things. First, they have realised, as Arne Rasmusson has put it, that 'to think

---

[53] Meeks, *The Origins of Christian Morality*, 5.
[54] Meeks, *The Origins of Christian Morality*, 11.
[55] *Confession of Faith: In a Mennonite Perspective* (Scottdale, PA: Herald Press, 1995), 81. This was in 1995 a new confession of faith for the two largest Mennonite bodies, the Mennonite Church and the General Conference Mennonite Church, which are currently moving toward merger.

outside a given hegemonic cultural imagination you need an alternative community that tells another narrative, forms other practices, extols other virtues. Thinking is a bodily and social activity.'[56] And, second, they have realised, as the above quotation from a recent statement of faith indicates, that a commitment to peace is integral to the Christian faith, not simply the hobby of a sub-set within the Church.

There are various ways to be a peace church. Any Church, local or denominational, could become one. Let me indicate some of what I think it means to move toward being a peace church.[57]

1. The first thing is simple and yet needs to be said: concern about peace and justice in the world should be on the agenda of a peace church. It needs to be said partly because there are probably still many who continue to label Stanley Hauerwas (or John Yoder) a sectarian. Having the Church as our first community, the community that provides our mother tongue, does not entail having it as our only community and certainly not as the only community with which we engage and with which we have dialogue. The brief discussion, above, of the negotiations between Judah and Assyria should make that clear. Like Judah we too should engage in 'negotiations at the wall'.

'If peacemaking as a virtue is intrinsic to the nature of the church, what are we to say about those without the church?' asks Stanley Hauerwas.[58]

First, I think we must say that it is the task of the

---

[56] Arne Rasmusson, 'Historicizing the Historicist: Ernst Troeltsch and Recent Mennonite Theology', in *The Wisdom of the Cross*, p. 235.
[57] For a complementary essay on becoming a peace church, see Alan Kreider and Eleanor Kreider, *Becoming a Peace Church* (London: London Mennonite Centre, 2000). This booklet is available from the LMC, 14 Shepherds Hill, London N6 5AQ.
[58] Stanley Hauerwas, 'Peacemaking: The Virtue of the Church', in *Christian Existence Today: Essays on Church, World, and Living in Between* (Durham, NC: Labyrinth Press, 1988), 95.

Church to confront and challenge the false peace of the world which is too often built more on power than truth. Second, Christians are prohibited from ever despairing of the peace possible in the world. We know that as God's creatures we are not naturally violent nor are our institutions unavoidably violent. As God's people we have been created for peace. Rather, what we must do is to help the world find the habits of peace whose absence so often makes violence seem like the only alternative. Peacemaking as a virtue is an act of imagination built on long habits of the resolution of differences. The great problem in the world is that our imagination has been stilled, since it has not made a practice of confronting wrongs so that violence might be avoided. In truth, we must say that the Church has too often failed the world by its failure to witness in our own life the kind of conflict necessary to be a community of peace. Without an example of a peace-making community, the world has no alternative but to use violence as the means to settle disputes.'[59]

It also needs to be said that having peace and justice on the agenda does not mean that everyone or most everyone within such a church need be a peace and justice activist or have the right positions on a set of social issues. What one does with one's time is dependent on talents, gifts, and callings. Our Christian convictions and commitments should decisively shape how we live, including how we use our time and what jobs we choose. But clearly not all of us are called to be activists. The other matter regarding social issues is quite complicated. It is not as if social issues don't matter. Some matter tremendously. I am not neutral about many issues. Nonetheless, relating Christian convic-tions to social issues is a complicated task. Christians with nearly identical concerns for the poor, for instance, may

---

[59] Hauerwas, 'Peacemaking', 95. Also see Yoder, *The Christian Witness to the State*, John Howard Yoder, *For the Nations: Essays Public and Evangelical* (Grand Rapids, MI: Wm B. Eerdmans, 1997), and, in addition to the writings already named by Hauerwas above, see Stanley Hauerwas, *After Christendom?* (Nashville, TN: Abingdon Press, 1991).

nonetheless differ on how that concern best relates to public policies. Furthermore, I have sometimes noticed an attitude about social issues among some friends and acquaintances over the years that has caused me concern. Christina Sommers says it well:

> Because morality has been sublimated into ideology, great numbers of people, the young and educated especially, feel they have an adequate moral identity merely because they hold the 'right' views on such matters as ecology, feminism, socialism, and nuclear energy.[60]

This struck me one day, not long after I had met my wife, Mary. I was relatively sure that I had known some Christian peace and justice activists who would think more highly of people who protest once in a while at a nuclear arms facility, at a prison, or against capital punishment, than they would of someone, like Mary, who gave eighteen years of her life living in south central Los Angeles being a missionary. This is because of the premium placed on having the right positions on issues. When my wife lived in inner-city Los Angeles she would not have had 'positions' on many of the political issues of the day. She was too busy trying to share Christ with others. She was too busy helping people survive in a neighbourhood where drug addiction, prostitution, murder, and various other afflictions were not 'issues' about which to have 'positions', but realities with which Pat, Theresa, and others she knew by name were confronted frequently. There is something wrong when we care more about correct 'positions' than lives well lived.

Now, don't get me wrong. There is no reason why it needs

[60] Christina Sommers, 'Where Have All the Good Deeds Gone?' in *Vice and Virtue in Everyday Life*, eds. Christina Sommers and Fred Sommers (San Diego, CA: Harcourt, Brace, and Jovanovich, 1989), 580. In a more recent essay Shelby Steele also has some interesting comments to make on what he refers to as 'a virtuousness that could be achieved through mere identification' (Shelby Steele, 'Baby-Boom Virtue', in *Judgment Day at the White House*, ed. Gabriel Fackre [Grand Rapids, MI: Wm B. Eerdmans, 1999], 178).

to be either/or. Though Mary was extremely busy, working day and night, and therefore might not have had room in her life for more activities, nonetheless it would have made sense for her – or her mission organisation – to have realised the connection between what she did and social policy issues on, say, capital punishment or racism. Moreover, it is precisely those who are serving faithfully day to day – working in hospices, befriending the poor, being with drug addicts, working in soup kitchens, raising children with handicaps, attending the victims of war – who should be significant participants in conversations about 'social issues' that affect people such as the ones they serve.

2. 'The first word Christians have to say about [violence] is church', says Hauerwas. Does that mean that church should be centred around peace and justice? Not at all. Church and our worship of God is about worshipping and serving God with the whole of our lives.[61] This means that it is inappropriate on one hand to exclude concerns about peace and justice from the life of the Church and on the other to reduce the life of the Church to concerns about peace and justice. Our lives are lived in the presence of a gracious and wondrous God, One who is worthy of our worship and who is the God of peace.[62]

One can see what I am referring to by glancing at various dimensions of the New Testament. Many Pauline scholars have come to recognise that a central component of most of the Pauline corpus is the reconciliation of Jews and Gentiles.[63] The New Testament (e.g., in Ephesians

---

[61] For two helpful discussions of this see Rodney Clapp, *A Peculiar People: The Church as Culture in a Post-Christian Society* (Downers Grove, IL: InterVarsity Press, 1996) and Marva J. Dawn, *A Royal 'Waste' of Time: The Splendor of Worshiping God and Being Church for the World* (Grand Rapids, MI: Wm. B. Eerdmans, 1999). Also see William T. Cavanaugh, 'The World in a Wafer: A Geography of the Eucharist as Resistance to Globalization', *Modern Theology* 15 (1999), 181–96, and David McCarthy Matzko, 'The Performance of the Good: Ritual Action and the Moral Life', *Pro Ecclesia* 7 (1998), 199–215.
[62] This is a repeated assertion in the New Testament.
[63] For one statement on this, within a large volume of literature, see James D. G. Dunn, 'The Justice of God: A Renewed Perspective on Justification by Faith', *The Journal of Theological Studies, NS* 43 (1992), 1–22.

and Colossians) often employs cosmic and doxological language to refer to the extraordinary reconciling acts of God wrought through Jesus the Christ. We should not reduce such rich, worshipful language to social ethics. But neither should we ignore the social ethical dimensions of such language. We should see, for instance, the validity of the analogy that has sometimes been drawn between 'there is neither Jew nor Greek' and the white/black situation in the USA. Or someone could look at a specific text like Galatians 5.16–26 on the 'works of the flesh' and the 'fruit of the Spirit'. Again, it is hardly adequate to imagine that the vices and virtues listed here have only to do with peacemaking.[64] On the other hand, it is difficult to imagine that there would not be a drastic re-thinking of the Church and violence (including military service) if the Church taught (as Paul suggests) that 'love, peace, patience, kindness, generosity, gentleness, and self-control' were to be fruit of the Spirit (virtues) embodied daily by Christians and that 'enmities, strife, anger, and factions' were works of the flesh (vices) to be avoided. Furthermore, Richard Hays, in what is probably the most thorough book on New Testament and ethics, claims that community, cross, and new creation come the closest to being central, unifying themes in the New Testament.[65] For some Christians whose primary identity is drawn from peace activism it may not be immediately obvious how these 'focal images' relate to Christian peacemaking. But for those of us wanting seriously to be Christian we need to live with these

---

[64] Or for that matter to imagine that virtue and vice language is quite adequate to describe the fruit of the Spirit and the works of the flesh. See Frank J. Matera, *Galatians* (Collegeville, MN: Michael Glazier, 1992); but see also Harry Huebner, 'A Community of Virtues', in *Church as Parable*, by Harry Huebner and David Schroeder (Winnipeg, Manitoba: CMBC Publications, 1993), 171–95.

[65] Richard B. Hays, *The Moral Vision of the New Testament: A Contemporary Introduction to New Testament Ethics* (New York: HarperCollins, 1996), 193–205. It is also worthwhile to note that he claims (200–5) that concepts like love and liberation are not central, unifying themes in the New Testament.

'central, unifying themes' as we attempt to live lives of Christian peacemaking.[66]

Or in relation to education in the Church, some words of Walter Brueggemann are instructive at this point. In his book, *The Creative Word*, he says that as we approach education within the life of the Church we need all three parts of the canon (referring to the Old Testament canon):

> [We need] the Torah [which is] a statement of community *ethos*, a definitional statement of the character of the community which is a given and is not negotiable among the new generation. In this first part of the canon, it is clear that the community precedes the individual person, that the community begins by stating its parameters and the perceptual field in which the new person must live and grow. In the Prophets, we deal with the *pathos* of God and of Israel, with the sense of fracture and abrasion between what is in hand and what is promised. This part of the canon expresses the conviction that such abrasion is not overcome by power or force, but by hurt. Therefore this part of the canon reflects on indignation and also on the anguish which belongs to this community and its perception. Third, in the Writings, we cannot in fact generalise for the whole. In the Proverbs at least, that is, in the 'counsel of the wise,' we may speak of the *logos*, of the conviction that there is sense and order and meaning to life. That logos is hidden and revealed. Education is the cat and mouse game of discovering and finding it hidden.[67]

---

[66] It is instructive to observe how Hays himself offers such reflections on peacemaking (*Moral Vision of the New Testament*: 313–46). And given his quite positive assessment of Yoder's work (239–53), it is also worthwhile to see how Yoder approaches these issues by reading the various works mentioned in footnotes, above (in relation to Scripture, especially *The Politics of Jesus*).

[67] Walter Brueggemann, *The Creative Word: Canon as a Model for Biblical Education* (Philadelphia: Fortress Press, 1982), 12–13.

Or, again, Brueggemann says,

> There have always been those who preferred the Torah of *certitude* from the scribe or the *freshness* of word from the prophet or the *hunch* of counsel from the wise. Always in Israel, these folks had to listen to each other and be reminded that not any one of them could author the entire tradition. It is the invitation of canon to educators that we should have a varied repertoire of both mode and substance, and that we should have a keen sense of which season requires which part of the canon.[68]

Yes, worshipping and serving the God revealed in Jesus Christ is much more than caring about peace and justice, but because of who this God is – and who we are called to be in Christ – it is not less than that.

3. Denominational peace fellowships should work to put themselves out of business, at least as they have often existed. By saying this, I do not by any means intend to belittle the value peace fellowships have been and continue to be. I am sure that such groups have done many wonderful things over the years both for their own members and for their denominations. Nonetheless, I believe peace fellowships have also sometimes made it less likely that peace and justice would be integrated into the life of the Church. That is because peace fellowships are often viewed by the Church as a whole as fringe groups and they often come to view themselves that way and carry on their existence in that mode. To take but one example: it is quite predictable that peace groups are theologically on the fringe; the members rarely identify with whatever their particular denomination defines as orthodox. Why is that? And how could a group that defines itself that way ever

---

[68] Brueggemann, *The Creative Word*, 12. I hope it is obvious that what Brueggemann says relates not only to education, but to how we think about life in the Church generally.

become considered a natural outworking of the theology
of that church? I would argue that every denomination
could, with proper instruction and moral training,
come to see peacemaking as part and parcel of its
core theological identity. How do we help that to
happen? This is the central task of those who would help
their church become a peace church. Then, the tasks of
peace groups become facilitating further education,
informing about relevant issues, and co-ordinating
certain responses to pressing issues. However, it is
important to realise that if a significant portion of a local
church or a denomination is on board with an identity as
a peace church this makes the work of peace groups, in
some ways, more complicated. It is relatively easier to be
comprised of a, more or less, self-selected group of like-
minded people. Truly to integrate peacemaking into the
life and convictions of the Church is quite difficult
and requires a significant commitment of time and
resources.

4. Finally, it is possible that the approach urged by
   Hauerwas and affirmed in this essay might break the
   impasse that sometimes develops between those willing
   and those unwilling to say they are pacifists. Because
   what Hauerwas has helped us to see is that what we
   want centrally is for Christians to embody Christian
   virtues, including virtues such as reconciliation, forgiveness, and peacemaking – virtues that will sometimes lead us, like Jesus, to love our enemies in a way
   that scandalises.[69] Perhaps we can see this by again
   briefly discussing Dietrich Bonhoeffer.

---

[69] Those who do not, like Hauerwas, see this implying a commitment to
nonviolence, need to wrestle seriously with ways in which the use of
violence would be disciplined (without forgetting the ways in which our
lives are shaped by our life within the Church). This is, of course, a
complicated subject. But one might begin by reading Stanley Hauerwas,
'Whose "Just" War? Which Peace?', Reinhard Hütter, 'Be Honest in Just
War Thinking! Lutherans, the Just War Tradition, and Selective
Conscientious Objection', in *The Wisdom of the Cross*, and John Howard
Yoder, *When War Is Unjust: Being Honest in Just War Thinking*, revised
edition (Maryknoll, NY: Orbis Books, 1996).

Back to Bonhoeffer

Often when people find out that I am a pacifist *and* that I
have a deep interest in Dietrich Bonhoeffer they want to
know whether I think Bonhoeffer was a pacifist. And,
generally, they want to make sure that I know that of
course he wasn't because he was involved in one or more
of the plots to kill Hitler. Because I am a person who enjoys
intellectual debates, I can be drawn into the debate about
whether or not Bonhoeffer was a pacifist. But I have come
to realise that though there might be some purpose in
discussing the whethers, whys, and wherefores of
Bonhoeffer's involvements in assassination attempts on
Hitler, such a discussion is mostly a distraction. For it is
much more important to look at the whole of Bonhoeffer's
life and teachings rather than focusing on whether and
why, in his extreme circumstances, he might have been
involved in any attempts to assassinate Hitler.

This is not the place to outline Bonhoeffer's life and
views regarding peacemaking; I have done that elsewhere.[70] But, let me say three things, briefly. First, it is an
injustice to Bonhoeffer's legacy to use him as an argument
against pacifism. He had no qualms about referring to
himself as a pacifist and much of his short adult life was
devoted to studying the Sermon on the Mount and training
ministers so they could live by and encourage other
Christians to be shaped by the Sermon on the Mount,
including the call of Jesus to the scandalous love of
enemies.

Second, in the midst of Nazi Germany, as the quote at
the beginning of this essay illustrates, Bonhoeffer looked to
some observers like 'a pacifist and an enemy of the state'.
Furthermore, within the context of Nazi Germany the
contrast was not so much between Bonhoeffer and
pacifism. It was rather the contrast between Bonhoeffer's

---

[70] In addition to my essay mentioned in note 1 above, also see, more
recently, Mark Thiessen Nation, 'Discipleship in a World Full of Nazis:
Dietrich Bonhoeffer's Polyphonic Pacifism as Social Ethics', in *The Wisdom
of the Cross*, 249–77.

life and convictions and those of the average Christian and theologian in Nazi Germany. It needs to be recalled, in the year 2000, that during Bonhoeffer's life more than 90 per cent of the German population belonged to churches that in various ways were ostensibly rooted in the just war tradition.

And third, Bonhoeffer could not but care about the question that has become the stock question for pacifists: 'But what about Hitler?' Of course he did; as would Hauerwas. But it was not central for Bonhoeffer. Rather, what he agonised over was a church that could so easily (and often eagerly) follow Hitler. His central question – as with Hauerwas – was 'But what about the Church?' 'How do we shape Christians so that their lives are determinatively shaped by the Gospel of Jesus Christ, so that they witness to Christ with the way they live, and so they can resist an Adolf Hitler in a Christian manner?' Are members of our churches committed enough to discipleship and to peacemaking that we would be willing to be so out of sync with the dominant culture or with our nation-state that we could be in danger, like Bonhoeffer, of being labeled 'pacifists and enemies of the state' or, like Hauerwas, 'sectarians' and enemies of the good of the state? When these sorts of questions become centrally defining within a church then it might truly be a peace church, following Jesus the Prince of Peace, himself accused of 'perverting' the nation.

6
No Abiding Inner City:
A New Deal for the Church

Samuel Wells

'What has Hauerwas' work to say to a deprived urban community in East Anglia?' This is a question I am often asked. The question generally arises from two sources. One supposes that Hauerwas' world is an intellectual one, seldom entered by those engaged in the pragmatic rhythm of parish ministry. The second supposes that Hauerwas' emphasis on the identity of the Church is hard to sustain when one's adult congregation is around fifteen people. This essay gives me an opportunity to answer the question by gently querying the assumptions that bring the question about.

One of the most forceful criticisms of Hauerwas' work is that it disables the social and political involvement of the Church in issues of freedom and justice. This is perhaps most fully articulated by Gloria Albrecht.

> Hauerwas' labelling of all work for justice as symptomatic of a universal and sinful will-to-power is itself an expression of white middle-class cynicism and despair. ... Faithfulness and submission to an absolute, nonviolent God, who alone is absolutely in control of history, legitimates a self-interested, middle- and upper-class pessimism and paralysis. ... Those with the benefits of work, influence, education, leisure, health care, housing, recreation, vacations, and resources are comforted in their belief that because they cannot unilaterally control and solve complex, modern issues, their finite and partial actions would be

unacceptable expressions of the sinful human desire for control.[1]

I feel the force of Albrecht's critique, because my temperament is not one that takes easily to 'solving complex, modern issues'. Stanley Hauerwas' arguments for nonviolence and politics must be read in the context of his passionate and combative character. Do they still apply when transferred to a character more 'pessimistic and paralysed' than his?

For many who have sought to live and to minister in the Church that Hauerwas describes, the image that has captured the imagination is not from Hauerwas but from MacIntyre. It is the image of the Church as a community of a new St Benedict, keeping the flickering flame of faith alive amid the gathering gloom of the new Dark Ages.[2] This may well be an appropriate view, one that is true to a strain in Hauerwas' thought, and one that appeals to the tongue that frequently sings the line 'Change and decay in all around I see'. It is a view that suits my own character. But it is not a view that makes a robust response to Albrecht – and in truth it does not do justice to my present circumstances, which I shall now explain.

A New Deal

When I began to live in Norwich, in 1997, I explored ways of getting to know the dynamics, the passions and the

---

[1] Gloria Albrecht, *The Character of Our Communities: Toward an Ethic of Liberation for the Church* (Nashville, TN: Abingdon Press, 1995), 115–16. Much of Albrecht's language is clearly inappropriate – one can hardly imagine Hauerwas using a phrase like 'universal will-to-power', for example. But it nonetheless constitutes a substantial criticism. For Hauerwas' initial response, see Stanley Hauerwas, 'Failure of Communication or a Case of Uncomprehending Feminism: A Response to Gloria Albrecht', *Scottish Journal of Theology* 50 (1997), 228–39. For my own engagement with Albrecht, see Samuel Wells, *Transforming Fate Into Destiny: The Theological Ethics of Stanley Hauerwas* (Carlisle: Paternoster Press, 1998), 68–73.

[2] Alasdair MacIntyre, *After Virtue: A Study in Moral Theory* (second edition, London: Duckworth, 1985), 263.

stories of the community I had entered. The bad reputation of the estate was mentioned by everybody, inside and outside the community: and various statistics indicated that it was perhaps the most deprived community in East Anglia. Yet I found that both of the local authorities – the County Council and the City Council – were setting about respective initiatives in encouraging and resourcing local people to articulate the needs and aspirations of their own community. In the City's case this was to establish a more appropriately-derived direction for Council policy; in the County's case it was a modest attempt to form a partnership between business, statutory agencies, the voluntary sector, and local residents. In a culture where the vicar has to earn any right of entry into people's homes, I began to realise that attending such gatherings was a form of corporate pastoral care. Sitting quietly listening at these and other meetings was the most direct way of learning what mattered to local people, and communicating that what mattered to them, mattered to God and to the Church.

And then an unexpected thing happened. In September 1998 the Labour Government announced that seventeen cities were to have the opportunity of choosing a Pathfinder estate to participate in the New Deal for Communities programme. It soon transpired that Norwich was to be one of the selected cities, and that my parish, North Earlham, together with a smaller, neighbouring community, the Marlpit, was to be Norwich's Pathfinder estate.[3] Overnight my situation was transformed. From being the priest of a deprived, neglected estate in a backwater of Britain, I found myself part of, indeed initially chair of, a holding group, at the heart of the

[3] The New Deal for Communities programme comes in three phases. Phase 1 runs for a few months and gives the community time to form a partnership with other interested parties and articulate a broad vision. Phase 2 runs for 6–9 months and is concerned with making detailed plans and proposals to enhance employment, health, education and community safety in the area. Phase 3 is a 7–10 year period of delivering projects worth around £40 million. The budget for the seventeen Pathfinder projects runs to over £800 million.

political agenda, with potentially many millions of pounds at its disposal. No one was in charge – the usual power-brokers having been deliberately excluded – and for a few months there was a remarkable opportunity for any forceful personality in the community to have enormous influence.

The philosophy behind the New Deal for Communities programme is simple. Give deprived communities the opportunity to regenerate themselves. Offer them support, encourage them to form partnerships with business and statutory agencies, make funding dependent on evidence of inclusive working and general propriety; but insist that key decisions affecting the future of the community are taken in and by the community. The goal of this new programme is that people in deprived communities become agents of their own destiny.[4] One might say that a difference between the rich and the poor is that the rich suffer from their own mistakes, whereas the poor suffer both from their own mistakes and from the mistakes of the rich. The New Deal plea is a cry that one could imagine coming from the pages of the First Book of Samuel: 'Let us be like other communities – let us make our own mistakes, rather than constantly feel subject to the mistakes of others.'[5]

By now you will understand why I am not saying that the Church's role is simply to keep the character of the faithful as the world enters a new Dark Age. For someone

[4] The similarity of this language with the language of liberation theologians is no coincidence. The reason why the scheme is so attractive is that it is open to these kinds of interpretations. Gutiérrez's description of 'a humankind that wants to take hold of the reins of its own life and be the artisan of its own destiny' (Gustavo Gutiérrez, A Theology of Liberation: History, Politics and Salvation second edition, trans. by Caridad Inda and John Eagleson, London: SCM Press, 1988, 30) sounds particularly appealing in a culture of dependence such as has been widespread in North Earlham since the estate was built.

[5] One feature of Hauerwas' writing is that he has never been frightened of making mistakes. He sees his work as maintaining a conversation, rather than establishing a definitive position. Considering his doctoral thesis, he says, ten years after its publication, 'I think this book was enough on the right track that its mistakes have proved fruitful. For finally I think this is the best most of us can do: make interesting mistakes.' (Stanley Hauerwas, Character and the Christian Life: A Study in Theological Ethics (third printing with a new Introduction, San Antonio, TX: Trinity, University Press 1985), xxxii.

who has drunk as deep at the well of Hauerwas as I have, New Deal for Communities offers an acute challenge.[6] Hauerwas offers a tragic account of the world, a tragedy to which those schooled in virtue may become accustomed, but a tragedy nonetheless subverted by the irony of the Gospel, an irony played out in the victory of the cross and in eschatological hope.[7] The Hauerwas student therefore imbibes a profound scepticism towards 'comic' stories, that is, stories with a conventionally happy ending.[8] New Deal for Communities offers itself as a comic story: give people in impoverished communities what they have never had, power over their own lives, and see wonderful things come about. This is not a Hauerwas way of telling a story. How then should the story be told?

In the face of an optimistic humanist story, one reflex reaction jumps straight to original sin and the corrupting effect of power. It is all very well to exalt the humble and meek, but how long will the meek keep the earth after they inherit it? One can continue in this vein with a certain cynicism: the programme is part of a general shift away from local authorities to central Government control. If the programme works, Government gets the credit for dealing direct with deprived communities, and local authorities are shown to be dispensable. If the programme fails, Government and the deprived communities will probably be able to blame the familiar bungling bureaucrats in local government.

Despite these instinctive reactions, I am committed to viewing the programme as a remarkable opportunity. The

[6] I might add that I was initially attracted to Hauerwas by his willingness to criticise the progressive forces in the Church with which I had always been frustrated but from which I had never previously seen an alternative. I describe this story in the preface to my *Transforming Fate Into Destiny*, xiii–xiv.

[7] For extended reflections on the way the irony of the Gospel subverts the tragedy of life, with particular reference to Hauerwas' work, see *Transforming Fate Into Destiny*, 164–79.

[8] For an extended exploration of comedy, romance, tragedy and irony, see Northrop Frye, *The Anatomy of Criticism: Four Essays* (Princeton: Princeton University Press, 1957), 131–239. Frye's magnificent essay is considered at length in a local church context by James Hopewell, *Congregation: Stories and Structures* (London: SCM Press, 1984).

opportunity is a challenge to the Church to leave to one side its diagnosis of human failure, and to sit around the table, along with everyone else, bringing its remedy for sin and its story of salvation. The establishment of the New Deal for Communities programme has included the scheduling of large public meetings, the writing of an outline bid, the election of a Community Partnership, the setting-up of sub-groups to cover issues like health, education and employment, the appointment of a project manager, field workers and office staff, the formation of sub-committees covering matters such as finance, personnel and project appraisal, and the carrying-out of a baseline survey. These activities have involved a profound self-examination by the community, one in which deep questions of identity, aspiration and purpose have been raised and considered. This is not a time for the Church to bury its talent in the hillside, aware that its Master is harsh on those who perceive salvation in secular terms. The Church brings its talent into the marketplace: it comes to the table with its faith on its sleeve. But what is the faith that speaks to this context, what is the talent with which it trades? In what follows I address these questions in terms of outlook and of action.

Outlook

Status

The three Earlham churches are all named after women of the holy family. The medieval church is St Mary's. In the 1930s, when Norwich expanded to the west and absorbed Earlham, St Anne's was built as the daughter church of St Mary's. Soon after, St Elizabeth's was founded in a small hall on the new local authority housing estate of North Earlham. When the new St Elizabeth's was built in 1991, North Earlham became a parish in its own right.

The new church experienced a terrible spate of vandalism for its first five years. Windows were smashed, cars torched, stones thrown at the congregation, motor bikes driven round and round the church during services,

services frequently disrupted. Three complementary approaches have helped St Elizabeth's congregation to emerge from these troubled times. One is patience. Much of the unrest came from a relatively small number of young people, who gradually grew up, expressed their anger differently, found an alternative focus for their energy, or moved away. A second is youth work. The church has put most of its energy into offering a great number of local children and young people a mixture of hospitality and constructive projects to engage their energy and interest. There have been youth clubs, football teams, dance clubs, trips away, sleepovers and discos. Over time these have helped many to see the church as 'theirs'.

The third approach concerns status, and has more direct links to Hauerwas' work. A teenager said to me, 'I knew the last vicar: I used to throw stones at his house.' This was volunteered, not in a hostile way, but as if it were an inevitable and unremarkable part of local life. 'What was it that led you to want to do that?' I asked her, gently challenging the force of inevitability. 'Because, you see, I don't believe in God', she said, simply and conclusively.

St Elizabeth's has undergone a gradual alteration in its perception of its own status. Supporting the values of a traditional institution, surrounded by young people who felt that they had little stake in mainstream society's hierarchy of rewards, appealing for order while no one seemed to be taking any notice, the church was in the condition of a hopelessly failing parent. Gently the church has come to see that the young person who threw the stone is in fact more representative of a widespread view, and thus more like a 'parent', whereas the church, being small and not taken seriously, is in fact more like a child. The power of the church is not that of the parent – greater resources, more experience, greater physical strength; instead, the church's power is that of the child – stubbornness and doggedness, and the tendency to ask awkward or embarrassing questions. So when the time comes to sit down with other groups in the community, the church sits down as a child, still learning, potentially disruptive, rather than as a parent, saying 'come to where we already are'.

Hauerwas refers to the distinction between the Church as strategy and the Church as tactic.[9] A strategy 'postulates a *place* that can be delimited as its *own* and serve as the base from which relations with an *exteriority* composed of targets or threats (customers or competitors, enemies, the country surrounding the city, objectives and objects of research, etc) can be managed'. This is 'the typical attitude of modern science, politics, and military strategy'. It is about making oneself safe from contingency. Any effort by St Elizabeth's to implement a strategy can clearly be seen as a failure. A tactic, by contrast, has no place of its own. It always lives in another's space, and must abide within another's rules. It has no general strategy, but makes *ad hoc* engagements as occasions arise. This is the experience that St Elizabeth's has come to see as its vocation.

Hauerwas also commends the character of the L'Arche communities. Development approaches sometimes distinguish between three models – working for, working with, and being with.[10] Jean Vanier employs similar distinctions when he describes the ethos of his differently-abled communities. 'We are trying to live in community with people who are mentally handicapped. Certainly we want to help them grow and reach the greatest independence possible. But before "doing for them", we want to "be with them." ' ' "To live with" is different from "To do for." It doesn't mean simply eating at the same table and sleeping under the same roof. It means that we create relationships of gratuity, truth and interdependence, that we listen to the handicapped people, that we recognise and marvel at their gifts.'[11] It is central to the tactic of St Elizabeth's that 'being with' comes before 'working with', while 'working for' is

[9] See Michel de Certeau, *The Practice of Everyday Life*, trans. Stephen Rendall (Berkeley, CA: University of California Press, 1988), 35–7, quoted in Stanley Hauerwas, *After Christendom?: How the Church is to Behave if Freedom, Justice, and a Christian Nation are Bad Ideas* (Nashville, TN: Abingdon Press, 1991), 16–18.

[10] See, for example, Sarah White and Romy Tiongco, *Doing Theology and Development: Meeting the Challenge of Poverty* (Edinburgh: St Andrew Press, 1997), 13–15.

[11] Stanley Hauerwas, *Sanctify Them in the Truth: Holiness Exemplified* (Nashville, TN: Abingdon Press and Edinburgh: T&T Clark, 1998), 143.

part of the parental role that has been largely set aside as unsatisfactory, inaccurate and unsustainable in equal measure.

Story

One of the things I found most difficult to get used to on moving to Norfolk was the kind of stories that local people tell. I had been accustomed to the culture of Tyneside, in the North-East of England: a culture of heavy industry, trade unions, working men's clubs and plenty of energy and humour. The abiding story was a profoundly tragic one: things used to be great (a thriving shipyard) but nothing lasts forever; we may have lots of talent (the footballer Paul Gascoigne) but let a morsel of hubris in, and somehow the feet of clay are revealed. Though surrounded by ghosts of golden eras, the community had plenty of enthusiasm for celebration and respect for institutions.

The culture of North Earlham, by contrast, is dominated by one institution only: the extended family. Participation in institutions outside the family – clubs, unions, churches – is low. There are thus relatively few places where a common story is established and rehearsed. The principal shared experience is that of the City Council as landlord, and of the co-dependent relationship that has developed between corporate landlord and individual tenant. The people I know here are much more cautious than the people I knew in the North-East when it comes to articulating a shared story. The consequence of a reluctance to articulate a story is that the present tense is elevated in significance: meanwhile the past is something of a foreign country and the future a closed book. Life for many people is largely a matter of survival, and the tools of the future – diaries, bank accounts and formal education – are accordingly downgraded.

In this culture I have come to understand the value of institutions. Institutions are bodies that pass on wisdom from one generation to another, that take the charisma of a founder and sustain that vision in the years after the founder has gone, that train people in public relationships, that redeem failures by learning from mistakes, and that establish trust by their openness to public scrutiny. To use MacIntyre's language, institutions embody traditions, foster practices, and train people in virtue.[12] Without institutions, it is hard for a community to gain a sense of its own story, to step out of the perpetual present tense. To return to a theme of Hauerwas' early work, decisions are made in view of a shared past and a perceived future; living in a perpetual present therefore underlines the insoluble nature of crises of decision. The community simply has fewer resources for making decisions. When, moreover, the principal common experience is that the important decisions are taken elsewhere (that is, in City Hall), the community loses not only the resources for making choices but also the reward for making good choices.[13]

St Elizabeth's has found perceiving itself as a child in relation to its surrounding culture a liberating experience. It has also come to see its gift to its surrounding culture as also about being a child – but this time a child in relation to history. It is a child because it knows it is small in relation to the great heritage that lies behind it – a heritage of creation, Israel, and Jesus, and all the missionaries, saints, martyrs and faithful of the Church over the centuries. It is a child because it is yet young in relation to the great destiny that lies before it, a destiny of kingdom and promise, of the healing of wounds and the drying of tears, of the fullness of the glory of God and the exaltation of the humble and meek. It is a child because it stands before the fatherhood of God, able to be there because of the baptism which has grafted it into God's story and has given it a share in that story's heritage and destiny. And so the good news that St Elizabeth's offers to its community,

---

[12] See MacIntyre's discussion in his *After Virtue*, 204–25.

[13] For the shortcomings of 'decisionism' see, for example, Stanley Hauerwas, 'From System to Story: An Alternative Pattern for Rationality in Ethics', *Truthfulness and Tragedy: Further Investigations in Christian Ethics* (Notre Dame, IN: University of Notre Dame Press, 1977), 15–39, and the summary of Hauerwas' argument in *Transforming Fate Into Destiny*, 13–39.

the good news of Jesus Christ, is news that offers to free its community from the tyranny of the perpetual present. The good news is that through baptism God offers his people a past and a future.

What the Christian story offers North Earlham is memory and hope.[14] Memory means looking on the past without resentment; hope means looking on the future without fear. Both memory and hope stem from the faith which professes that time is on our side and that the truth sets us free. The God of Jacob and David and Peter is a God who has a place and a purpose for those who know they have lied and cheated and stolen. There is no need any more to exaggerate one's trials, fabricate one's successes or hide one's failures. If God knows the secrets of all souls, if God can forgive sin and heal broken hearts, bind up wounds and restore to community, then there is no need to perpetuate false stories or pretend that there is no story.[15] One can accept shared responsibility for the mistakes of earlier generations, one can challenge the paralysis of the story that says it has always been so. One can move from the bitterness of telling the story with oneself always as the victim, to the wonder of realising that one has been included by grace as a small character in a glorious drama in which the

---

[14] On memory, see Stanley Hauerwas, 'Self-Deception and Autobiography: Reflections on Speer's *Inside the Third Reich*', *Truthfulness and Tragedy*, 82–98; 'Memory, Community, and Reasons for Living: Reflections on Suicide and Euthanasia', *Truthfulness and Tragedy*, 101–15: 'Resurrection, the Holocaust, and the Obligation to Forgive', *Unleashing the Scripture: Freeing the Bible from Captivity to America* (Nashville, TN: Abingdon, 1993), 140–8. On hope, see Stanley Hauerwas, 'Hope Faces Power: Thomas More and the King of England', *Christian Existence Today: Essays on Church, World, and Living in Between* (Durham, NC: Labyrinth Press, 1988), 221–36; Stanley Hauerwas and Charles Pinches, 'On Developing Hopeful Virtues', *Christians among the Virtues: Conversations with Ancient and Modern Ethics* (Notre Dame, IN: University of Notre Dame Press, 1997), 113–28.
[15] See Stanley Hauerwas, *A Community of Character: Toward a Constructive Christian Social Ethic* (Notre Dame, IN: University of Notre Dame Press, 1981), 12, and *Sanctify Them in the Truth*, 177–90 on the liberal 'story that we have no story'.

central character is not oneself or one's antagonists, but always God.[16]

Meanwhile, with God as the central character, the future becomes a different story. In a culture where the extended family is dominant, friendships outside the family are fragile, and the future is secured only by having more children.[17] Baptism presents a rival model of community to that offered by friendship or family. Baptism offers membership of a body, the body of Christ.[18] No longer does one have to carve out one's own destiny: destiny is now a gift, rather than an achievement. One's own success is no longer the goal or security of life. A project is worthy if it points to Christ, not if it secures independence. Possessions are valuable to the extent they can be shared, not to the extent they can be kept. Even death can be faced, if it is seen as an event in God's story, rather than as the end of one's own. I have already suggested one definition of the distinction between the rich and the poor. Here is another. Imagine the eschaton were coming tomorrow. The rich are those who say, 'Couldn't we have just a bit more time? I'm only just getting used to e-mail, I haven't tried out my new car, and I'm so looking forward to my daughter's graduation.' The poor are those who say, 'Yes, please.' Hope means facing the future without fear.

When a church believes it is part of a story, a story of memory and hope, it can know better when to challenge its community, and when to comfort and affirm. The North Earlham estate is 60 years old. St Elizabeth's, old and new, is 60 years old too. The church bears the name of a saint, Elizabeth, who was past the age when any fruit (of the kind

---

[16] For a discussion of the difference between a hero, who is always seeking to be the centre of the story, and the saint, who is always a peripheral character in a story that is always about God, see Samuel Wells 'The Disarming Virtue of Stanley Hauerwas', *Scottish Journal of Theology* 52 (1999), 82–8.

[17] Compare Hauerwas' own understanding of having children – see a summary in *Transforming Fate Into Destiny*, 172–8.

[18] For a profound understanding of the body of Christ in relation to human cloning, see Stanley Hauerwas and Joel Shuman, 'Cloning the Human Body' in Ronald Cole-Turner (ed.), *Human Cloning – Religious Responses* (Louisville, KY: Westminster John Knox Press, 1997).

most valued by her culture) was expected of her. Let us say she was about 60. The miracle of grace is that Elizabeth found a place in the story of salvation. She became fruitful, and her fruit spoke the truth which unsettled the proud and pointed towards the saviour. The faith of the church that bears her name keeps alive the faith that it too, and the community that shares Elizabeth's age and sense of frustration and rejection, may find a remarkable place in God's gracious story.

The story teaches us that the miracle of Elizabeth happened 2000 years ago. St Elizabeth's has chosen to celebrate this joyous anniversary by creating two stained-glass windows, of the pregnant Elizabeth and the babe inside her greeting the pregnant Mary and her newly-conceived babe. The windows proclaim the faith of the Church that God was the mighty who came down from his seat to become the humble and meek who was then highly exalted. It is a story that proclaims to the mighty that they will not be exalted unless they become humble and meek, and to the humble and meek that they too may hope to be exalted. It is a story that promises us our souls will be filled with joy when we sing to God our saviour.

Action

If, as Hauerwas maintains, the principal social ethical activity of the Church is to be the Church, then the most significant social witness of St Elizabeth's is to gather together on a Sunday.[19] Given the fragility of institutions in the community, the regular and frequent voluntary

---

[19] Perhaps Hauerwas' most widely-quoted words are these: 'The first social-ethical task of the church is to be the church: ... The church does not have a social ethic: the church is a social ethic.' *The Peaceable Kingdom: A Primer in Christian Ethics* (Notre Dame, IN: University of Notre Dame Press, 1993), 99. From time to time, Hauerwas reflects on congregational life and worship and their ethical dimensions. See 'The Ministry of a Congregation: Rethinking Christian Ethics for a Church-Centred Seminary', *Christian Existence Today*, 111–31; 'In Defence of Cultural Christianity: Reflections on Going to Church', *Sanctify Them in the Truth*, 157–73.

gathering of people who have no blood relationship, financial gain, or common pastime, and no particular economic or racial identity, is the most remarkable thing about the Church. The assembly comes about through geographical location,[20] a shared commitment to the Christian tradition, and a common identity which one member describes as 'a bunch of misfits who somehow fit together'. As Hauerwas himself says, 'The church, as a society of the liberated, is thus the necessary paradigm that can offer us imaginative possibilities of social relations otherwise not thought possible'.[21]

The 'imaginative possibilities of social relations' at St Elizabeth's are perhaps most in evidence in the interaction of adults and children. Several factors contribute to making St Elizabeth's unusual in this respect. Children outnumber adults at the Sunday morning service by about four to one. Not a single one of these children brings a parent with them. The church has adults, and the church has children – but the church has no nuclear families. Those adults who endured the time of persecution the church went through some years ago emerged with a remarkably positive, try-anything approach. Thus all who come are prepared to interact with whoever walks through the door. The building is modern and flexible, with no fixed seating and a comfortable floor. These four factors have made it possible to develop a particular style of worship in which children and adults together explore God's word and mystery. For example, at Epiphany adults and older children discussed in groups where was the darkness, where was the manger, and how we could be the star in relation to Iraq, Ethiopia, and a street near the church respectively, while the younger children cut out shapes representing darknesses, mangers and stars. A shared enquiry and shared discovery helps the adults break out of

---

[20] Almost everyone can or could walk to church. I have never known there to be more than three cars parked outside during a Sunday morning service.
[21] Stanley Hauerwas, 'Some Theological Reflections on Gutiérrez's Use of "Liberation" as a Theological Concept', *Modern Theology* 3 (1986), 67–76, at 76.

comfortable modes of thought, and offers the children adults who listen to them and take their questioning journey of discipleship seriously. This is not a 'family service', for there are no families: it is the body of Christ in communal discernment.[22] By learning to be friends with people very different from themselves, old and young learn more about what it means to be friends with God.[23]

A second 'imaginative possibility' is in the way the church has reconstrued its notion of glory and of the communion of saints.[24] The new St Elizabeth's is a square modern building in which immanence has triumphed over transcendence. Where is one therefore to direct one's eyes in worship? The bare emptiness of the new building has given hospitality to large artistic collages of provocative themes – Easter, Christmas, the Exodus, Noah's Ark – devised and produced by local schools. Thus in a physical way the church celebrates that in the community which turns to God. Extending this principle to adults, a dozen young mothers have taken, developed and mounted photographs of characters in the local community. These photographs have then been placed on the walls of the church as a reminder to the community that their needs and longings are at the heart of the church's prayers, and as a reminder to the congregation of those who are not with them as they come into God's presence. This is a church that knows instinctively the distinction between church and world, but does not mistake that awareness for sectarianism. By articulating its vulnerability and neediness, seeking and valuing the gifts of outsiders, and giving hospitality to the true character of its community, it

---

[22] Of course there are occasions when the children and adults worship separately. But on these occasions it is the adults, not the children, who leave the main worship space and go into a smaller room, later to return and report on what they have discovered in their 'group'.

[23] On friendship, see Stanley Hauerwas and Charles Pinches, *Christians Among the Virtues*, particularly 31–51 and 70–88; and Stanley Hauerwas, 'Timeful Friends: Living with the Handicapped', *Sanctify Them in the Truth* 143–56.

[24] On the significance to Hauerwas' theology of the communion of saints, see *Transforming Fate Into Destiny*, 29–31.

has subverted the conventional notions of service and turned a conflict of stories into a shared search for beauty.

A third 'imaginative possibility' lies in liturgy. This community has as low a literacy rate as any in the country. Actions, pictures, music and spoken words provoke, artic- ulate, and communicate in a way that the written word seldom does. It is a place where worship is much more about actions than about words. If the principal social witness of the Church is to be the Church – to meet together week by week to worship the God of Jesus Christ – then the principal form of its gospel is in the practices rehearsed in its liturgical life. Four of those practices may be appropriate to offer here.

One is confession. Few people in this community need to be reminded of their failure. Many, however, need to be reminded that they are neither uniquely guilty nor uniquely innocent, that they are loved unreservedly and that they are not written out of the story. A frequent form of confession at St Elizabeth's is to invite two members of the congregation to form a human sculpture. They kneel upright facing one another, heads resting on each other's shoulder, hands on one another's upper arms.[25] The statue proclaims that there is no reconciliation with God without reconciliation with neighbour, and yet that each neighbour is as broken and needy as the other. Few words need be said, but adults and children may walk around and touch the statue if they wish to. The ritual is a performance of the Gospel of grace, a call to repentance, an assurance of sins forgiven, a demonstration of the liberating power of a truthful story, and an offering of hope to the community.[26]

Another simple liturgical action is to stand for the reading of the Gospel. This is common to most Anglican churches. One small difference at St Elizabeth's is that the chairs are generally arranged in a horseshoe, with the altar

[25] The sculpture is inspired by one called 'Reconciliation', carved by Josefina de Vasconcellos, which stands in the ruins of Coventry Cathedral. An identical sculpture stands in the Peace Gardens, Hiroshima.
[26] On forgiveness and reconciliation, see William H. Willimon and Stanley Hauerwas, *Lord, Hear Us: The Lord's Prayer and the Christian Life* (Nashville, TN: Abingdon Press, 1996), 78–86.

at the open end, and the lectern facing the altar at the top of the horseshoe. It is sometimes difficult to persuade all the congregation to stand for the Gospel: it is part of the culture that few if any people are worthy of that kind of respect. But to turn to the back and face the Gospel is not only to turn around, not only to be attentive to the shocking news of Jesus' story, but to realise that the Gospel comes in from the outside, through the same door as the stranger, and that openness to the one means openness to the other. The two can be equally demanding. For a long time the congregation were used to looking to the back and trying to imagine how they could welcome teenagers with rollerblades on their feet, stones in their hands, and anger in their heads. The church has been profoundly shaped by these experiences. There is no sentimentality about the 'stranger'. Yet the small congregation includes a high proportion of 'strangers': this is not an easy place to be of mixed race, for example. Openness to the stranger is a key gift St Elizabeth's offers to its community – and it learns this openness by the liturgical act of turning to the door to hear the Gospel.[27]

A third simple gesture that shapes the worship of St Elizabeth's is the practice of two children baking the eucharistic bread on the morning of the holy communion service. These two children then bring up the bread during the service as the table is prepared. It does not occur to the congregation to say 'How sweet!' any more than it occurs to God to say 'How sweet!' when he receives the other fruits of creation and human labour. The act is a reminder that all bring different things to God's table, but all receive back the same thing. It is an education that all good gifts around us come with a cost to somebody, most often God. And it is a reversal of the expectation that adults give while

---

[27] Hauerwas is quite sure that the preacher's job is to tell us something we do not want to hear. See 'Practice Preaching', *Sanctify Them in the Truth*, 235–40; see also Stanley Hauerwas and William H. Willimon, *Preaching to Strangers: Evangelism in Today's World* (Louisville, KY: Westminster John Knox Press), 1992, 1–15. Hauerwas' concern with the stranger is embodied in the fourth of his 'Ten theses for the reform of Christian social ethics' – see *A Community of Character*, 9–12.

children receive. The practice forms the congregation to be a particular kind of gift to their community: they are shaped to be better at receiving the hidden gifts that so many in the community have longed so deeply to give to someone. The pride on the children's faces as they offer the bread is an inspiration that often the best way the Church can serve its community is by finding ways to receive.

A final practice that is by no means unique to this church but which speaks to its context is the way communion is received. The chairs are pushed back and all stand shoulder to shoulder in a loose circle. All stand silently, permitted to stand in God's presence only by his grace, and wait as each part of the body is nourished. This is not a substitute family for those whose nuclear families have fallen short. It is not a circle of friends, gathered to encourage and affirm and enjoy one another. It is the body of Christ, finding its wholeness in the broken heart of God. Family and friendship are both noble and worthy institutions, endorsed, in general, by Scripture. But the body of Christ, joined in baptism, is the unique way in which the community understands its dependence on God through the incarnation, death and resurrection of Christ, and its interdependence, one on another.

Conclusion

How can one blend together two stories?[28] How does a church set the energy and optimism of the humanist New Deal for Communities story alongside Hauerwas' deeply ironic story of human tragedy and divine comedy?

I have suggested three dimensions in which the relationship may be fruitful. The first concerns status. New

---

[28] Hauerwas considers this key question in 'A Tale of Two Stories: On Being a Christian and a Texan', *Christian Existence Today*, 25–45. I cannot hope in this short essay to address all the issues that arise from the encounter of stories – issues ranging from the mediating role of the parish priest to the potential tensions between the story of the local church and that of the universal Church. I am grateful to Stephen Platten for pressing me on these points.

Deal for Communities tells a story which may sound faintly familiar to some ears. It offers redemption to deprived communities. To find redemption, each of the partners in the community's welfare – statutory service providers, local businesses, voluntary groups, and residents themselves – must to some extent acknowledge their own failure. By working together, listening to one another, and maintaining a shared vision, each can hope for a gradual improvement in the economic and social well-being of the community. The 'Pathfinder Community' thus looks suspiciously like the Church – formed in repentance and reconciliation, maintained by mutual support.

If the local church is to be part of this redemption, it must come to the table in humility, recognising, like everybody else, its own failure. No one has a *right* to be at the table: everyone is invited to bring to the table what they can offer for the improvement of the community. The local church's response to this invitation depends on the kind of story it tells about itself. If it tells a purely tragic story, in which all human striving turns to dust, its story will paralyse not only its own action but also the activity of the community as a whole. It would be a refusal of the invitation to sit at the table. If, by contrast, it tells a purely comic story, in which greater knowledge, healthy listening and good working practice can overcome all obstacles to the well-being of all, it will be coming to the table with little significant to say. Christians must come to the table, but must come with their story of grace and truth, treasure in clay jars, servant kings and empty tombs. Like all partici-pants, Christians have had to recognise they have no *right* to be at the table: the question is, what do they *bring* to the table? Like a child who has been waiting to speak for a long time – and like many in the community who feel like such a child – the local church has a great deal to say.

The second dimension is that of story. The local church is a fellow child at the table, fragile and needing help yet with much to offer. It is distinguished by the story it has to tell. It is a story of purpose, failure, cost, forgiveness, reconciliation and resurrection. Together these elements offer back to the community a past that might otherwise be lost in recrimination and mistrust, and promise to the community a future that might otherwise be closed by fear or despair. The local church can enter the planning process with the grace of knowing that failure is not the worst thing that can happen, with the wisdom of knowing that others have walked this way before, and with the freedom of knowing that the creativity, compromise, friendship, and perseverance of the process rest in the power of the Spirit. What members of the New Deal for Communities process appear to value most about the Church is its tradition of trust. This trust, as Hauerwas is fond of saying, can only arise from a community whose story shows that it has nothing to fear from the truth.

The third dimension lies with the practices developed by the worshipping church. If the community is to develop, it needs not only structural change but also new habits, new ways of relating, new skills, new friends. I have described a number of commonplace practices of one local church in a deprived community in order to show the significance of such practices in reflecting and shaping faith and in offering that faith to the wider community. Hauerwas makes even larger claims: 'My account of such practices, moreover, entails my "metaphysics", since I believe that such a practice not only describes how Christians must act in relation to one another but reveals the very character of God's creation'.[29] Such practices bear out another concern close to Hauerwas' heart, the way a congregation learn their morality from the habits formed by their liturgy.[30] One is only aware of the significance of such practices when one notices their absence. To take the simplest example, church meetings start with a prayer: New Deal meetings never do. For church regulars saying a prayer at the start of a meeting may have become a habit given scant consideration. But at a New Deal meeting, sensing

[29] Stanley Hauerwas, 'Foreword', in Samuel Wells, *Transforming Fate Into Destiny*, x–xii, at xi.
[30] On the ethical dimensions of liturgy, see Stanley Hauerwas, 'The Liturgical Shape of the Christian Life: Teaching Christian Ethics as Worship', in *In Good Company: The Church as Polis* (Notre Dame, IN: University of Notre Dame Press, 1995), 153–68.

something curiously missing which one has elsewhere taken for granted, one becomes slowly aware that this gathering is taking upon itself an enormous task – and is seeking to perform it in its own strength alone. How awesome is the sight! The spectacles that discern this are those given by the habit of corporate prayer.

The first form of society, and the 'imaginative possibility of social relations' *par excellence,* is of course God the holy Trinity. In Rublev's icon of the Trinity, depicted in the form of Abraham's three visitors, the three dimensions – of status, story, and practice – coalesce in one picture. What is shown in the icon is a paradigm of grace, a model of society, in which each person is able to offer completely while at the same time being able to receive completely. This is a picture of what St Elizabeth's wants for its community under the New Deal for Communities programme. It wants every person in the community to be able to give all that they have in them to offer, and to receive all that others are longing to give.[31]

What the Church brings to the table is its perception of its status – its realisation that it is not a powerful benefactor but a humble child with much to offer and in need of help. It brings its faith in its story – its heritage and destiny, its memory and hope. And it brings its habits and practices, worn into shape through ritual and experience, embodying the offering and receiving that underlie all shared life, centred on eucharist, baptism and the reading of Scripture. This is the way the local church serves its community most faithfully and fully: and it does so by being the Church.

---

[31] For an extended reflection on theological ethics shaped by the Trinity, see L. Gregory Jones, *Transformed Judgement: Towards a Trinitarian Account of the Moral Life* (Notre Dame, IN: University of Notre Dame Press, 1990). Jones does discuss Trinity and community (120–9), but he does not refer to Rublev's icon.

TESTING HAUERWAS

7
Is Stanley Hauerwas Sectarian?

Nigel Biggar

The standard charge levelled against Stanley Hauerwas, and the most common reason for dismissing what he has to say, is that he is 'sectarian'. By 'sectarianism' what is usually meant is a retreat into the private world of the Church and into personal spirituality, and what is assumed to be a correlative disengagement from public concerns and debate. If the sectarian does not simply abandon the (public) world to its fate, then the most he does is to address it uncompromisingly in his own language and in the form of a monologue, saying, in effect, 'There's the Gospel: take it or leave it!' Here the sin of sectarianism takes the specific form of a 'confessional' (as distinct from 'dialogical') mode of address.[1]

This, for example, is the gist of the criticism made of Hauerwas by one of his most eminent critics, Max Stackhouse. In a review of *Dispatches from the Front*,

---

[1] The concept of sectarianism that Hauerwas' critics use is more or less the one classically defined by Troeltsch. According to Troeltsch, the sect renounces any idea of ruling the world, adopts a stance of opposition to worldly powers, aspires after personal moral and spiritual perfection and the building and maintenance of a 'radical fellowship of love', and is eschatologically oriented (Ernst Troeltsch, *The Social Teaching of the Christian Churches*, trans. Olive Wyon, 2 vols, Chicago and London: University of Chicago Press, 1976, vol. I, 331–43). Troeltsch, however, is more sensitive than Hauerwas' critics to the critical role that the sect plays by embodying a radical alternative to the political and social status quo. This is implied, for example, by his description of the typical alternative to the sect – the church – as 'overwhelmingly conservative' (330) and characteristically involved in 'compromise with the State, with the social order, and with economic conditions' (335). Taking one step further in this direction, H. Richard Niebuhr admits that the Christ-against-culture type of Christian (his equivalent to Troeltsch's sectarian) has often had a reforming effect on the world's culture, but only inadvertently (*Christ and Culture*, New York: Harper and Row, 1975, 66–7).

Stackhouse emphatically characterises the liberal
Christianity, which Hauerwas is held to repudiate, as
'engaged': 'Christianity has a liberal element at its core....
It has engaged philosophies and cultures from beyond its
own roots.... It demands ... socially *engaged* theology in
which philosophy and ethics and social analysis play
decisive roles'.[2] Further, Stackhouse suggests that, whereas
liberal Christians believe in the possibility of rational
conversation across boundaries that distinguish religious
and philosophical traditions, Hauerwas is an 'ideologist'
demanding 'conformity of conscience' from his disciples,
who 'simply assert their beliefs against any who challenge
them'.[3] In this critic's eyes, at least, Hauerwas is sectarian
(because disengaged) and, more specifically, confessional.

But Stackhouse's view is distorted; and in this particular
cross-boundary 'conversation' his liberal ears have been
less than wide open. It is true that Hauerwas does not
believe that the primary task of the Christian Church is to
support the American liberal democratic status quo.[4] It is
true that he does believe that the Church's primary task is
to be faithful to its own theological norms of practice and
speech, and to grow in accordance with them. But this does
not amount to irresponsible indifference to the fate of the
world and disengagement from the task of promoting its

[2] Max Stackhouse, 'Liberalism dispatched vs. liberalism engaged',
Christian Century (18 October 1995), 962. My emphasis.
[3] Stackhouse, 'Liberalism dispatched', 963.
[4] Responding to Oliver O'Donovan's book, *The Desire of the Nations:
Recovering the Roots of Political Theology*, Hauerwas in effect makes the
revealing admission that what appears to be his general repudiation of
attempts to Christianize the political or social order is, more exactly, a
repudiation of the assumption, widespread in the context of *American*
Christianity, that the liberal status quo is already Christian: 'If heard in
places like Britain ..., where Christianity is more or less perceived by
many as a curious but largely antiquated cultural oddity, ... in such
contexts a hopeful reminder of God's ultimate conquest of ungodly
powers is salutary.... But for Christians in America, who see themselves
very much in control ... what is most helpful, indeed necessary, is a
reminder that they too, even in America, continue to live in exile' (Stanley
Hauerwas, with James Fodor, 'Remaining in Babylon: Oliver
O'Donovan's Defense of Christendom', in *Wilderness Wanderings: Probing
Twentieth-Century Theology and Philosophy* [Boulder, CO and Oxford:
Westview Press, 1997], 214).

good. On the contrary, as Hauerwas sees it, it is the only way in which the Church can serve the world properly: 'As Christians we will not serve such a world well if we pretend that the church is only incidental to the world's salvation.'[5] Maybe for the Troeltschian sectarian, more certainly for the Niebuhrian Christ-against-culture type, the practice and cultivation of spiritual life is seen as an alternative to political engagement;[6] but for Hauerwas prayer is 'our most important *civic* responsibility'[7] and the Church's worship of Christ its 'main *political* task'.[8] Hauerwas is far more Barthian than Pietist. He is convinced that the Christian Church has something to communicate to the world that is vital to its well-being, corporate and individual. He is sure that the Christian story of the God who raised Jesus from the dead, and who is even now working toward the eschatological completion of the world's redemption, inspires and sustains the virtues of faith and hope, and thereby those of gratitude for life,[9] honesty in argument,[10] patience in uncertainty and suffering,[11] and nonviolence in the face of aggression.[12] This is why he is so relentlessly insistent that the Christian Church concentrate on thinking and living out its own story, instead of squandering itself in merely repeating in religious tones the moral platitudes that the world already takes quite for granted. He really believes that the Church has news about the human and public good to proclaim to secularist liberals.

In spite of the apparent implications of his polemical rhetoric, Hauerwas is therefore interested in having the

[5] Stanley Hauerwas, *After Christendom?* (Nashville, TN: Abingdon Press, 1991), 43.

[6] See note 1 above.

[7] Stanley Hauerwas, 'A Christian Critique of Christian America', in *Christian Existence Today: Essays on Church, World, and Living in Between* (Durham, NC: Labyrinth Press, 1988), 185. My emphasis.

[8] Stanley Hauerwas and William H. Willimon, *Resident Aliens: Life in the Christian Colony* (Nashville, TN: Abingdon Press, 1989), 45. My emphasis.

[9] E.g., Hauerwas and Willimon, *Resident Aliens*, 55.

[10] E.g., Hauerwas and Willimon, *Resident Aliens*, 63.

[11] E.g., Hauerwas and Willimon, *Resident Aliens*, 66.

[12] E.g., Hauerwas and Willimon, *Resident Aliens*, 62.

Church shape society-at-large – albeit in a fashion that is true to its own norms. Those who have listened carefully to him will not be very surprised to find him endorsing Oliver O'Donovan's assertion that the idea of Christendom – namely, that secular authority should be fashioned to serve the advancement of the Gospel – is an aspect of the Church's proper understanding of its mission: 'It was the missionary imperative that compelled the church to take the conversion of the empire seriously and to seize the opportunities it offered' – and opportunities not just for wielding power, but also for Christianising politics.[13] However, in a society where it is blithely assumed that the dominant moral and political norms are Christian, in spite of the fact that these are understood in rigorously secularist terms, it is time for the Church to stand back from the business of trying to shape the world and for it to reflect on *how* it is trying to shape it. It is time for the Church to think again about what it means to be the *Church*, about what its particular vocation is – and to do this, not because it has ceased to care about the wider world, but precisely because it cares to discharge its own peculiar and vital service to it properly. This is the context in which, according to Hauerwas, the Christian Church in the USA now stands.

As Hauerwas sees it, the eagerness of liberal Christians to be effective in shaping society-at-large has moved them to jettison anything that liberal secularists might find objectionable. Consequently, the impact that they have succeeded in having has been essentially conservative, at least confirming what the world already assumes, and at most deepening it. Liberal Christianity has succeeded in bending the world's ear only by being careful to avoid saying anything radically unfamiliar; it has been 'persuasive' only in so far as it has ceased to have anything very original to communicate.

For Hauerwas, the paradigmatic liberal Christian is Reinhold Niebuhr. For it was Niebuhr who came to exercise widespread cultural influence by effectively reducing theology to anthropology. In his hands, theology's role is

---

[13] Hauerwas, 'Remaining in Babylon', 206–7.

basically restricted to that of illuminating the human condition, specifically in terms of the concept of sin,[14] thereby justifying political 'realism' – that is, acceptance of the inevitability of the political use of (violent) force.[15] In spite of his criticism of the optimism of liberal politics, Niebuhr remained firmly within the secularising tradition of liberal theology, especially in his programme of 'translating' the story of God's redemption of the world into symbols of constant features of human existence. Accordingly, Niebuhr strips the cross of Jesus of its decisive soteriological role and reduces it to the symbol of 'the perfection of agape which transcends all particular norms of justice and mutuality in history'.[16] In Niebuhr's defence, it might be pointed out that this symbol is not merely illuminating, but also somewhat morally effective; for it presents an ideal that, though impossible to realise fully in history, nevertheless moves sinful humans to raise their moral sights.[17] But even if Niebuhr's understanding of the cross is not entirely lacking 'salvific' content, and even if he did understand it as a morally inspiring 'revelation', it is still not unequivocally theological; that is to say, it is not at all clear that it refers either to a decisive act of *God* in the course of the history of his redeeming work, or to an act that is effective in transforming the relationship of human beings to *him*. If we add to this equivocation Niebuhr's deep suspicion of eschatology,[18] we might well see fit to join Hauerwas in judging him to be 'functionally atheistic'.[19]

---

[14] Stanley Hauerwas, 'No Enemy, No Christianity', *Sanctify Them in the Truth: Holiness Exemplified* (Edinburgh: T&T Clark, 1998), 193–4; Hauerwas, *After Christendom?*, 109, 183 n. 17.

[15] Stanley Hauerwas, 'The Irony of Reinhold Niebuhr: the Ideological Character of "Christian Realism"', *Wilderness Wanderings*, 48f.

[16] Reinhold Niebuhr, *The Nature and Destiny of Man*, 2 vols, vol. 2: *Human Destiny* (New York: Scribners, 1964), 74, quoted by Stanley Hauerwas in 'On Keeping Theological Ethics Theological', *Against the Nations: War and Survival in Liberal Society* (Minneapolis: Winston Press, 1985), 48 n. 26.

[17] In Hauerwas' own words: 'religion illuminates this condition [of the basic self-interestedness of human collectivities] and provides some inspiration to do better, even though the full realization of its ideals are [sic] impossible in history' (Hauerwas, 'The Irony of Reinhold Niebuhr', 51).

[18] Hauerwas and Willimon, *Resident Aliens*, 86–7.

[19] Hauerwas, *After Christendom?*, 31, 166 n. 12.

Hauerwas stands to Niebuhr and the American tradition of Protestant liberalism much as Barth stood to the German neo-Kantian tradition represented by Ritschl and Harnack. Both champion a theistic realism over and against a 'religious' humanism.[20] Both challenge the easy identification of liberal humanist culture with Christianity. Both urge the Church to take its own special vocation seriously, and to concentrate on being faithful to its own 'story' or dogmatic principles, not merely to preserve its identity, but precisely in order to perform its own unique and vital service to the world. Consequently, both share a deep suspicion of the 'apologetic' mode of trying to win over non-believers, and for similar reasons.

For Barth, 'apologetics' begins from some generally demonstrable human capacity, religious or moral, and seeks to argue for Christianity as its necessary fulfilment. The paradigm here is Schleiermacher's theological method, which argues from general religious self-consciousness to specifically Christian self-consciousness as its supreme realisation.[21] Barth's objection to this procedure is that the historical self-realisation of the free God in Jesus Christ is made to fit the terms set *a priori* by a non-Christian anthropology: 'from ... some general knowledge of God and

---

[20] I say this, notwithstanding my impression that Hauerwas has generally been much shyer than Barth to talk directly of God, preferring instead to focus on the distinctive, character-forming 'story' of the Christian Church. Indeed, elsewhere I have implicitly criticised him for permitting ecclesial sociology to eclipse theology (see Nigel Biggar, *The Hastening that Waits: Karl Barth's Ethics*, Oxford: Oxford University Press, 1993, 1995); and he himself has acknowledged the cogency of this criticism, as least with regard to his work up to 1986 ('In spite of everything I was trying to do to sustain the integrity of Christian speech, ... I may have done nothing more than reproduce Durkheim, albeit with an ecclesiological twist' ['The Truth about God: The Decalogue as Condition of Truthful Speech', *Sanctify Them in the Truth*, 37]). Still, the central place that eschatology occupies in Hauerwas' thought (see, e.g., Hauerwas and Willimon, *Resident Aliens*, 86ff), together with his description of the task of the Church as that of bearing witness before the world 'that God really is busy redeeming humanity' (*Resident Aliens*, 92), makes it clear enough that when he talks of the Christian 'story', he is not talking of a morally useful fiction.
[21] Karl Barth, *Church Dogmatics*, trans. G. W. Bromiley (Edinburgh: T&T Clark, 1975), I/1, 192–3.

man, it is known beforehand, known *a priori*, what revelation must be, may be, and ought to be'.[22] In the field of
ethics, then, 'apologetics' amounts to 'the attempt to
establish and justify the theologico-ethical enquiry within
the framework and on the foundation of the presuppositions and methods of non-theological, of wholly human
thinking and language'.[23] Against this human domestic-
ation of God, Barth calls for polemics rather than
apologetics, insisting that theology must let God's self-
revelation grasp human language, and not language
revelation.[24] Accordingly, theological ethics must 'annex'
general ethics, rather than surrender to it;[25] and, above all,
it must not 'try to eliminate from its own task the alien
element which ... necessarily characterises it. ... [It] must
not and will not disarm its distinctive Whence? and
Whither? in order to assure itself a place in the sun of
general ethical discussion. ... [It] must always be absolutely resolved to stick to its own colours and not to allow
itself to be hindered in the fulfilment of its own task'.[26]

Here, Hauerwas is a companion, indeed a follower, of
Barth.[27] Taking Tillich's theology as typical, Hauerwas
describes apologetics as seeking to render Christian
thought credible by translating it into terms intelligible to
modern people. The problem with this, however, is that the
flow of interpretative traffic has tended to move only in
one direction – *from* Christianity *to* modernity – and that
'modern interpreters of the faith have tended to let the
"modern world" determine the questions and therefore
limit the answers'.[28] But unlike Barth, and to his credit,

[22] Karl Barth, *Church Dogmatics*, trans. G. T. Thomson and Harold Knight
(Edinburgh: T&T Clark, 1956), I/2, 4.
[23] Karl Barth, *Church Dogmatics*, trans. G. W. Bromiley *et al.* (Edinburgh:
T&T Clark, 1957), II/2, 520.
[24] Barth, *Church Dogmatics*, I/1, 340–1.
[25] Barth, *Church Dogmatics*, II/2, 522–4.
[26] Barth, *Church Dogmatics*, II/2, 524.
[27] For evidence of Hauerwas' indebtedness to Barth on this point see,
e.g., Stanley Hauerwas, *The Peaceable Kingdom: A Primer in Christian Ethics*
(Notre Dame, IN: University of Notre Dame Press, 1983), 55; and
Hauerwas and Willimon, *Resident Aliens*, 19–24.
[28] Hauerwas and Willimon, *Resident Aliens*, 20.

Hauerwas distinguishes between Christian apologetics of the second century AD and that of the modern period. He admits that, since Christian doctrine posits 'a strong continuity between the God who redeems and the God who creates', Christians should expect to find something in common with non-believers; and, indeed, they 'should not be surprised to find their specific religious beliefs confirmed by the best humanistic alternatives'.[29] However,

> the apologist of the past stood in the Church and its tradition and sought relationship with those outside. Apologetic theology was a secondary endeavour because the apologist never assumed that one could let the questions of unbelief order the theological agenda. But now the theologian stands outside the tradition and seeks to show that selected aspects of that tradition can no longer pass muster from the perspective of the outsider. ... Ironically, just to the extent this strategy has been successful, the more theologians have underwritten the assumption that anything said in a theological framework cannot be of much interest. For if what is said theologically is but a confirmation of what we can know on other grounds or can be said more clearly in non-theological language, then why bother saying it theologically at all?[30]

Clearly, then, Hauerwas' objection to 'apologetics' is not indicative of a lack of interest in engaging with non-believers, in communicating with them, in persuading them, in trying to render the Christian view of reality intelligible and credible and plausible to them. On the contrary, what he objects to is a particular form of apologetics that seeks to communicate by abandoning constitutive features

---

[29] Hauerwas, 'On Keeping Theological Ethics Theological', 24. Cf. Barth, *Church Dogmatics*, I/2, 4: 'This reversal [of the priority of theology to anthropology] is the great temptation of all theology. We shall therefore not be surprised to meet traces of it here and there as early as the Apologists of the second century of the Church ...'.
[30] Hauerwas, 'On Keeping Theological Ethics Theological', 24.

of Christianity that non-believers are likely to find immediately alien; that is 'persuasive' only in the sense that Christian faith accommodates itself to unbelief, and not in the sense that unbelief is attracted to faith; that achieves intelligibility only by requiring the faith to adapt itself to the non-believer, and not by requiring the non-believer to adapt herself to faith. It is for this reason that Hauerwas describes the theologian's job as 'not to make the gospel credible to the modern world, but to make the world credible to the gospel'.[31]

Hauerwas' insistence that, in dialogue with non-believers, Christians should not assume that they are the only ones who need to do the rethinking, the adapting, the moving, hints at a second objection to certain apologetic strategies; namely, their assumption that unbelief is basically a theoretical, rather than a practical, problem. I take it that this is what Hauerwas is suggesting when he tell us that, whereas 'the theology of translation' assumes that Christianity comprises an ideal essence that can be abstracted from an implausible ancient Near Eastern world-view and relocated in an acceptable modern one, '[i]n Jesus we meet not a presentation of basic ideas about God, world, and humanity, but an invitation to join up, to become part of a movement, a people';[32] and 'we are not Christians because of what we believe, but because we have been called to be disciples of Christ ... [which] is not a matter of a new or changed self-understanding, but rather ... [of becoming] part of a different community with a different set of practices'.[33]

The case is overstated. The point should not be that becoming a Christian involves no change in one's understanding of oneself or of reality; surely it does. Rather, the point should be that this intellectual change is not brought about just, or mainly, by thinking, but by doing. Hauerwas characteristically specifies this 'doing' straightaway as

---

[31] Hauerwas and Willimon, *Resident Aliens*, 24; see also Stanley Hauerwas, 'Theology and the New American Culture', in *Vision and Virtue* (Notre Dame, IN: Fides, 1974), 243.
[32] Hauerwas and Willimon, *Resident Aliens*, 21.
[33] Hauerwas, *After Christendom?*, 107.

participation in the Christian community and engagement in its practices. Barth, in contrast, speaks of it first of all as the act of acknowledgement by the sinful human self of the commanding God – Creator, Reconciler, and Redeemer – who has revealed himself in Jesus Christ. But Hauerwas need not be at serious odds with Barth here, if we read him along Pascalian lines. For Pascal, unbelief is only superficially a matter of reason, far more deeply a matter of habitual passion. So,

> if you are unable to believe, it is because of your passions, since reason impels you to believe and yet you cannot do so. Concentrate then not on convincing yourself by multiplying proofs of God's existence but by diminishing your passion.[34]

Belief must take root in the heart as well as the mind; and for this to happen, *'les vieux mécanismes'*[35] of desire must be broken down and new ones put in their place:

> For we must make no mistake about ourselves: we are as much automaton as mind. As a result, demonstration is not the only instrument for convincing us. How few things can be demonstrated! Proofs only convince the mind; habit provides the strongest proofs and those that are most believed. It inclines the automaton, which leads the mind unconsciously along with it. ... In short, we must resort to habit once the mind has seen where the truth lies, in order to steep and stain ourselves in that belief which constantly eludes us, ... We must therefore make both parts of us believe: the mind by reasons, which need to be seen only once in a lifetime, and the automaton by habit, not allowing any inclination to the contrary.[36]

---

[34] Blaise Pascal, *Pensées*, trans. A. J. Krailsheimer (Harmondsworth: Penguin, 1966), no. 418.
[35] Philippe Sellier, *Pascal et St Augustin* (Paris: A. Colin, 1970), 546: 'the old mechanisms'.
[36] Pascal, *Pensées*, no. 821.

But how does this happen? How does one restructure the unbelieving automaton with the habits of faith?

> You want to be cured of unbelief and you ask for the remedy: learn from those who were once bound like you and who now wager all they have. These are people who know the road you wish to follow, who have been cured of the affliction of which you wish to be cured: follow the way by which they began. They behaved just as if they did believe, taking holy water, having masses said, and so on.[37]

Put in other, more Hauerwasian terms: if you want to believe, then become a disciple, join the Church, learn its practices. If Hauerwas is understood thus, there is no real quarrel here between him and Barth. Becoming an apprentice in the Christian community, and opening the heart of oneself to the living reality of the loving and commanding God, are not alternatives: the one is a practical means to the other.

Hauerwas recognises, then, that conversion to Christian faith is not simply an intellectual matter, but also – and primarily – a practical one; and he is critical of those modern apologetics that suppose otherwise. And if it is right – and I think it is – to read modern atheism as having its roots, not so much in theoretical problems to do with epistemology and theodicy, as in an indignant assertion of moral autonomy against traditional Christian notions of sin and of salvation by divine grace,[38] then this practical bias is entirely appropriate.

Notwithstanding all this, Hauerwas implicitly acknowledges that intellectual apologetics has a role to play, although it is not quite clear how he would describe that role.[39] At least, he would see it in the first place as a matter of explicating moral and political views in terms governed

---

[37] Pascal, *Pensées*, no. 418.
[38] See Stephen N. Williams, *Revelation and Reconciliation: A Window on Modernity* (Cambridge: Cambridge University Press, 1995).
[39] That is to say, I know of no statement by Hauerwas about it.

by the Christian 'story', in order to present liberal secularists with the fact of an alternative viewpoint. By its very presence, this raises questions about liberal assumptions – questions that those who are genuinely liberal, and therefore really open to considering different points of view, will let themselves entertain. Among the questions raised is a basic one about the assumption that liberal rationality simply *is* rationality, and whatever demurs from it is ipso facto irrational.[40] For what seems self-evidently rational to liberals, is, to a significant extent, shaped by their own particular 'story' or reading of the human situation.[41] Here, of course, Hauerwas is borrowing from Alasdair MacIntyre's concept of the tradition-based nature of human rationality; but he is not thereby espousing ideological relativism (and in that sense, 'sectarianism'); for he also endorses MacIntyre's affirmation of the possibility of critical dialogue between traditions, in which one can prove itself superior to another by its capacity to resolve questions or tensions that have proven intractable in terms of that other's framework.[42]

Beyond simply presenting an implicitly challenging, alternative, Christian 'story', Hauerwas does go on to bring it into explicit, critical engagement with political liberalism. For example, he specifies the liberal ideal of freedom as consisting in a Kantian-Romantic liberation of the individual from the stifling constraints of tradition and historical community, and into creativity and universal fellowship.[43] He observes, however, that far from realising this ideal, liberal emancipation has led to disenchantment and alienation. Bereft of given moral and social contexts, the individual is burdened with the constant demand to make choices for himself, but without any external

[40] Hauerwas and Willimon, *Resident Aliens*, 101.
[41] Hauerwas and Willimon, *Resident Aliens*, 79–80; Hauerwas, *Where Resident Aliens Live* (Nashville, TN: Abingdon Press, 1996), 80–1; Hauerwas, 'No Enemy, No Christianity', 197–8.
[42] Hauerwas, 'The Non-Violent Terrorist: In Defence of Christian Fanaticism', *Sanctify Them in the Truth*, 183–7.
[43] Hauerwas, 'Theology and the New American Culture', 253; Hauerwas and Willimon, *Resident Aliens*, 79, 89.

guidance as to what might make one choice better than another. Thus disoriented, he becomes prey to the tyranny of his own fears and desires;[44] and since among these are the fear of insignificance and the correlative desire for status, he then becomes a slave to fashion:

> But as we are thrown back upon ourselves, when we lose the sense of moral and social involvement, we become prey to sensations of anxiety and guilt. ... There appears to be no external reality strong enough to call us from the monad-like form of our existence, for value has become privatized. Morally, it is assumed that our ethical positions are but subjective preferences. The only way of establishing the best preference is by observing which are held by the largest number of individuals, ... [45]

Individualism begets fashion-conscious consumerism, which begets conformism:

> In a highly cooperative and traditional society variety and eccentricity can be tolerated. It is assumed the social order is a going concern. In a highly individualistic society, however, eccentricity represents to the individual the threat of societal chaos and anarchy that he cannot bear to contemplate.[46]

In response to the oppressive illusion of this liberal 'freedom', Hauerwas argues that 'true freedom arises ... in our being linked to a true story', and especially to the Christian story, wherein life ceases to be 'the grim, just-one-damn-thing-after-another sort of existence we have known before', and 'the little things of life ... are redeemed and given eschatological significance'.[47] In addition, he suggests that the idea of moral authority deserves to be

---

44 Hauerwas and Willimon, *Resident Aliens*, 32.
45 Hauerwas, 'Theology and the New American Culture', 257.
46 Hauerwas, Theology and the New American Culture', 256 n. 26.
47 Hauerwas and Willimon, *Resident Aliens*, 67.

recovered out of the general denigration into which liberal
'freedom' has cast it, on the ground that the Aristotelian
and Christian assumption that some people are more
virtuous than others makes good sense.[48]

Hauerwas also goes some way toward a critical analysis
of the liberal ideal of political pluralism; that is, of a polity
whose common good consists of the balance of power
achieved by the free bargaining of competing interest
groups, all of whom have agreed to follow established
procedures for resolving disagreements. He observes that
this ideal presupposes basic alienation between the
competing groups, whose relations are therefore naturally
characterised by mutual distrust;[49] whereas, he asserts,
human beings are essentially social, not only in the
descriptive sense that community of some kind is necessarily the matrix of human individuals, but also in the
normative sense that, in order to become fully individual,
we must enter fully into community.[50] From this it follows
that human individuals and human groups share in a
common good that is far more than just the utilitarian
aggregate of private goods, and is genuinely common or
public; but this is something that the pluralist ideal cannot
admit.[51]

Liberalism's lack of a substantive concept of the
common good has helped to corrupt public debate from
genuine dialogue between alternative opinions with a view
to approximating more closely to the truth (about the
common good), into mere negotiation between competing
interests.[52] Postmodernism has then intensified this
process by abandoning the epistemologically realist

[48] Hauerwas and Willimon, *Resident Aliens*, 98–9; Hauerwas, *Where
Resident Aliens Live*, 62–3.
[49] Stanley Hauerwas, 'The Church and Liberal Democracy: The Moral
Limits of a Secular Polity', *A Community of Character: Towards a
Constructive Christian Social Ethic* (Notre Dame, IN: University of Notre
Dame Press, 1981), 81; Hauerwas and Willimon, *Resident Aliens*, 68:
'eternal hostility among subgroups'.
[50] Hauerwas, 'Politics, Vision, and the Common Good', *Vision and Virtue*,
236.
[51] Hauerwas, 'Politics, Vision, and the Common Good', 234–5.
[52] Hauerwas, 'Politics, Vision, and the Common Good', 237; Hauerwas,
After Christendom?, 29.

conviction that there exists an objective truth to be (more or less) grasped, in favour of a constructivist concept of 'truth' as designating the 'upshot' of encounters between persons or groups.[53] In turn, the corruption of dialogue has led to the degeneration of the classic liberal virtue of tolerance from an active readiness to entertain alien points of view in the course of dialogue undertaken in the faith and hope that (more of) the truth will out, to a passive post-modern letting-be of alternative views so long as they do not get in the way of the individual's liberal 'freedom' to pursue his own private interests.[54] As an alternative to this degenerate liberalism, Hauerwas presents the Christian Church as a genuine community, where there is an engaged tolerance of difference in the course of dialogue that understands itself as aiming at closer approximation to the truth:

> We rejoice in the difference and diversity of gifts among those in the church, as that very diversity is the condition of our faithfulness. Discussion becomes the hallmark of such a society, since recognition and listening to the other is the way our community finds the way of obedience. ... Christians do not believe that there is no truth; rather truth can only be known through struggle. That is exactly why authority in the church is vested in those we have learned to call saints in recognition of their more complete appropriation of that truth.[55]

A further, related complaint that Hauerwas makes against

---

[53] Hauerwas, 'Politics, Vision and the Common Good', 237; Hauerwas, *After Christendom?*, 31–3.
[54] Hauerwas, *Against the Nations*, 83 n. 21. 'Too often tolerance becomes a formula for condemning anyone who demands that their difference be taken morally and politically seriously.' For my own attempts to develop a distinction between the tolerance of care and the tolerance of indifference, see Nigel Biggar, *Good Life: Reflections on What We Value Today* (London: SPCK, 1997), ch. 7, 'Tolerance ... not Indifference'; and my response to Alastair Campbell's paper, 'Euthanasia and the Principle of Justice', in *Euthanasia and the Churches*, ed. Robin Gill (London: Cassell, 1998), 109–13.
[55] Hauerwas, 'The Church and Liberal Democracy', 85.

liberal 'tolerance' is that it extends to religion only in so far as the latter remains private and politically insignificant, and that it amounts to an absolute intolerance as soon as religion tries to speak in public in its own, theological terms.[56]

A quite different front on which Hauerwas engages liberalism is over the role of the state, though here his thought displays either change or inconsistency. For on one occasion he complains (in 1974) that the liberal state does not 'plan or act in the interest of forming the good society';[57] but on others he criticises liberalism's strengthening of the state in the name of defending the rights of the individual and at the expense of intermediate institutions (1985, 1992),[58] claims that the Christian story prefers charity to be offered through an intermediate institution like the Church rather than by way of government aid (1992),[59] and reckons that '[i]nvariably, politicians tend to be totalitarian ... because bureaucrats are bureaucrats' and are more self-interested than other people (1996).[60] To my British ears, the last two complaints sound a lot more like expressions of American libertarianism than of Christianity.

The last criticism that Hauerwas levels against liberalism is the most characteristic, and one of the most contentious: namely, that liberal democracies, more than other states, 'are heavily dependent on war for moral coherence'.[61] His argument is that in an age of secularism, the destiny of the nation-state, and especially one that stands for high humanist ideals such as 'freedom', offers deracinated individuals a Grand Cause to which to devote, and for which to martyr, themselves, thereby gaining for

[56] Hauerwas, *After Christendom?*, 72; Hauerwas, 'A Christian Critique of Christian America', 187 n. 21.
[57] Hauerwas, 'Politics, Vision, and the Common Good', 234.
[58] Hauerwas, *Against the Nations*, 123–5; Hauerwas and Willimon, *Resident Aliens*, 33–4.
[59] Hauerwas and Willimon, *Resident Aliens*, 82.
[60] Hauerwas, *Where Resident Aliens Live*, 53.
[61] Hauerwas and Willimon, *Resident Aliens*, 35. I say that this is the 'most characteristic' criticism, because it draws most directly on Hauerwas' pacifist reading of the Christian story.

their little lives a self-transcendent significance.[62] I have no quarrel with the characterisation of modern nationalism as a kind of secularist religion offering a quasi-immortality to its devotees,[63] nor with the claim that liberal values have in fact served to idealise the nation-state and reinforce its religious status. What I do doubt, however, is whether liberalism is *necessarily* tied to belligerent nationalism; for it seems to me that liberal democracies in Europe have shown a marked decline in nationalism and an increased reluctance to go to war since 1918.[64] Moreover, I am not convinced that it is impossible – or always wrong – for a nation to go to war genuinely in defence of liberal values and human rights.[65]

Hauerwas' engagement with liberalism is invariably ad hoc rather than systematic. The points he makes, telling though they be, are accordingly limited in their development. So, for example, he makes the worthwhile assertion that freedom is better conceived in terms of participation in a 'true' story than of 'emancipation' from it, and he makes it clear enough that the story he has in mind is the Christian one; but he does not go on to answer the questions that naturally spring to mind here: How are we to tell a true story from a false one? And how can we know that the Christian story is *the* true one? He might respond that the only real answers to such questions are to be found in practical engagement. But a non-believer has to have some prior reason to *begin* to live according to the Christian story rather than according to another, even if it is the case that only by so living will that reason – and the

---

[62] Hauerwas and Willimon, *Resident Aliens*, 35, and 62; Hauerwas, *Against Christendom*, 33.

[63] See Benedict Anderson, *Imagined Communities: Reflections on the Origin and Spread of Nationalism*, rev. ed. (London and New York: Verso, 1991), 9–12.

[64] Even if Hauerwas is talking only of American liberalism – and his remarks on page 62 of *Resident Aliens* suggest that he is – my point still stands: that liberal democracy as such is not necessarily bound up with belligerent nationalism.

[65] As I understand it, that is largely why the NATO democracies intervened in Kosovo. See my 'Kosovo: Taking Stock', *Church Times* (18 June 1999); and 'On Giving the Devil Benefit of Law in Kosovo', in *Kosovo*, ed. William Buckley (Grand Rapids, MI: Wm B. Eerdmans, forthcoming).

truth of the story – be confirmed. Even though Pascal saw the commitment to practice as the decisive moment in the process of conversion, he nevertheless recognised the value of neutralising intellectual objections to the faith and advancing arguments for it (for example, that Christianity gives a superior account of the human situation – that it 'outnarrates'[66] rival anthropologies), in order at least to establish that making a wager in favour of faith is not an unreasonable thing to do. It is not clear that Hauerwas sees the need for this.

Again, Hauerwas suggests that there is more to be said for the notion of moral authority than meets the liberal eye, but he does not develop his suggestion. He also points out the need for a substantive concept of the common good, for the formation of public virtue, and for the opening up of secularist public discourse, but he does not go on to explore and explain how these needs could be met in a plural society replete with rival accounts of the human good. Maybe he would retort that the deficiencies of the liberal polity can only be met within the Christian Church; and therefore, having pointed out the corruption of the liberal ideals of tolerance and virtue, he is content to present the Church and its 'story' as the contexts in which these can be regenerated. This policy certainly concurs with remarks he has made in several places to the effect that political liberalism depends on religious presuppositions that it is (constitutionally?) unable to acknowledge.[67]

---

[66] The term, of course, is John Milbank's, not Pascal's. See, for example, John Milbank, *Theology and Social Theory* (Oxford: Blackwell, 1990), 330: 'this stoic-liberal-nihilist tendency, which is "secular reason" ... cannot be refuted, but only out-narrated, if we can *persuade* people ... that Christianity offers a much better story'. Author's emphasis.

[67] See, for example, Hauerwas, 'The Church and Liberal Democracy', 74: 'genuine justice depends on more profound moral convictions than our secular polity can politically acknowledge'; Hauerwas, *After Christendom?*, 35: 'America continues to rely on religious presuppositions for its public ethos that cannot be acknowledged'; and Hauerwas, 'Remaining in Babylon', where he seems to endorse Oliver O'Donovan's argument that 'because liberal culture has lost its theological horizon, modern political theory finds itself hopelessly entangled in self-inflicted incoherence and unintelligibility' (p. 203).

So, in sum, Hauerwas' message to liberalism appears to be: *extra ecclesiam nulla salus*.

So be it and Amen. Nevertheless, although it is constitutionally accountable to the theological story in terms of which certain crucial 'liberal' values alone make full sense, and although it therefore has the resources to overcome the incoherence into which liberalism has fallen, the Christian Church itself is still in the process of learning what a properly Christian politics would look like under the conditions of sin. It wrestles just as much as wider liberal democratic politics with questions of unity and diversity, authority and dissent, the limits and possibilities of tolerance and dialogue. Plenty of scope remains for further ecclesiological work in describing the proper shape of human community obedient to God before the eschaton; in which case, telling liberals that their salvation lies in the Church by no means marks the end of the discussion.

Further, Hauerwas draws here a sharp distinction between liberalism and Christianity that is not sustainable. This is because, on the one hand, there are considerable respects in which liberalism is rooted in Christianity;[68] and on the other, it is largely from liberalism that Christianity has learnt some of the (more liberal) political implications of its 'story'. There are good theological reasons why Christians should own liberalism, albeit in a qualified sense.

Given this, it seems to me quite wrong to say baldly, as Hauerwas does, that Christians have no stake in the continuation of Western civilization,[69] or 'that Christians would be ill advised to try to rescue the liberal project either in its epistemological or political form'.[70] If to

---

[68] See, for example, L. A. Siedentop, 'Liberalism: The Christian Connection', *Times Literary Supplement* (24–30 March 1989), 308: 'The birth of the individual was ... a Christian achievement. Christian ontology is the foundation for what are usually described as liberal values in the West – for the commitment to equality and reciprocity, as well as the postulate of individual freedom'. Hauerwas himself, early on in his career, endorsed A. D. Lindsey's claim that 'the basis of democracy ... arose from the experience of the Puritan congregation as a fellowship of equals' (Hauerwas, 'Politics, Vision, and the Common Good', 239).

[69] Hauerwas, *Against the Nations*, 40.

[70] Hauerwas, *After Christendom?*, 35.

'rescue' liberalism here means simply to shore it up as it stands, then I would agree. But if it means to transform and regenerate it, then I would not. In so far as Christians recognise – and I would be very surprised if Hauerwas thinks that they should not – that liberal politics represents a significant advance both on the religious wars in sixteenth- and seventeenth-century Europe out of which it was born, and on the 'Christian' *anciens régimes* that it replaced, then Christians do have an interest in its survival – in *some* form.

To conclude, let me give a direct answer to the central question with which this essay has been concerned: Is Hauerwas sectarian? No, he is not: first, in that he does not insist that the Christian Church live and think according to the norms of its own story as an alternative to politics, but precisely as the basic condition of the Church's discharge of its proper political responsibility; second, in that he recognises the possibility of properly theological apologetics, both practical and intellectual; and, third, in that he engages in intellectual apologetics in the form of ad hoc criticism of political liberalism. It is true that a sectarian quality attends the sharpness with which Hauerwas is wont to distinguish between the (liberal) world and the Church. But I wonder whether his recent endorsement of Oliver O'Donovan's concept of 'Christendom'[71] signals a certain softening here, and thereby a warming to the project of recovering liberalism's lost theological horizon and rescuing it in non-secularist form?

---

[71] Hauerwas, 'Remaining in Babylon'. See note 4 above.

8
Can Women Love Stanley Hauerwas? Pursuing an Embodied Theology

Linda Woodhead

> There is no ideal church, no invisible church, no mystically existing universal church more real than the concrete church with parking lots and potluck dinners.
>
> The names Blacks, Indians, and women too often sound like stories told by others, rather than how those people would tell their stories.
>
> I try to do theology in a manner that exposes the politics, the material conditions, of Christian speech.[1]

Can women love Stanley Hauerwas? The short answer has to be 'Yes'. For evidence I look no further than myself, for Hauerwas has long been my favourite contemporary theologian and ethicist. I admire his directness, his honesty, his lack of pomposity, and his compelling insistence that the Church matters. Above all, as I hope to show in this essay, I admire the way in which he has pioneered a new way of doing theology. My criticisms relate to the same area, for I shall also argue that he has not yet followed through some of the more radical implications of his own pioneering theological project. This I try to show in relation to gender.

I am not the first to consider Hauerwas' work from a

---

[1] Quotations from Stanley Hauerwas, *The Peaceable Kingdom: A Primer in Christian Ethics* (Notre Dame, IN: University of Notre Dame Press, 1983), 107; *After Christendom? How the Church is to Behave if Freedom, Justice, and a Christian Nation are Bad Ideas* (Nashville, TN: Abingdon Press, 1991), 136; *Sanctify Them in the Truth: Holiness Exemplified* (Edinburgh: T&T Clark, 1998), 5, respectively.

162   FAITHFULNESS AND FORTITUDE

gendered perspective. An interesting critique has already
been offered by Albrecht.[2] The latter does not, of course,
exhaust the enterprise, for there is no single gendered
perspective. The meanings, representations and possibilities of gender vary in different times and places. Gender is
not a passively received identity, but is actively interpreted, appropriated, performed, and negotiated at both a
social and an individual level. It is negotiated in relation to
given social, economic and political situations, as well as
specific race and class locations. In what follows I therefore
consider Hauerwas' work not in terms of some abstract
essence of womanhood, but from the perspective of a very
specific gender position: that of the group of working-class
women in a town in northern Britain who are the subject of
a remarkable long-term study by Beverley Skeggs.[3] I could
have chosen this study not only because of the quality of its
research and analysis, but because it unsettles a number of
theological and sociological presumptions.[4] Whilst Skeggs

[2] Gloria Albrecht, *The Character of Our Communities: Towards an Ethic of
Liberation for the Church* (Nashville, TN: Abingdon Press, 1995). Unfortunately
I did not come across Albrecht's important book until this essay was almost
complete. There are many points of convergence between Albrecht's
approach and my own: above all both of us seem to be calling for a similar
reinterpretation of the theological task and to be criticising Hauerwas for what
Albrecht trenchantly refers to as an 'inability to see the particularity of its own
social and historical location ... [which] results in a defense of white male
social privilege against the stirrings of subjugated voices' (137). There are also
points of difference. Unlike Albrecht I do not attend to Hauerwas' sexual
ethics, though I do, like her, consider his interpretation of violence and his
totalising interpretation of Christian tradition and community. I am less
critical than Albrecht (and Hauerwas) of liberalism – or rather, I am more
inclined to recognise the diversity of liberalism and the value of some of its
strands from both a gendered and a Christian point of view. I think I am more
open than Albrecht to the authority of Scripture and tradition, and tend to
incorporate them in my work to a greater extent. And in general my criticisms
of Hauerwas tend to be less harsh than hers because I view his work as
containing a number of conflicting themes and arguments, some of which
support the 'embodied theology' I am advocating, whilst others undermine it.
[3] Beverley Skeggs, *Formations of Class and Gender: Becoming Respectable*
(London: Sage, 1997).
[4] Within sociology the text has become well known for the way in which
it undermines much current identity theory by showing that there simply
is no identity which working-class women in Britain can inhabit (instead
their lives are shaped by a constant struggle not to fall below the
threshold of 'respectability').

does not address theological questions explicitly, I hope to show how her attentive study of the actual lives, hopes, roles and relationships of working-class women offers an interesting perspective from which to view some key themes in Hauerwas' work.

Whilst my primary aim is to explore Hauerwas' work from a fresh angle of vision, I also hope to show what is at stake for theology in admitting a gendered perspective. I have myself been critical of some forms of feminist theology because of their dismissal of the richness of Christian tradition in favour of an essentialised notion of 'women's experience'.[5] Here I hope to show that it is possible to adopt a gendered perspective without oversimplifying the complexity of women's experience, without attempting to trump Christian faith with some higher authority, and without invoking the moral high ground of victimhood. At the same time I also hope to expose the untenability of the position which views the entrance of gender into the arena of theology as the unwelcome and inappropriate intrusion of a wholly secular concern. What the latter view overlooks is that the theological enterprise is already embodied and situated – by gender as much as by class, race and so on. To offer a gendered perspective on a theological position is not to judge it by an alien standard, but to force awareness of the gendered presuppositions which it already carries without acknowledgement.

An additional argument I wish to develop is that despite Hauerwas' failure to adopt a gendered perspective, the enterprise is validated by the theological revolution which his work has set in train. Not only is the adoption of a gendered perspective wholly congruent with Hauerwas' insights into the contextual nature of theology and faith, it is also true to his attempt to take Christian belief in human finitude, limitation and sinfulness with proper seriousness. As I attempt to show in the next section, Hauerwas already allows these insights to shape his theological project through a reflexive

---

[5] Linda Woodhead, 'Spiritualizing the Sacred: A Critique of Feminist Theology', *Modern Theology* 13 (1997), 191–212.

awareness of the importance of race, ethnicity and class. In the section which follows, I therefore consider some of the more general reasons why he fails to extend the same treatment to gender (general in the sense that the reasons apply to the contemporary theological establishment more widely). The main part of this essay looks in more detail at specific relations between gender and key themes in Hauerwas' work. Finally, I return to the issue of theological method, and try to draw out the ways in which this essay's adoption of a gendered perspective might propel the theological revolution which Hauerwas has initiated still further.

Race, Class and Gender in Hauerwas' Work

To insist, as does Hauerwas, that all ethics and theology is 'determined by the particularities of a community's history and convictions'[6] is to recognise the importance of the social, material and cultural aspects of life for theology and the Christian life. The central emphasis in Hauerwas' work on the importance of Church does not signal a desire to escape from these realities (as some liberal critics charge), but to take them with utter seriousness. So seriously does he take them that he wants the Church to create its own political and economic context rather than to compromise itself by accommodating to those of a secular world. Thus the theological revolution which Hauerwas has initiated involves the recognition that theology is not an exercise in which the disembodied mind of the theologian gazes on the timeless, Platonic truths of text and tradition and interprets them for an abstract essence called 'Church'. Instead, Hauerwas shows an unusual willingness to reflect on his own formative contexts, to make reference to the institutional constraints of the theological enterprise, to reflect sociologically on contemporary society, and to speak of and for actual Christian communities and the men and women who belong to them. He criticises a false objectivity

---

[6] Hauerwas, *The Peaceable Kingdom*, 1.

in theology and ethics which tries to occupy a 'midair place' and 'has the peculiar effect of alienating the moral agent from his or her projects',[7] and he denies that theology can be 'systematised', preferring to see it as 'ad hoc', 'inherently practical', and 'a pastoral discipline'.[8] In all these ways he is, I believe, a pioneer of a new theological approach which I shall refer to in what follows as 'embodied theology'.

Given his embodied approach, it is not surprising to find that Hauerwas is sensitive to the theological relevance of issues like race and ethnicity. This sensitivity is part and parcel of his belief that Christianity has to do not with abstract propositions but with the historical realities of a God made known in the life of Israel, Jesus Christ, and the continuing life of the Church: 'The church and Israel are two people walking in the path provided by God; they cannot walk independently of one another, for if they do they both risk becoming lost.'[9] Hauerwas is acutely aware of the realities of anti-Semitism. Not only does he acknowledge Christianity's culpability in its relation to the Jews, but he proposes a theology which aims to overcome Christian anti-Semitism through repeated insistence that salvation comes from the Jews.[10] Also in relation to race and ethnicity, Hauerwas displays some awareness of the violence done to the native peoples of North America and of Christian complicity; is actively interested in the Irish situation; and makes frequent reference to ethnic conflicts such as that in Bosnia.[11] With his usual honesty and courage he is even prepared to admit that 'my early life was constituted by practices that allowed me to treat African-Americans in a manner that can only be called racist'.[12]

---

[7] Hauerwas, *The Peaceable Kingdom*, 18.
[8] Hauerwas, *The Peaceable Kingdom*, xvi.
[9] Hauerwas, *The Peaceable Kingdom*, 107.
[10] See, in particular, Stanley Hauerwas, *Wilderness Wanderings: Probing Twentieth-Century Theology and Philosophy* (Boulder, CO: Westview Press, 1997).
[11] See, for example, Hauerwas, *After Christendom?*, 131–40, 153–61.
[12] Hauerwas, *Sanctify Them in the Truth*, 102.

To some extent class, and the significance of money and economic status more generally, also registers on Hauerwas' theological horizon. For example, he frequently mentions his own background as the son of a bricklayer, and shows some sensitivity to the ways in which theology's class entanglements present a danger. Whilst he offers no systematic critique or analysis of current economic conditions or of the Church's proper relationship to them, he comments that 'something has gone wrong when questions about Trinity have no purchase on how we make as well as what we do with our money',[13] and notices that 'the high humanism of [modern] theology and preaching ... hid the class interest intrinsic to such preaching'.[14] I also take Hauerwas' irreverence toward many of the polite conventions of theological debate as, in part, a subversive recognition of the importance of certain markers of cultural and social status. Occasionally though, Hauerwas' awareness of the importance of class in relation to the theological enterprise slips. In *Christian Existence Today*, for example, he claims that, 'The nobility of the university is not ... established by birth. Rather, those who occupy the hierarchy of the university are there because they are distinguished by willingness to expose themselves to the truth by developing the skills of critical intelligence.'[15] The unfortunate implication is that the failure of women, blacks, and members of the working class to attain adequate representation on university faculties can be explained in terms of their lack of virtue, rather than that of the societies and institutions which exclude them.

It is in relation to gender, however, that Hauerwas is most silent. Compared to his frequent references to the fate

[13] Hauerwas, *Sanctify Them in the Truth*, 158.
[14] Hauerwas, *Sanctify Them in the Truth*, 194. Stanley Hauerwas also makes the wonderfully frank acknowledgement in *Christian Existence Today: Essays on Church, World and Living in Between* (Grand Rapids, MI: Baker Books, 1995), vii, that he writes for money. On Hauerwas' views on the market economy, see Arne Rasmusson, *The Church as 'Polis': From Political Theology to Theological Politics as Exemplified by Jürgen Moltmann and Stanley Hauerwas* (Lund: Lund University Press, 1994), 253–7.
[15] Hauerwas, *Christian Existence Today*, 228.

of the Jewish people, his references to the fate of women are practically non-existent. Whilst Hauerwas is much better read than many theologians in the social sciences, he makes little reference to the literature of gender studies. (There are some sporadic exceptions – he cites both Catherine MacKinnon and Jean Bethke Elhstain, for example.[16]) On the rare occasions that he refers to feminism or feminist theology he tends to be dismissive. This does not, however, mean that his work is ungendered, as I will argue below. Rather, it means that it tends to be informed by largely unconscious male interests and agendas. To give a fairly trivial example at the outset, not only bricklaying but also baseball and cricket are important tropes in Hauerwas' writing, and are used to image not only theology but the Christian life itself. Whilst not wholly incomprehensible, these are the sorts of metaphors which induce in women a common sense of standing under signs to which they do not belong.[17]

Some General Causes of Gender-Blindness in Contemporary Theology

Hauerwas is by no means exceptional amongst modern theologians in his reluctance to admit gender as a significant issue. This reluctance is greatest, of course, in theologians of a more conservative hue – those who, like Hauerwas, are critical of liberal theology and who wish to reinscribe God's transcendence, the authority of Scripture and tradition, the importance of the Church, and the exclusiveness of Christian truth.[18]

How is this reluctance to deal with gender to be

---

[16] Both are referred to in *After Christendom?*, 9; 116–17; 130; 177n, for example.
[17] Judith Butler, 'Contingent Foundations: Feminism and the Question of "Postmodernism"', in J. Butler and J. Scott (eds), *Feminists Theorize the Political* (London: Routledge, 1992), 3–22.
[18] For more on this 'type' of modern religion, see Linda Woodhead and Paul Heelas, *Religion in Modern Times: An Interpretative Anthology* (Oxford and Malden, MA: Blackwell, 2000) on 'religions of difference'.

explained? A number of factors seem relevant, all of which apply to Hauerwas as well as to other theologians of conservative conviction. One of the most important is simply the rhetorical and structural difference which conservative theology must constantly maintain with liberal theology (as well as with alternative spiritualities like the New Age). Both conservative and liberal theology are products of the modern (post-Enlightenment) era, and both are constituted in part through mutual opposition. This opposition has increased in the post-World War II era as what Robert Wuthnow calls the 'great fracture' between liberals and conservatives has opened to such an extent that the liberal–conservative schism has become the most important structuring dynamic of contemporary Western Christianity.[19] The fracture is now one which runs within rather than simply between different denominations, and the ferocity of the battle has often intensified as a result. In this context gender often becomes a marker of liberal difference to the extent that liberals have tended to be much more willing than conservatives to admit women to positions of institutional power and, at least in recent times, to take seriously a feminist critique of religion. What is more, much feminist theology has drawn on liberal theological presuppositions (such as the authority of experience). This alliance between liberalism and attention to issues of gender is in itself a reason for conservative theologians to be suspicious of the latter.

Failure to attend to issues of gender may also be explored in terms of a sociology of knowledge. Until very recently theology has been an activity reserved for men. Women's attempts to do theology in the nineteenth century were blocked not only by their exclusion from the positions in academia and the Church which would have made this possible, but by the practical impossibility of publishing works of theology qua theology.[20] Male

---

[19] Robert Wuthnow, *The Struggle for America's Soul: Evangelicals, Liberals, and Secularism* (Grand Rapids, MI: William B. Eerdmans, 1995).
[20] Julie Melynk, *Women's Theology in Nineteenth-Century Britain: Transfiguring the Faith of Their Fathers* (New York: Garland, 1998).

opposition to women's theology was explicit, and often couched in terms of ridicule. As Ruskin said, for example, 'Strange, and miserably strange, that while [women] are modest enough to doubt their powers, and pause at the threshold of sciences where every step is demonstrable and sure, they will plunge headlong, and without one thought of incompetency, into that science in which the greatest men have trembled, and the wisest erred.'[21] Whilst the situation varies from place to place, theology at the end of the twentieth century remains a largely male preserve. Men continue to outnumber women on theology faculties throughout Europe and the USA, often to a greater extent than would be true in other subjects in the humanities and social sciences. One effect is to render the issue of gender invisible, for when men remain in positions of unques- tioned dominance it remains possible to view a male agenda as 'natural' and neutral.

Related to this situation is a reluctance amongst many theologians to take issues of methodology seriously. In much theology the question of method is still approached in terms of traditional questions about the relative authority of Scripture, tradition and reason. What is not discussed (as it is in the social sciences and, increasingly, in the humanities), are broader questions about the relations between our social and institutional placements and the way we think. But to ignore such questions is to assume that knowledge comes from nowhere and to obscure the role of cultural, social, educational and economic capitals in the production of any knowledge. To put it bluntly in relation to theology: since most academic theology is still written by white middle-class males for other middle-class males (consult the contributors' page of any collection of theology), there is little to challenge or contextualise the legitimacy of the knowledge produced.

Yet we are positioned in our locations, not determined by them. Male dominance of theological institutions and practices does not then preclude sensitivity to issues of

---

[21] John Ruskin, 'Of Queen's Gardens', in *Sesame and Lilies* (Philadelphia: Henry Altemus, 1899, [orig. 1865]), 73.

gender – it just makes it harder to achieve. A counterbalancing pressure in recent times has been the increased visibility of women, feminism, and gender studies in both Church and academy. One effect has been to make it harder for theologians, even those of conservative persuasion, to ignore gender completely. Increasingly, their rejection of its importance has to be made explicit, and to be justified theologically. One approach is to argue, against 'the feminists' or other 'contextual' theologians, that gender has little or no relevance in the economy of salvation. As John Milbank puts it in *Theology and Social Theory*, for example:

> The supernatural perspective of charity reveals that from every finite position, within every social situation, an advance to perfection remains possible. This perspective does not simply agree with the Aristotelian insight about 'moral luck', by the way in which our moral capacities are restricted by our social situation and fortune. For the perspective is only possible as a new social perspective, which is that of the Church. To be part of the Church (insofar as it really is the Church) is to have the moral luck to belong to the society which overcomes moral luck.[22]

From this perspective issues such as class, gender and race become irrelevant for the Christian community (interestingly, Hauerwas cites this passage with general approval).[23] This move is similar to that made by those theologians who argue that the use of masculine tropes in talk of God is not limiting or oppressive, since in their application to the infinite their sense is transformed. The Church becomes a socio-linguistic zone in which the

---

[22] John Milbank, *Theology and Social Theory* (Oxford: Blackwell, 1990), 231.
[23] Hauerwas notes in *After Christendom?*, 172, however, that despite a 'fundamental agreement' with Milbank, 'how this is to be worked out in detail is not an easy matter'. Part of Hauerwas' hesitation appears to relate to the potential of such talk of the 'real' Church to feed an abstract ecclesiology which makes no contact with actual Christian communities.

power-relations which apply elsewhere cease to do so, and a hermeneutic of suspicion can therefore be suspended.

This leads to the final and possibly the most widespread criticism of the gendering of theology by conservative theologians: that it represents the incursion of a secular agenda into the territory of the theological. Just like talk about issues of race and class, concern with gender is assumed to be part of a wider discourse of rights, liberation and individual self-realisation which is characterised by conservative theologians as part of a much-despised 'Enlightenment project'. As the following section shows, this too is a view which Hauerwas seems to share and which goes some way towards explaining and justifying his gender-blindness.

Gender-Blindness in Relation to Hauerwas' Theological Agenda

As well as being related to some more general causes of gender-blindness in contemporary theology, I believe that some of the more specific themes of Hauerwas' theological project serve to render gender invisible. Equally, these themes and their interpretations are symptomatic of a lack of gendered awareness. Three seem particularly significant.

Preoccupation with violence

Hauerwas' theology is structured around an opposition between violence and peace.[24] The former becomes the defining characteristic of 'the world'; the latter of the Kingdom. The meaning of each term is given not only through their mutual opposition, but by the discursive contexts in which they occur. Quite often the idea of violence seems to be filled out with greater detail than that

---

[24] For an excellent discussion of these themes, see Rasmusson, *The Church as 'Polis'*, 303–30.

of peace in Hauerwas' work. One reason, no doubt, is that so much of this work is devoted to a critique of contemporary society, and that it is in the course of Hauerwas' repeated analyses of the sins and failings of this society that the notion of violence gains much of its content (equally, of course, the notion of violence gives direction and focus to such analysis).

The examples which Hauerwas invokes in his characterisations of violence are particularly telling. The primary example is war. Hauerwas has written extensively about the wars of the twentieth century, including the world wars, the wars of Vietnam and Korea, the Gulf War, and the war in the former Yugoslavia. He has also addressed the Cold War, and the build-up of nuclear weapons in the post-war world. In Hauerwas' view violence is inherent in all modern nation-states, not only because they were founded through violent struggle, but because their continued existence is underwritten by the exercise, or threat, of violence. 'States,' he and Will Willimon write, 'particularly liberal democracies, are heavily dependent on wars for moral coherence ... war for us liberal democracies is special because it gives a sense of worth necessary to sustain our state'.[25] Within this context it becomes clear why the Holocaust becomes the chief symbol of the violence of modern times for Hauerwas, and the Jews its exemplary victims.

It is in terms of war and martial activity then that Hauerwas interprets violence. What is interesting from a gendered perspective is what this leaves out. For whilst active involvement in war has undoubtedly been a, if not the, major male mode of participation in violence in the twentieth century (both in reality and in the cultural imagination), it is not clear that the same has been true for women. One thinks in this context of the way in which a number of women writers spoke of the war(s) through which they lived as products of male agency and as indications of the bankruptcy of male-dominated cultures.

[25] Stanley Hauerwas and William H. Willimon, *Resident Aliens: Life in the Christian Colony* (Nashville, TN: Abingdon Press, 1989), 35.

Such comments came from both the right and the left of both the religious and the political spectrums. One example would be Virginia Woolf. In *Three Guineas*, for example, she addressed the question 'How in your opinion are we to prevent war?', and answered, in part, through an ironic gendered distancing:

> Though many instincts are held more or less in common by both sexes, to fight has always been the man's habit, not the woman's. Law and practice have developed that difference, whether innate or accidental. Scarcely a human being in the course of history has fallen to a woman's rifle; the vast majority of birds and beasts have been killed by you, not by us; and it is difficult to judge what we do not share.[26]

Woolf went on to explore the 'violences' done to women in a society in which economic and cultural capital were largely controlled by men, and to relate them to the violence of war. In doing so she reminds us that for most women violence is related to the private not the public realm, and to forcible exclusion from the public realm. Woolf's point could be reinforced by reference to women's experience of domestic violence and sexual abuse within the family. Such violence inflicted by an intimate or a family member is, however, eclipsed in Hauerwas' writing by violence within the public realm inflicted not by intimate but by enemy.

The broader point which emerges from Woolf's essay, however, is that violence is not necessarily encountered by women in physical terms at all, nor related to traumatic events. Skeggs' study reinforces this point in the contemporary context and in relation to working-class women. One of her findings is 'that it is not the singular [traumatic experience] but the unremitting emotional distress generated by the doubts and insecurities of living [their] class that working-class women endure on a daily basis ...

---

[26] Virginia Woolf, *A Room of One's Own and Three Guineas* (London: Chatto and Windus, The Hogarth Press, 1984), 113.

whereas an event can produce explanations of identity, the mundane reiterative everyday experiences of living degradation and negative value positioning often cannot'.[27] Skeggs also notes that '[These] experiences are rarely considered worthy of study and knowing' – a point which is unfortunately borne out by Hauerwas' theological writings, as by many other works of modern theology, ethics and social commentary.

It may, of course, be objected that a theological preoccupation with violence, and a construal of such violence in terms of war, physical brutality, and the actions of the powerful state derives not from a normalised masculine experience, but from a proper Christian concentration upon the cross. In this context it is interesting to refer to Florence Nightingale's *Suggestions for Thought* (1850–52) in which she expatiates upon the plight of Victorian women. Like both Skeggs and Woolf she speaks of contemporary women's lives in terms of fragmentation, self-division, frustration and a dissipation of energies created by exclusion from significant public work, intellectual endeavour and religious involvement. It is in relation to the cross, however, that her thought is most revolutionary. Nightingale begins by drawing a central contrast between physical and spiritual suffering, and deploring modern society's over-concentration upon the former – a symptom, she says, of the fact that 'we set the treatment of bodies so high above the treatment of souls'.[28] But physical robbing and murdering are, she says, no worse than their spiritual equivalents:

> 'Robbed and murdered' we read in the newspapers. The crime is horrible. But there are people being robbed and murdered continually before our eyes, and no man sees it. 'Robbed' of their time, if robbing means taking away that you do not wish to part with, slowly 'murdered' by their families. There is scarcely any one

[27] Skeggs, *Formations of Class and Gender*, 167.
[28] Mary Poovey (ed.), *Florence Nightingale: Cassandra and other Selections from Suggestions for Thought* (London: Pickering and Chatto, 1991), 217.

who cannot, in his own experience, remember some instance where some amiable person has been slowly put to death at home, aye, and at an estimable and virtuous home.[29]

From there Nightingale takes a short but significant step to compare Christ's suffering on the cross unfavourably with that of women like herself. As she says in one of her most theologically shocking passages, 'Suppose one says, How much worse not to strive to save thousands from a crucified spirit than to crucify one body, thereby trans-ferring that lofty spirit to some other reign of God's universe!'[30]

Nightingale's apparently blasphemous reflection will hardly be welcomed by a traditional theology of the cross. It does, however, serve to illustrate not only some of the more dangerous implications for theology of the adoption of a differently-gendered perspective, but also the diffi-culty of maintaining that gender plays no part in theological interpretation. Both points are acknowledged by most feminist theologians, and have often been used to justify the enterprise of feminist theology as this has developed since the 1970s. In the context of this discussion of Hauerwas on violence, it is interesting to note that such theology has generally favoured the notion of 'oppression' to that of violence, and has often given the same structural and rhetorical prominence to the former that Hauerwas gives to the latter. The implication is not just that feminist theologians believe violence to be differently experienced by women than by men in the ways I have been suggesting, but they believe that the category of violence to be much less well suited to describing sin and evil viewed from women's perspectives than this alternative. To identify the anti-Kingdom with violence, in other words, may be to mask the reality of sin as it is encountered by many women. The corollary is that many feminist theologians believe the Kingdom is better described in

[29] Poovey, *Florence Nightingale*, 70.
[30] Poovey, *Florence Nightingale*, 202.

terms of liberation than peace – a suggestion which, as we
will now see, Hauerwas explicitly repudiates.

The attack on liberalism

Hauerwas is well known for his attacks on liberal society.[31]
His theology presents modern Western society (of which
the USA is generally taken to be representative) as a
product of the liberal ideal. This ideal is viewed by
Hauerwas as deriving directly from the Enlightenment
project, and as being a chief cause of the moral poverty of
contemporary society. Hauerwas characterises liberal
society in terms of the conviction that individual freedom
of choice is the overriding moral imperative. He links this
to an inadequate anthropology in which persons are
viewed as atomised autonomous individuals, and argues
that such a view gives rise to a false picture of society as the
product of a contract between freely-choosing, pre-social
individuals. For Hauerwas, such an understanding is
inadequate on every front. Above all, it fails to recognise
the primacy of community. Human beings are formed by
the communities to which they belong and the stories and
practices of those communities rather than by their
individual choices. Indeed, they are incapable of making
real choices at all if they have not been formed by strong
communities and traditions. We do not shape ourselves,
society shapes us – for good or ill. What is particularly
pernicious about modern societies in Hauerwas' view is
that they obscure this truth from themselves. Not only are
they individualistic, proud and violent, therefore, but they
are also dishonest and self-deluded. Their fate, Hauerwas
often seems to suggest, is already sealed, for by encouraging a rampant individualism they undermine their own
foundations.

Hauerwas presents Christianity as the mirror-image of
such liberalism. Here it is community which has primary

---

[31] Again, a helpful and detailed discussion of Hauerwas' views on liberal
society can be found in Rasmusson, *The Church as 'Polis'*, 248–302.

importance; love and humility which replace freedom; and the building-up of the body of Christ which supplants the vain ideal of self-realisation. Yet not every form of Christianity has remained true to this standard. Not surprisingly, Hauerwas views liberal Christianity as the chief dissident. In his view the mainline churches have uncritically reinforced the ideals of liberal society and tried to present them as Christian. In their desire to present Christianity as fully compatible with the modern state, liberal Christians have downplayed the concrete and distinctive elements of faith which appear to threaten freedom of choice. In this sense, liberal Christianity is in Hauerwas' view still 'Constantinian', still concerned to ally itself with the nation-state rather than devoting its energies to building up its own community in faithful witness to the God made known in Jesus of Nazareth.

One of the reasons why Hauerwas criticises 'those working for women's liberation' is because they seem to him to buy uncritically into this liberal package. As he says in *Christian Existence Today*:

> Generally, I think most of the charges made against male-dominated culture are both fair and just. My interest is not that particular issue but the assumption that lies behind the recommendation that freedom means rejecting the limits of our birth – either culturally or sexually. Put more strongly, I want to argue that there is something very misleading and self-deceiving about the description many have accepted that they are or should try to become free from all the stories except those they have 'freely' chosen.[32]

Hauerwas criticises liberation theology – which he appears to bracket together with feminist theology – in strikingly similar terms. His chief criticism is of reliance on 'the metaphor of liberation'.[33] Speaking of Gutiérrez's *A*

---

[32] Hauerwas, *Christian Existence Today*, 29.
[33] Hauerwas, *After Christendom?*, 53.

Theology of Liberation,[34] for example, he comments that, 'Though perhaps not intending it, phrases such as "free from all servitude" and "artisans of our own destiny" have the ring of the Enlightenment', and asks:

> Has Gutiérrez, perhaps unwittingly, underwritten a sense of liberation at odds with the gospel? For the salvation promised in the good news is not a life free from suffering, free from servitude, but rather a life that freely suffers, that freely serves, because such suffering and service is the hallmark of the Kingdom established by Jesus. As Christians we do not seek to be free, but rather to be of use, for it is only by serving that we discover the freedom offered by God. We have learned that freedom cannot be had by becoming 'autonomous' – free from all claims except those we voluntarily accept – but rather freedom literally comes by having our self-absorption challenged by the needs of another.[35]

Considered from a gendered perspective these quotations raise a number of important issues. One is the accuracy of Hauerwas' account of feminist theology (or of feminism) in terms of its dependence on the 'metaphor of liberation'. Whilst it is true that some feminism and feminist theology has made central use of this theme, I hope this essay shows that a gendered and feminist perspective often involves a good deal more. Another issue is the extent to which Hauerwas' remarks about freedom reflect his own situation as a white, middle-class, fully enfranchised citizen of the most powerful nation in the world. In other words, is Hauerwas reporting neutrally on the Christian way for all, as he sometimes seems to suggest, or do his remarks in fact have rather less relevance for those who find themselves in situations where economic, social, cultural and symbolic capital is much less readily

---

[34] Gustavo Gutiérrez, *A Theology of Liberation* (Maryknoll, NY: Orbis, 1972).
[35] Hauerwas, *After Christendom?*, 53–4.

available? To be more concrete still, what would it mean to tell a working-class mother whose days are spent earning money as a 'care-worker', and whose evenings are taken up with looking after her children and elderly mother that 'freedom literally comes by having our self-absorption challenged by the needs of another'?

To approach this same point from another angle, a gendered perspective casts doubt on Hauerwas' guiding assumption that the world outside the Church is structured in terms of the assumptions and priorities of liberalism. To return to Skeggs' study of working-class women once more, what she found after nine years of intensive involvement, observation and interview was that the ideal of freedom played little or no part in these women's lives, and that their 'selves' were constructed chiefly through concrete caring practices and investments in these practices. Far from idealising this situation, Skeggs makes it perfectly clear that caring was the only avenue to social respectability available to the women she studied. Our society, it seems, is still one in which few other avenues are open to working-class women, and in which 'the panoptical gaze of the good, moral carer enables disciplinary practices to be enacted upon themselves'.[36] From this perspective, not only does it seem unfortunate that many Christian moralists have made a major investment in this gaze, but it appears far more questionable that our society is uniformly characterised by possessive individualism. Far from being the free, autonomous, independent selves which Hauerwas criticises, the 'selves' of the women studied by Skeggs, 'were full of duty and obligation generated through their relationships to others ... Here I am not romanticising the kinship networks of the working class but rather suggesting that historically they have been so excluded from full citizenship which promoted discourse of individualism that they have never been positioned by it in the same way as the middle classes.'[37]

In the course of a discussion of Robert Bolt's play *A Man*

---

[36] Skeggs, *Formations of Class and Gender*, 72.
[37] Skeggs, *Formations of Class and Gender*, 164.

for All Seasons, Hauerwas proposes 'to offer an account of
the character necessary to maintain what Bolt's [Thomas]
More called "that little area in which I must rule myself" '.[38]
Despite his strictures against liberalism he appears to
accept the legitimacy of this 'little area'. What Skeggs'
study reminds us is that there are those whose social
positioning and individual circumstances still makes the
achievement of such an area hard or impossible. Despite
conservative theologians' strictures, I believe that for them
the liberal insistence on each individual's ability, duty, and
indeed right to a 'little area in which I must rule myself' is
both legitimate and properly Christian, and need not
necessarily involve the individualism and selfishness of
which Hauerwas is properly critical. Christianity is, after
all, a religion distinguished by its address to each
individual, its belief in the importance of individual
conversion, its pervasive practices of scrutiny and discipline of the self, and its vision of judgement as focused on
individuals, not communities. It is no coincidence, I think,
that Christianity's power to create a sense of a 'little area in
which I must rule myself', and to engender a sense of
power and control over otherwise out-of-control lives is
clearly central to the current success of evangelical-charis-
matic Christianity in transforming lives in many of the
poorest parts of the world. And as some evangelical and
Pentecostal (as well as liberal) churches demonstrate, such
an emphasis need not be incompatible with belief in the
sovereignty and power of God, or with the building up of
strong communities.

One truth, one tradition, one Church

A final feature of Hauerwas' theology which seems to have
particular significance from a gendered point of view is
what some postmodernists would undoubtedly refer to as
its 'totalising' tendencies. In his typically provocative style,
I suspect that Hauerwas would happily embrace the

---

[38] Hauerwas, *Christian Existence Today*, 199.

description. In a recent reflection on postmodernism, for example, he argues that 'the Christian difference' is that it unashamedly asserts there is only one way to God and to truth – through Jesus Christ.[39] Hauerwas underlines this assertion in conscious opposition to the currently fashionable embrace of 'difference', and in defiance of postmodernism's belief in the oppressive and coercive powers of such 'totalising' discourses.

From his very earliest writings, one of the most important and distinctive features of Hauerwas' theology has been its emphasis not only on the importance of narrative, but on the Christian narrative which tells the story of God. As he says in *The Peaceable Kingdom*, for example, 'Christian convictions are [not] of significance only for the church, for Christians claim that by learning to find our lives within the story of God we learn to see that world truthfully'.[40] It is interesting to note that this was written around the same time that writers like Foucault and Lyotard were attacking any idea that there might be a meta-narrative, meta-language, or meta-theory through which all things can be represented. Lyotard in fact defines the postmodern simply as 'incredulity towards meta-narratives'.[41] These attacks were made on moral as well as epistemological and sociological grounds. As alternatives, Foucault speaks of a plurality of 'power-discourse' formations, and Lyotard of a plurality of 'language games'.

Of course Hauerwas is not untouched by a postmodern turn, for he shares its rejection of an Enlightenment meta-narrative and the belief in context- and narrative-independent truths which it generates. Yet Hauerwas shows no hesitation in speaking repeatedly of *the* truth of *the* Christian meta-narrative. So he writes of '*the* story that we claim is truthful to the very character of reality';[42] '*the*

---

[39] Stanley Hauerwas, 'The Christian Difference: Surviving Post-modernism', *Cultural Values* 3.2 (April, 1999).
[40] Hauerwas, *The Peaceable Kingdom*, 34.
[41] Harvey, *The Condition of Postmodernity: An Enquiry Into the Origins of Cultural Change* (Cambridge, MA and Oxford: Blackwell, 1990), 45.
[42] Hauerwas, *Christian Existence Today*, 102.

concrete people who acknowledge the authority of the Bible';[43] 'the Christian faith';[44] and of 'reclaiming the church as a disciplined body of disciples'[45] (all italics mine). Nor is this style of singularity reserved for Christianity; as we have seen above Hauerwas' work is similarly characterised by talk about the secular world. Thus Hauerwas and Willimon speak, for example, of 'the world [which] has declared war upon the gospel'.[46]

In other words, whilst Hauerwas is happy to accept that the truth can only be known and spoken from within particular contexts, traditions and communities, his language betrays his belief that there is only one valid Christian context, narrative and community within which the truth can be known and embodied. From a gendered point of view this begs the question 'Whose Church and which narrative?', and obscures the way in which talk of 'true doctrine', 'orthodoxy' and 'the Church of God' can and has been used by those with ecclesiastical and theological power (usually men) to exclude visions and embodiments of Church with which they have disagreed (sometimes women). And given what Hauerwas calls the Constantinian captivity of the Church, it is obvious that the communities and stories which have tended to be excluded by such a strategy have been those which have most threatened the legitimating relations between Church and state by, for example, suggesting a radical re-ordering of social relations (either of class or gender, either within or without the Church).

Unusual amongst academic theologians, Hauerwas is well aware of these issues. Heir to a Radical Reformation trajectory (as Rasmusson[47] has argued so persuasively),

---

[43] Hauerwas, *Christian Existence Today*, 55.
[44] Hauerwas and Willimon, *Resident Aliens*, 152.
[45] Hauerwas, *Sanctify Them in the Truth*, 80. At other times, however, Hauerwas speaks of tradition as 'a lively argument' (Hauerwas and Willimon, *Resident Aliens*, 72, for example), and suggests that 'the nature of Christian ethics is determined by the fact that Christian convictions take the form of a story, or perhaps better, *a set of stories'* (*The Peaceable Kingdom*, 24, my italics).
[46] Hauerwas and Willimon, *Resident Aliens*, 152.
[47] Rasmusson, *The Church as 'Polis'*, 174–382.

Hauerwas is also well aware that it has been those churches labelled heretical and dissenting by monopolistic and mainline churches which have often been the most prophetic in witnessing against the violences and injustices of the state. Why then does he continue to employ the totalising discourses typical of the established churches? My guess is that he does so because he believes that such language can have subversive as well as conservative uses, and that its abandonment would lead to a shallow relativism which lacks the power to challenge the contemporary socio-economic order.[48] The danger, however, is that in using the language of the enemy one becomes the enemy. One begins to disenfranchise all those whose vision of the Gospel differs from one's own, and to present a picture of the Church as a fortress of unity and truth besieged by heretics rather than as an ongoing struggle and debate between different groups with different visions of Church. What is more, those who take this route often end up with a deeply abstract and idealised picture of the Church – something which also sits uneasily with Hauerwas' desire to be a theologian not of 'the Church', but of and for real churches and actual Christian people.

Hauerwas' tendency to use a homogenising discourse not only for Church, but also for 'world' can have an equally distorting effect. Just as the Church is not one thing, so modernity is not one thing – it too represents a complex co-existence and struggle between different cultural trajectories and different political and economic configurations. By making 'the world' seem all of a piece ('a world of mendacity and fear'),[49] Hauerwas and his collaborators often sound remarkably like the modern (post-1789) popes in the way in which they position whatever falls outside their jurisdiction as 'error' (in sociological terms, both surely represent reactions to the Church's loss of socio-political power). Yet in truth, Church and world have never been this hermetically

[48] Hauerwas, 'The Christian Difference', develops an argument along these lines.
[49] Hauerwas, *The Peaceable Kingdom*, 100.

sealed from one another. This is true in relation to individual lives too. Hauerwas sponsors the idealised view that we only find true community in the 'colony' of the Church. Yet most of us participate in many communities (families, workplaces, neighbourhoods, clubs, associations, charitable bodies, music festivals and raves, alternative religious communities, self-help groups, etc.) in which we glimpse something of the true community of which the Church should be the highest representation. The fact that it is not always so is, of course, because we generally find the vices which inhibit community in our churches as well as in the other forms of community to which we belong.

As we also see in relation to 'fortress' Catholicism, one effect of distinguishing too harshly between Church and world is to condemn all initiatives that do not win the approval of those with power in the Church.[50] One problem with this is that it condemns those outside the Church to a realm which is wholly ungodly. Yet the fate of many women (as, for example, of many working-class people, people of colour, and gays) has always been to be both in and out of the mainline churches. Structural arrangements have left them unable to make a full investment even if they would have wished to. For such people, talk about 'the Church', 'the tradition', 'God's truth' can be heard as legitimisation of that which prevents their being ordained, disruptive, single, or uninterested in families and children – in other words, as legitimisation of that which excludes them from full membership of the body of Christ. And for those of us who find ourselves in this position, a language not of the Church, but of many churches, many Christianities, and many traditions often seems a liberating possibility. It need not imply 'relativism', irony or self-distancing, nor that there is no truth to pursue (or to be pursued by). Rather, a move away from totalising discourses can enable a greater awareness

[50] See Bill McSweeney, *Roman Catholicism: The Search for Relevance* (Oxford: Blackwell, 1980) and Tom Buchanan and Martin Conway, (eds.), *Political Catholicism in Europe, 1918–1965* (Oxford: Clarendon Press, 1996).

of one's own situatedness, and of the realities of struggle for the truth and for power. It can enrich the search for truth and for God or (as Hauerwas rightly prefers to say), can open us more fully to the dangerous God who searches for us and unsettles our perceptions of truth. In less theological language, it is in the 'gaps' opened up by the existence of conflicting discourses that resistance to dominant and idolatrous discourse can sometimes begin. As Sharon Welch puts it, 'We can see the foundational flaws in systems of ethics only from the outside, from the perspective of another system of defining and implementing that which is valued ... Pluralism is required, not for its own sake, but for the sake of enlarging our moral vision.'[51] But this will be resisted because it is unsettling to those who believe they already have the truth, and who identify that truth with existing institutions. In some cases, that includes theologians. For the sort of gendered standpoint I have been exploring begins to undermine the self-understanding of the theologian as uniquely empowered to represent God to Church and world, and prompts us to consider alternatives.

Embodied Theology

This essay represents an attempt to push Hauerwas' insistence that theology is always a view from somewhere, and to follow where this leads in relation to some key themes in his own work. I have suggested that Hauerwas sometimes betrays the radical implications of his own insights by acting and speaking as if membership of the Church abstracts theologians from wider material and social struggles and contexts. Against this view, I have tried to show how Hauerwas' theology clearly reflects its classed and gendered – as well as ecclesiastical – positioning. I am not, of course, suggesting that we should embrace a new (or old) error by trying to take a view from

---

[51] Sharon Welch, *A Feminist Ethic of Risk* (Minneapolis: Fortress Press, 1990), 126.

everywhere. Rather, I am pressing Hauerwas' description of the Church as 'a community capable of being critic to every human pretension', and of theology as its handmaid.[52] My suggestion is that a properly embodied theology must be reflexive about its own positioning, and take steps to try to avoid some of the exclusions and abuses to which they can lead. Rather than identifying our views with God's truth (a professional danger for all theologians), I am suggesting that we need to develop a healthy awareness of the view from elsewhere, and in particular from those locations which are least likely to be represented in theology.[53] This is not a plea to bow down before what is currently on the agenda of the politically correct, but to take seriously the Christian proclamation of a kingdom in which the first will be last and the last first.

In arguing for such an embodied theology, I am merely following hints in Hauerwas. Hauerwas has already expressed his dissatisfaction with traditional modes of systematic theology.[54] More than most, he is aware that theologians in late modernity cannot continue in their old tracks as if nothing has happened. Above all, he has made us aware that responsible theology must be done in, for and with the Church. Whilst this slogan has been popular at least since Barth, it is Hauerwas who has had the courage and imagination to follow it through. This is particularly clear in his insistence that Christian truth is embodied not just in texts but in the lives of Christian men

[52] Hauerwas, *The Peaceable Kingdom*, xviii. This view of the task of theology is related to Hauerwas' characterisation of the 'fundamental form' of sin as 'self-deception' (46).
[53] 'One of the great tragedies of being poor and white in the South ... is that the poverty is of the sort that the people are not produced who are later able to say what it means' (Hauerwas, *Christian Existence Today*, 44, n. 17).
[54] In a new introduction to *Character and the Christian Life: A Study in Theological Ethics* (Notre Dame, IN: University of Notre Dame Press, 1995; orig. 1975), for example Hauerwas comments, 'Systematics is often where theologians retreat ... when they forget that the intelligibility of their work depends on people who actually believe and live the life which God has made possible' (xxxii). Compare his earlier comment in *The Peaceable Kingdom* that systematic theology has 'distorted the ad-hoc character of theology as a discipline of the church' (xx).

and women, that theology must proceed through attentiveness to these lives, and that to 'know what Scripture
means, finally, we must look to those who have most
nearly learned to exemplify its demands through their
lives'.[55]

In faithfulness to this belief, Hauerwas has developed a
form of unsystematic theology which is responsive to the
particular needs, requests, worries and invitations of
particular people and communities. What is more, he
develops this theology in dialogue with the actual
situations he has encountered in the churches of which he
has been a member, and in attentiveness to the lives of
saints in those communities. Sometimes he uses fiction to
inform his embodied theology, sometimes anecdote,
sometimes personal confession.[56] All this is new, courageous and important. Its theoretical counterpart is the
increasing stress which Hauerwas has placed upon the
importance of narrative in the course of his theology. He is
interested in narrative not because he likes stories, but
because his embodied theology finds its authority in a
historical particularity which is better conveyed through
narrative than theoretical abstraction. As he says,
'narrative formally displays our existence and that of the
world as creatures – as contingent beings'.[57]

Hauerwas' theological sensitivity to the embodied and
material nature of creaturely existence is thus the cue to
which I have been responding in this chapter. Not only
have I tried to push its implications for gender further than
he has, but by using Skeggs' study I have also tried to show
that the social sciences may have a more important role to
play in a properly embodied theology than Hauerwas

---

[55] Hauerwas, *The Peaceable Kingdom*, 70.
[56] Hauerwas made extensive use of fiction in *A Community of Character:
Towards a Constructive Christian Social Ethic* (Notre Dame: University of
Notre Dame Press, 1981) when he developed his reflections on a story-
formed community through dialogue with Richard Adams' *Watership
Down* (9–35). More recently he has made equally extensive use of the
novels of Anthony Trollope (*Dispatches from the Front: Theological
Engagements with the Secular* [Durham, NC: Duke University Press, 1994],
31–79).
[57] Hauerwas, *The Peaceable Kingdom*, 28.

admits. I am particularly thinking of empirically-based studies like Skeggs' rather than the more abstract social theory which is the subject of John Milbank's theological excoriations.[58] Of course Hauerwas does indeed make use of the social sciences, but he chiefly uses them as a tool with which to describe the secular-liberal world he rejects. What he does not do is to refer to studies like Skeggs' or, more surprisingly, to the many excellent studies of congregational life in the United States. Even if one believes, as Hauerwas sometimes seems to, that the Church is the only proper object of the theologian's attention, the best of these sociological studies share his concern to understand and represent the lives and beliefs of actual Christian people and actual churches.[59] A number also offer reflections on the embodiedness of the theological enterprise itself which help develop the responsible reflexivity I have been advocating. To rely solely on personal and fictional accounts of Christian lives whilst ignoring a growing body of disciplined research seems a strange exclusion and one which, like the exclusion of gender, sits oddly with Hauerwas' revolutionary theological project.[60]

---

[58] For criticism of Milbank's blanket dismissal of the social sciences, and a more constructive analysis of the relations between theology and sociology, see David Martin, *Reflections on Sociology and Theology* (Oxford: Clarendon Press, 1997).

[59] I say sometimes because, particularly in Hauerwas' later work, we find comments like the following: 'It may even be the case that Christians will discover in those who are not Christians how we might live more faithfully and truly' (*Sanctify Them in the Truth*, 58). A number of the exemplary sociological studies to which I allude are extracted in Woodhead and Heelas, *Religion in Modern Times*.

[60] I am not, of course, suggesting that theology should uncritically accept the methods and findings of social science, nor that the latter is itself immune from some of the limitations and self-deceptions of which I have been accusing disembodied theology. On the failure of the sociology of religion to adopt a gendered perspective, for example, see Linda Woodhead , 'The Impact of Feminism on the Sociology of Religion', in Richard K. Fenn (ed.): *A Companion to the Sociology of Religion* (Oxford and Malden, MA: Blackwell, 2000).

9

The Church and the Concentration Camp: Some Reflections on Moral Community

Duncan B. Forrester

A Journey of Moral Enquiry[1]

We were returning home from holiday in Austria with our children some years ago. After Munich we began to notice road signs pointing to Dachau. These signs and that word brought back for Margaret and me a host of dark memories – of the news of the concentration camps that became public in the latter years of the Second World War, of the films of the liberation of the camps that were shown in British cinemas for a time after the war 'Lest We Forget'; of the stories that were told to us by a German Jewish family that stayed with us in St Andrews in 1939 before going to safety in the USA. The road-sign brought back old feelings of anger, shock and dismay that human beings could be so wicked, that evil of a cataclysmic sort should flourish in 'civilised' and 'Christian' Europe, that such awfulness should come to pass in the twentieth century after an epoch of what we had believed was progress.

As we drove past a section of the perimeter fence and glanced at the ominous huts and edifices preserved intact inside the boundary, our children seemed to sense that something was wrong, that their parents were distressed, that this place stood for something that seemed to inspire horror. They asked, as children do, the obvious questions: What is this place? What happened there? Why did it take place? Couldn't good people have stopped it?

We told them as honestly as we could about the

---

[1] I am indebted to various friends and colleagues for helpful comments on drafts of this essay, especially to Peter Hayman, Michael Northcott, and my wife, Margaret.

concentration camps, about Nazism, about the Holocaust, about what happened there. We always felt that it is important to tell truth to children, not to shield them from reality, even if that reality is appallingly evil and ugly. We always tried to answer their questions directly, to ensure that they received from their parents the truthfulness they are entitled to expect.

But this time it was peculiarly difficult to be truthful. Dachau and Auschwitz and the other camps were and are a problem not just for sunny, over-optimistic liberals who have a cheery confidence in moral progress, but for everyone, and particularly for Christian believers. We did the best we could to respond to our children's questions and explain how it all happened, and why it wasn't nipped in the bud, and how many ordinary people like us knowingly or unknowingly colluded in what was going on. We described what went on in the camps in relation to Jews, and gays, and gypsies, and Christians, and communists. We talked particularly about anti-Semitism, and we were at pains to pass on a lesson that we had learned in Christian homes during the War, that one mustn't blame the German people as a whole, and that we must honour those who courageously stood against the evil. We tried not to disguise the horror of it all. And I think we made clear that we felt that ultimately the only response possible to the horror of Dachau was a war of liberation, despite all the reservations and all the unease that Christians must have about violence.

The children picked up our unease. Somehow it didn't all add up, theologically or ethically. There were no satisfactory explanations for the horror. None of the responses seemed to be adequate. In some way we felt ourselves to be implicated. The evidence coming from the only part of the United Kingdom to be occupied, the Channel Islands, suggested that had Britain been occupied it would have been no different here. As we responded to their questions, the children knew us to be in turmoil.

The next day we drove across the plains of northern France. Here the unavoidable theme for discussion with the children was the significance of the acre upon acre of First World War military graveyards. Somewhere there, amidst the tens of thousands of tombstones and the vast number of unmarked graves lay the body of the uncle after whom I am named, killed aged nineteen in a vastly destructive, horrifying and muddy trench battle and now lying in a nameless grave. Once again, the children asked questions. They wanted to know what that war had been about, they wanted an explanation for this huge orgy of destruction and violence. I have a history degree. I have studied the origins of the First World War. I know about the assassination in Sarajevo of the Archduke Ferdinand of Austria. I tried explaining all this historical 'wisdom' to the children. But as I spoke, I knew it didn't add up to an explanation, let alone a justification of this vast orgy of destruction, violence and death. It certainly didn't make any Christian sense. And the children, aware of our embarrassment, must have wondered in what sort of world they were to grow up.

A few years later, we took the children to the only extermination camp the Nazis established in France, near Strasbourg. After seeing the barracks, the gas chamber, the ovens for cremating the bodies, the villa of the governor with its rose garden, fertilised with the ashes from the ovens, where the prisoners' orchestra played Mozart to entertain the governor's guests, our daughter was physically sick, and remained distressed for days. Our son bombarded us with questions: How could this happen? Who was responsible? Why did God allow it? After tortuous and inadequate attempts on our part to make sense of all this, we had to say, quite simply that Hitler and his associates were very evil men. What would you do about him? Does God love Hitler? Ought we to love him? – the questions poured out. And wrestling with such questions is what serious theological ethics is all about, for the questions of children more commonly go straight to the heart of the matter than do the convoluted and pretentious questions of adults, and particularly perhaps of academics.

Outside the Camp ... with Jesus?

Driving past Dachau, our children did not seem to notice what was glaringly obtrusive and problematic for

Margaret and me: just outside the perimeter wire there stood a graceful little eighteenth-century church, freshly painted and with a typical central European onion dome on the top of its tower. It was probably Roman Catholic, but it might possibly have been Evangelical; that really didn't matter. Here was a Christian church, almost certainly regularly used for worship, standing less than a hundred yards from the fence, visible to anyone moving about inside the camp.

Perhaps it was significant that it stood outside the camp. In most Western prisons the chapel is inside, signifying a religious involvement in what goes on in prison. That is the Christendom locale for a chapel, for in Christendom the Christian faith is involved in the discipline of the society, and often enough the prison was run by a troika of governor, chaplain and doctor. Perhaps it is healthier in normal circumstances for the location of the church to be outside the camp, a standing reminder of the impermanence of the camp, and the need to seek the city that is to come. After all, that place, outside the camp, was where Jesus bore the stigma and suffered for the sake of the life of the camp, of the city (Hebrews 13.12–14). But these Nazi days were no normal circumstances, and inevitably we had to ask what went on in that little church outside the camp when the camp behind the wire was active in its death-dealing ways of destruction.

Some things are almost certain. The Bible would have been read, Sunday by Sunday, or day by day. There would, at least from time to time, have been preaching, expounding and application of the message of Scripture. Bread would have been broken in the Lord's Supper, the Eucharist, the Mass, with the people receiving the Body and Blood of the Lord. From time to time children and even adults would have been received into the household of faith in baptism. God's praise would have been sung, and prayers offered for the Church and the world. All the ordinary central activities of a congregation of God's people within a hundred yards of Dachau concentration camp! And through the wire all the comings and goings of congregation and of concentration camp visible to one another, paraded before one another! But sometimes, of course, for a variety of reasons, people cannot see, or choose not to see what lies before them.

Here, presumably, was a congregation which had all 'the marks of the true Church', as the dogmaticians say, existing within a hundred yards of the concentration camp. Was the worship of that little congregation timeless, allowing the worshippers to step, or believe that they stepped, into a different reality in which Dachau concentration camp no longer existed? Did that church provide an escape from the awful reality so close by? Or did it engage in prayer, in protest, in action with what was going on, which could be seen and heard, and smelled and could have been touched had there not been a wire and a guard tower in between?

Who, I wonder, attended that church? Local villagers, no doubt, and probably older ones, for the young people would be away fighting the war. Did SS or Gestapo men ever happen to come into the little church? Did members of the staff of the camp, or their families worship there? Perhaps a doctor carrying out experiments on inmates, or even the governor might happen by. What would the worship and the life of that church say to them? Would it give them solace, allowing them to carry on their activities with a quiet mind? Would it transport them to a different world enabling them to evade responsibility for what they did in this world? Would they receive beneath that onion dome a premature and illusory forgiveness, cheap grace that makes no demands, at a knock-down price?

We will never know the answer to these questions. But what we do know without a shadow of doubt is that people engaged in unspeakably evil courses of action often find solace in religion. General Pinochet throughout the torture and repression of innocent people by his government was regular in his attendance at mass. Franz Fanon, in a different but not unconnected realm found himself, as a psychiatrist in Algeria, expected to treat and 'heal' government torturers who were suffering from remorse so that they could return with an equable mind to the torture of the innocent.

Did the congregation meeting in that little church in the shadow of Dachau raise up prophets who dared to denounce the system and confront the evil? Almost certainly the answer to that is 'No', as there is so little evidence of dissident voices from within the churches requiring to be silenced. Or was the Dachau church a quiet school of virtue and faithfulness, like the little congregation under Pastor Trocmé in the village of Le Chambon-sur-Lignon in the Cévennes, where, when a Jewish woman knocked on the door late at night and asked if she could come in, Madame Trocmé totally unselfconsciously answered, 'Yes'. And that, as is well known, started an escape route for several hundred Jews into safety in Switzerland – discipleship spontaneously in action. But that kind of faithfulness may perhaps not be possible, cheek by jowl with Dachau.

Or did the little church outside the wire proclaim an apocalyptic faith, denouncing Dachau as Babylon the great whore, and confidently foreseeing its destruction and the vindication of its victims? Or did it even sustain its people on apocalyptic imagery striving to be reborn, or to come alive in courageous critique of the camp and all it stood for? Was the congregation a peaceable community which by its very existence and walk presented an alternative to the violence being unleashed behind the fence? I wonder, and I hesitate to press my questions towards an answer because I fear the truth about that little church would not be as I might wish it to be. In all probability it was just a quiet little congregation meeting in a much loved building, and carrying on as if nothing unusual was happening behind the wire close by.

Let us press our speculations one step further. Suppose the prisoners in the camp could see the people coming and going around that little church; perhaps through an open door or window they see a little of what was going on, hear part of a chorale, perhaps on the wind catch phrases of a sermon or a prayer. Was it possible that they might glimpse the expression on people's faces as they came to church, and see whether it was changed or the same when they left? The prisoners would notice without a doubt whether the worshippers glanced towards the camp or kept their gaze averted. They would take the measure of the expression on their faces. Do they care about the camp, and us, and what goes on here? the prisoners would ask each other, I have no doubt.

And what would the prisoners make of all this? We have no evidence, apart from the wire and the watchtower and the little church, and the knowledge that there must have been prisoners, and guards, and worshippers, and pastors around these places when the camp was operating. What was the impact of all this on the prisoners? Was it in any sense a sign of hope to them? Did it affirm or destroy any faith they might have? Did it in any way lift up their hearts and minds to a coming day, which would be a day of judgement as well as of vindication? In its compromised mundane ordinariness did the life of that congregation suggest that the camp lacked ultimacy, and despite everything was doomed to destruction? Did its existence raise a question mark against the existence of the camp? Or was it a sign to the prisoners of sheer irrelevance?

We will never be able to answer these questions, but we have to ask them. For that church outside the perimeter fence at Dachau stands in a sense for every church although its locale is apparently so much more extreme and demanding. And if it is a church which neither has nor is a social ethic, its existence, and the existence of many another church just like it, raises awkward questions about one of Stanley Hauerwas' most suggestive and problematic epigrams: 'The church does not have, but is a social ethic.'

Inside the Camp ... with Jesus?

Dachau was the first concentration camp to be established by the Nazis, almost immediately upon their gaining of power in 1933. It was not at the beginning an extermination camp – those came somewhat later, but as a logical development of the purposes for which Dachau was established. Churchill proclaimed during a debate about the rebuilding of the House of Commons after it had been destroyed in the blitz, when some people were advocating moving from the traditional and rather adversarial layout to the more common semicircular legislature layout, 'We shape our buildings, and then our buildings shape us'. He was right. I taught for eight years in India in a Christian college the premises of which had been carefully designed in 1938 to enable and encourage the development of well-integrated and diverse community life, and good relations between staff and students. These buildings served their community-building purpose remarkably well.

Dachau was built to make a very different statement, and to be the prototype of a ruthless instrument for carrying through the grand design of the Nazis. The camp, Goldhagen says, 'was the first major distinctively new institution that Nazism founded after Hitler's accession to power'.[2] It symbolised and enabled a regime that depended on division, hatred and contempt to carry out its evil work, and it demanded that whole sections of the population, most notably the Jews, should be first systematically excluded, degraded and intimidated, and then eliminated in the 'final solution' in the extermination camps.

From 9 March 1933 at Dachau, in Martin Gilbert's words, 'terror found a hidden base behind barbed wire'. But the purpose was not that it should remain hidden; it was important that terror should spread from the camps throughout the population like ripples from a stone thrown into a pool. The fence was as it were calculated to enable outsiders to see a little of what went on inside, and to give inmates a tantalising glimpse of the outside world. The local SS, with a reputation for savagery, established the camp in a set of empty huts in a gravel pit. Within a month, the camp had expanded to house five thousand prisoners, Jews, gypsies, gays and critics of the regime. The camp started as a kind of crystallisation and intensification

---

[2] H. J. Goldhagen, *Hitler's Willing Executioners: Ordinary Germans and the Holocaust* (New York: Vintage, 1997), 170. Goldhagen gives a succinct and horrifying account of the development and scale of the camps, 167–78.

of the terror that was ruling the streets, and in a subtle way it conferred legitimacy on the terror and encouraged brutality outside.[3]

In October 1933 a new code of discipline and punishment was introduced to make Dachau a model of what was to become the central distinctive institution of the Nazi state. Absolute obedience to orders was ensured by the strictest of sanctions; 'agitators' were to be hung.[4] Large numbers of prisoners were killed through summary executions, erratic outbreaks of violence on the part of guards, or simply through exhaustion, sickness and overwork. The purpose of the camp from the beginning was degradation, destruction and death, all as an expression of the ideology of the Nazi regime. A Jewish prisoner who survived described the camp in February 1938:

> The Jewish prisoners worked in special detachments and received the hardest tasks. They were beaten at every opportunity – for instance, if the space between the barrows with which they had to walk or even to run over loose flints was not correctly kept. They were overwhelmed with abusive epithets such as 'Sow Jew', 'Filth Jew' and 'Stink Jew'. During the working period the non-Jewish prisoners were issued with one piece of bread at breakfast – the Jews with nothing. But the Jews were always paraded with the others to see the bread ration issued ... In February, March and April there were a number of 'suicides' and shootings 'during attempted escape'. The Jew Lowenberg was horribly beaten during a works' task, and committed suicide that night. In March two men were 'shot while attempting escape'. The Jew Lowy was shot dead for approaching closer than the regulation six metres to a sentry who had called him up. Another was ordered by a sentry again and again to approach until he

---

[3] Martin Gilbert, *The Holocaust: The Jewish Tragedy* (London: Fontana, 1987), 32–3.
[4] Gilbert, *The Holocaust*, 40.

stepped on the forbidden 'neutral zone' outside the barbed wire, whereupon he was shot dead.[5]

Goldhagen saw the camp as having four crucial features which are of relevance to our discussion:

1. It was a place of violence, where extreme violence was regarded as a laudable and necessary means of reaching goals.
2. It was a place where Germans could act as masters without 'the bourgeois restraints which Nazism was rapidly superseding with a new anti-Christian morality'.
3. In the camps the victims were refashioned to confirm the Nazi world-view and their hatred and contempt for their victims.
4. It was a new world, the harbinger of the Nazi hope, 'in which the social transformation and value transmutation that were at the heart of Nazism's program were being most assiduously implemented.'[6]

Thus Dachau and the other camps not only had, but exemplified and embodied a social ethic, albeit an ethic of almost unbelievable evil. In an essay, 'A Century of Camps?' in which he considers the camps as an appalling exemplar of a modernist project, Zygmund Bauman examines the camps as an extreme case of a perverse desire to have mastery over human nature, craving and needs. The camps in this context had their own 'sinister rationality', and were intended to fulfil three functions:

> They were laboratories where the new unheard-of volumes of domination and control were explored and tested. They were schools in which the unheard-of readiness to commit cruelty in formerly ordinary human beings was trained. And they were swords

[5] Gilbert, *The Holocaust*, 57–8.
[6] Goldhagen, *Hitler's Willing Executioners*, 172–3.

held over the heads of those remaining on the other side of the barbed-wire fence, so that they would learn not only that their dissent would not be tolerated but also that their consent was not called for, and that pretty little depends on their choice between protest and acclaim. The camps were distillations of an essence diluted elsewhere, condensations of totalitarian domination and its corollary, the superfluity of man, in a pure form difficult or impossible to achieve elsewhere. The camps were patterns and blueprints for the totalitarian society, that modern dream of total order, domination and mastery run wild, cleansed of the last vestiges of that wayward and unpredictable human freedom, spontaneity and predictability that held it back. The camps were testing grounds for societies run as concentration camps.[7]

So here, in Dachau and the other camps, we have, I cannot say a community or a society, but a structure for people to live and die together. The camps had and were a perverse social ethic, which expresses, exemplifies and promotes an understanding of human beings, of the world and of God or the ultimate reality which recognises itself as being radically at odds with Christian and Jewish faith. And just as when I was meditating on the Church, and in particular the little church close to the Dachau perimeter fence, I noted that there is often a jarring dissonance between the ethic that the Church proclaims and what the Church in a particular context actually stands for and how Christians behave, so here also we have to enquire about moral life within the camps, and the effectiveness of the camps in promoting evil and vice. This I intend to do through a discussion of Tzvetan Todorov's amazing book, *Facing the Extreme: Moral Life in the Concentration Camps*.[8]

Inside the camps there was a regime of degradation and

[7] Zygmunt Bauman, *Life in Fragments: Essays in Postmodern Morality* (Oxford: Blackwell, 1995), 201. See also his *Modernity and the Holocaust* (Ithaca: Cornell University Press, 1991).
[8] Tzvetan Todorov, *Facing the Extreme: Moral Life in the Concentration Camps* (London: Weidenfeld and Nicolson, 1999).

death, the reversal of all decent and humane values, an unveiling of the heart of darkness. It was explicitly intended to destroy self-respect, integrity, honour, responsibility and affection among the prisoners, and to train and encourage the guards and administrators in the ways of evil. The concentration camp was planned to be a school of dehumanising vice. Here structural evil reigned without check. And yet, even here, goodness and love were found to be present, surviving and even flourishing in a hostile climate.

Where keeping the prisoners at the edge of starvation was a matter of calculated policy, partly in the hope that hunger would turn prisoner against prisoner, and one would steal the other's food, there was to be found from time to time a virtually sacramental sharing of bread, which expressed just that basic human solidarity that the Nazis were determined to destroy. Robert Antelme, who survived Buchenwald, remembered 'the hungry old man who'd steal in front of his son, so that the son could eat. Father and son ... hungry together, offering their bread to each other with hungry eyes'.[9]

Eugenia Ginzburg remembered discovering some cranberries growing: 'I ate the first two clusters all by myself; only on finding a third one did I remember my fellow creatures.' She also remembered an old prisoner bringing her some oat jelly he had prepared but would not eat himself; he was simply happy to watch her enjoyment. After recounting a number of such instances of caring and sharing, Todorov concludes, 'In the end, there is not a single prisoner, male or female, who does not remember being cared for, counselled, or protected at least once by someone else'.[10] These were essentially expressions of solidarity, of responsibility for one another, of accountability to one another, or perhaps in some cases of accountability to God.

There was, however, the issue of particular solidarities conflicting with the universal claims of the neighbour. In

[9] Todorov, *Facing the Extreme*, 35.
[10] Todorov, *Facing the Extreme*, 72–3.

Auschwitz, we are told, the Poles would share among themselves but refuse to share with the French. The French, when they received food parcels, drove the hungry Russians away with clubs and blows. Christians cared for fellow Christians. Jews tended to share among themselves but were commonly shunned by the others – so far had the system worked, in setting group against group in a hierarchy of degradation and competition for meagre resources. Such solidarities with those like us, defined in antagonism to the other, are simply, of course, collective self-interest, what Primo Levi calls 'we-ism', the selfishness of a group. Yet Todorov concludes, rather optimistically perhaps, that 'people will generally help those whose need is greatest, whether or not they are of the same nationality'.[11]

Todorov makes an interesting and important distinction between caring and solidarity:

> Caring … differs from solidarity in that those who receive care cannot automatically count on it; they are, after all, individuals, not members of a group. Caring cannot include everyone, not everyone in the world or even everyone in the same camp. The choice is made according to criteria other than nationality, profession or political persuasion; each person who is cared for is deserving in and of himself or herself. Yet here, too, having a common language is important – how does one discern the individuality of a person one cannot understand?
>
> There is a second boundary that should also be defined, that between caring and charity (or any of its synonyms). Unlike solidarity, charity makes no distinctions; it excludes no one. The recipient of charity need only be suffering or be somehow in jeopardy. With charity, there is no danger of its being turned to the advantage of any particular group. It is incontestably a moral act. Charity differs from caring, then,

---

[11] Todorov, *Facing the Extreme*, 83.

precisely in its being directed toward everyone rather than toward particular individuals.[12]

Yet again and again there was the discovery that caring for others, even in the camp, brings its own rewards and is a way of caring for oneself as well.

Todorov has important things to say about believers in the camps as prisoners, and even Christians themselves involved in the process of extirpation of Jews and others. We need to ponder, awful as it is, the story of the Einsatzkommando operating within Russia that was ordered to kill three thousand Jews and Gypsies before Christmas so that they could celebrate the birth of Christ in peace. And when Christmas came, their leader preached to them a moving sermon about the incarnation.[13]

Within the camps among the inmates Christians and other believers in a religious system or a political ideology such as communism provided the largest numbers of martyrs, people willing to die for a cause, which gave some kind of meaning to their dying and their life. Todorov suggests that the true believer 'can so love God (or Communism ...) that he or she forgets to love people'. Love of God, it seems, does not translate in any simple and direct way into love of one's fellows. Jehovah's Witnesses, for example, refused to do any work which might aid the war effort because they believed Hitler to be the devil; but they had no interest either in helping their fellow prisoners who were not Witnesses.[14] For most inmates who gave their lives as martyrs, the dying was a heroic witness rather than an act of care for others:

> Father Kolbe gave his life to save that of another man. But more than that ... it was to proclaim his faith in God; it scarcely mattered to him who in particular it was whose life he saved. The mothers, daughters, fathers and sons who went to their deaths with those

[12] Todorov, *Facing the Extreme*, 84.
[13] Todorov, *Facing the Extreme*, 148–9.
[14] Todorov, *Facing the Extreme*, 57–8.

they loved acted in a very different spirit. Their attraction to the specific individuals whom they cared about was stronger than their desire to live. In a sense, these people are more selfish; they do not want to die so that the other may live; they would prefer that both survive, so that they can continue to enjoy each other, Since that is impossible, they accept death – with the other, and not in his or her stead.[15]

Thus Grossman may be right in characterising kindness, unqualified attention to the other, as involving an absence of doctrine. And evil is the mindless following of rules.[16]

Varlam Shalamov, a prisoner in the Soviet gulag for twenty-five years, declared, 'The camp was a great test of our moral strength, of our everyday morality, and 99% of us failed it.' And that included a multitude who bore the name of Christ. Yet even in such ultimately dehumanising conditions some could resist the ultimate demoralisation and degradation and leave a memory as heroes, saints or martyrs.

Remembering is important, and telling the story gives significance to the lives of those who have suffered and provides a warning lest the same things should happen again. In the camps telling the story became a main reason for staying alive. At the top of his manuscript, a prisoner, Zalmen Gradowski, wrote:

Dear discoverer of these writings! I have a request of you: this is the real reason I write, that my doomed life may attain some meaning, that my hellish days and hopeless tomorrows may find a purpose in the future.[17]

Anamnesis is at the core not just of sacramental life and faith, but gives significance to our lives, even in the hellish camps, and holds out hope for the future. The story must

---

[15] Todorov, *Facing the Extreme*, 86.
[16] Todorov, *Facing the Extreme*, 123.
[17] Todorov, *Facing the Extreme*, 96–7.

be told, and possessed and handed on if we are to have dignity and expectation. Especially for Christians the anamnesis of the Holocaust and the camps is important, for as Stephen Bonner has said: 'The holocaust manifests the latent potential of their history and reconfigures it. The holocaust is their story and "working through" the past is necessary for all of them, not just the Germans. They must lift the holocaust beyond the relative, beyond other atrocities, in order to understand themselves and what their civilisation made possible.'[18]

On Being the Church

There are interesting, and indeed alarming, similarities between the Church and the concentration camp, between Dachau and the onion-domed church just outside its perimeter fence. John Milbank makes a neat contrast between world and Church, the world represented by Aristotle's polis, ultimately founded on violence, and the Church, as the *civitas Dei*, the abode of peace. But when we turn to the world in which we live this contrast is shown to be dangerously facile. The little church outside the camp has a highly ambiguous relationship to the violence that is concentrated in the camp, and to the peaceableness of the Gospel. In some alarming ways it possibly gives tacit, but none the less effective, support to the violence of the camp. In the camp with all its awfulness faith, hope and charity somehow manage to survive, perhaps in purer, truer form than within the church outside the fence. Sam Wells argues that for Hauerwas the model of virtue was the martyr or the saint, as against the classical tradition which accorded primacy to the hero; the Church was to be a school of saints and martyrs.[19] And yet in our scenario it is in the camp rather than the church that the saints, martyrs and heroes

[18] Stephen Eric Bonner, 'Making Sense of Hell: Three Meditations on the Holocaust', *Political Studies* 47 (1999), 328.
[19] Samuel Wells, 'The Disarming Virtue of Stanley Hauerwas', *Scottish Journal of Theology* 52 (1999), 82–8.

are in all probability to be found; and it is not quite convincing to suggest that they can be so only because they have been nurtured for such a time as this within the Church or synagogue.

'What makes the church the church', we learn from Stanley Hauerwas, 'is its faithful manifestation of the peaceable kingdom.'[20] The camp, on the other hand, stands for the triumph of unbridled violence, the kingdom of darkness, if you prefer such terminology. Each is intended to be both a school and an instrument. And each was in certain ways strikingly unsuccessful in the fulfilment of its task. The only peace that the little onion-domed church offered was a temporary refuge from the violence of its context. In the concentration camp, despite an evil panoply of means to degrade, demoralise and reduce to despair, there still occurred caring, generosity, courage, nobility and hope. And in 1945 the concentration camps were abolished, and some decades later the gulag disappeared – although there still remain around the world foci of genocidal violence, and techniques of oppression developed in the camps have been copied elsewhere.

Hauerwas' epigram that the Church does not have but is a social ethic appears in many places in his writings. It is a very attractive notion, suggesting that Christian ethics must be embodied in the life of a community, that ethics is not a possession of the Church but the gift to the Church which constitutes it as Church. The Church, for Hauerwas, is a social ethic in as far as it is a 'faithful manifestation of the peaceable kingdom in the world'.[21] Its first task is to be the Church, a community which can clearly be distinguished from the world.[22] It is shaped by a story which is sharply different from the world's story. Its most important social function is to be itself.[23] It is called to be a

[20] Stanley Hauerwas, *The Peaceable Kingdom: A Primer in Christian Ethics* (London: SCM Press, 1983), 99.
[21] Hauerwas, *The Peaceable Kingdom*, 99.
[22] Stanley Hauerwas, *Christian Existence Today* (Durham, NC: Labyrinth Press, 1988), 101.
[23] Stanley Hauerwas, *Vision and Virtue* (Notre Dame, IN: University of Notre Dame Press, 1981), 240.

community of the cross, and an alternative to the hostilities and divisions to be found elsewhere.

This is all heady stuff to which one is tempted to say that the church and the camp at Dachau provide an empirical refutation: that church is not like the Church of which Hauerwas speaks, and paradoxically the virtues that he sees as central to the Christian community are exemplified in costly ways within the camp, far from the orbit of the church. And yet the tense and mood of Hauerwas' adage are perhaps part of my trouble with it. He writes in the present rather than the future eschatological tense, and in the indicative rather than imperative mood. And so it is easy to suggest the epigram does not correspond, is not relevant, to the Church as we know it, or the church near the Dachau wire. But is he not perhaps in fact discussing the calling of the Church today? And is Hauerwas not perfectly aware that this calling can differ in various contexts, and that the actual visible Church to which we belong falls far short of living up to its calling? If that is so, the Church must be a community of forgiven sinners who have learned to live by grace rather than a fellowship of moral heroes and virtuous achievers. Let Stanley speak for himself:

> I suspect that theologically today the most vital form of Christian social ethics must actually be a concern about the kind of community that Christians form among themselves. In other words, the church will serve the world best as it serves its Lord through the depth of its doctrinal affirmations, its liturgical experience, and the kind of moral concern the members of the church share with one another. If it does this well the church cannot be content with its institutional affairs as an end in themselves, for the content of its doctrine, liturgy and communal form will not let it forget that it exists only as a mission to the world.[24]

---

[24] Hauerwas, *Vision and Virtue*, 216.

In other words – and here, I think, is the nub of Stanley's epigram – the Church is called to be the Church in different ways in different contexts. We attend to the Dachau concentration camp and the little church outside, and to the complex and often terrible story of the Church down the ages, and above all to Scripture, not to find there some universally valid pattern of being the Church, but rather to learn from the failures and the triumphs of the past how God is calling us to be the Church, a fellowship of disciples, today, and in relation to today's opportunities and problems. And in this conversation we are seeking above all to attend to the Church's Lord who calls the Church to be a manifestation not so much of goodness as of grace, of achievement as of faithfulness.

CONVERSING WITH HAUERWAS

10
The Church as a School of Virtue?
Human Formation in Trinitarian
Framework

Colin Gunton

Contributing to the rediscovery of the centrality of the virtues for human being is one of the gifts of inestimable value that Stanley Hauerwas has given to the world. There is no escaping the concept of virtue, even though much modern moral philosophy and theology has sought to do so, with its individualistic idea of the person as naked, choosing will: the rootless I of existentialism and consumerism. Perhaps central amongst Hauerwas' contributions is to remind us that we are creatures who have our being in time, and that the temporal, or narrative, shape of our being is intrinsic.

> The virtues are timeful activities. This is not just because the virtues can only be developed through habitual formation, but because the virtues bind our past with our future by providing us with continuity of self.[1]

How are our selves formed in time? In this essay, it will be contended that an ethic of virtue need not be incompatible with a doctrine of justification, as is sometimes suggested by both Hauerwas and others. Without wanting to deny that we need the virtues, I hope to place the notion in the context of a doctrine of God, giving it a broader basis than it sometimes has. Some of the questions I am following up

---

[1] Stanley Hauerwas, *Christian Existence Today: Essays on Church, World, and Living in Between* (Durham, NC: Labyrinth Press, 1988), 265.

have been suggested to me by Ellen Charry's recent book, and here I want to argue first, in agreement, for the necessity of a doctrine of the immanent Trinity, and then enquire into the way in which such a doctrine might feed an understanding of what it is to be human.[2] The path there, however, is tortuous, somewhat as follows.

First, something about the nature of a trinitarian doctrine of creation, needed for an understanding of the framework for being a human being in the wider created order. Then, second, an introduction to the notion of virtue, and particularly in relation to human sinfulness. What are we to make of virtue in a fallen world? Third, 'remaking the human', will say something about salvation as the act of the triune God, and the way in which God's action in the economy is based in God's eternal triune being. Fourth, something about the place of the Church in the formation of human virtues. In all the sections a double question will form a background accompaniment: What is the relation between being – what God and we are – and act? Do our acts flow from our being, as is the emphasis of an ethic of virtue, of training people to be certain kinds of people, so that certain kinds of acts follow from what they are? Or is the act more important, so that we form our persons from what we do? That is on the whole a more typical modern view, although it is, of course, a much more complicated matter than that makes it seem. The two are so interdependent that it scarcely seems possible to disentangle them, so that the main question for us is: How might the Church be conceived to play a part in shaping the being of people so that they are free to act in a way that makes for life rather than for death?

God, Creation and Eschatology

On the relation of the economic and immanent Trinity, there is just a little to be said. Rather than presenting yet

---

[2] Ellen Charry, *By the Renewing of Your Minds: The Pastoral Function of Christian Doctrine* (New York: Oxford University Press, 1997).

another discussion of what has come to be called Rahner's rule, I would here simply reiterate the procedure of Karl Barth on the relations of the revealed and ontological Trinity: that one cannot say of the eternal being of God more than is licensed by his revelation. It does not however follow that, as is sometimes concluded, God is only the economy. Barth's and, more ambiguously, Rahner's proposal is that while economy betokens being – what God does reveals who he is – being is by no means reduced to it. The point of affirming an immanent Trinity in relative distinction from the economic is to allow for personal space between God and the world. If God does not enable the world to be other because and in as much as he is other than it, the being of the world risks being simply swallowed up in that of God. At this place, the doctrine of the Trinity and the ontology of creation it involves perform a crucial and necessary function. By showing that it is one thing to be God, another to be the world, they enable both to be themselves, in right relation. That is a far more important rule than Rahner's because any breach risks binding the world so much into God's being that it loses its own distinctive reality.

Why? Only if God has freedom of action do we also. To be sure, there is freedom and freedom: freedom as the modern world tends to conceive it, as individual autonomy, an indelible character of the person, unaffected or relatively unaffected by relation to others; and a more relational and biblical conception. Here a number of questions jostle for attention, including one that would perhaps take us too far afield, that of the sense in which we would wish to say that God is free.[3] Our question is that of human formation, and in respect to freedom the question is: Are we formed in freedom, or are we in some way automatically free? And if we have to be formed in freedom, does this involve that notion with which the modern world is most uncomfortable, that we have to receive our freedom from outside, from others? Suppose

---

[3] See Robert W. Jenson, 'An Ontology of Freedom in the *De Servo Arbitrio* of Luther', *Modern Theology* 10 (1994), 247–52, at 250.

that we examine the question with the help of the notion of autonomy. Autonomy appears to require that human beings are self-directed, in the strongest sense of being utterly responsible for the formation of our ethical principles and actions. What place here is there for being formed? Yet in assuming that that is what autonomy involves, we are begging a question, that namely, of what autonomy means. What is the law of our being? Indeed, what are we ourselves? Let me begin with the general question, already touched on, of the real and distinct existence of things in general before moving to people.

The key is to be found in that most disputed and often neglected of doctrines, that of the Holy Spirit. So dominated have we been with what can be called the religious functions of the Spirit – the early theologians, for example, often defended his divinity by appeal to little more than the fact that sanctification is a divine work – that we tend to forget that the Spirit is the Lord and Giver of Life universally. In so far as we can distribute forms of action among the persons of the Trinity, Basil of Caesarea should be our guide. While affirming that the Holy Spirit is 'inseparable and wholly incapable of being parted from the Father and the Son', he yet held that it is necessary to distinguish: 'the original cause of all things that are made, the Father; ... the creative cause, the Son; ... the perfecting cause, the Spirit'.[4] I would gloss: the Father originates; he creates through the Son; and he perfects through the Spirit. What we gain is the notion of the Spirit as the perfecting cause, something Calvin picked up, saying of the Spirit that 'in transfusing into all things his energy, and breathing into them essence, life, and movement, he is indeed plainly divine'.[5] Now perfecting might involve a number of things; two in particular. First, Calvin's point stresses the nature of the creating act: God sees all that he has made, and it is very good (Genesis 1), because it is perfected by the Spirit. In that sense, it is through the Spirit's action that we discern the basis of the world's distinction from God, its being itself, the

---

[4] Basil of Caesarea, *On the Holy Spirit* XV 36 and 38.
[5] John Calvin, *Institutes* I xiii 14.

world. As the 'perfecting cause' the Holy Spirit, the Lord and Giver of Life, gives reality to the world by perfecting what the Father does through his Son: originating what is truly other. Yet, because it is through the Son, the one who was to become incarnate, that the world was originated, it is not what it is outside a continuing relation to God.

The notion of a continuing relation of the world to its creator brings us to the second way in which the Spirit is perfecting cause. This is in the eschatological work, according to which the creation is finally brought to its perfection, its completedness, in the fullness of time. A side-swipe at one of the exponents of 'economy alone' trinitarians, Catherine Mowry LaCugna, will indicate something of what I mean. In one crucial passage, the author speaks of an

> emanation and return ... [which] express ... the one ecstatic movement of God outward by which all things originate from God through Christ in the power of the Holy Spirit, and all things are brought into union with God and returned to God. There is neither an economic nor an immanent Trinity; there is only the oikonomia that is the concrete realisation of the mystery of theologia in time, space, history and personality.[6]

The question raised here is so important that I must spell out its implications. An eschatology of this kind, with its suggestion of a symmetrical outflow and return of things from and back to God, risks suggesting the ultimate point-lessness of creation. Is the world made simply to return to the nothingness whence it came? That is certainly the suggestion of much eschatology since Origen, and of Western eschatology since Tertullian in particular.[7] Against this, a truly pneumatological eschatology will allow us to pay far more attention to the creation's interest for and in itself: to give more stress both to its particular reality as this universe, the one created by God for a purpose, and to the being of the particular things and

---

[6] Catherine M. LaCugna, *God for Us: The Trinity and Christian Life* (New York: HarperCollins, 1991), 223.
[7] Tertullian, *Against Hermogenes* 34.

persons of which it is constituted. To be sure, we are not yet here in the realm of freedom, but giving human freedom foundation in the fact that the Spirit confers otherness on things, the fact that things are created for an end which is something more than is given in the beginning. Creation through the Spirit is creation that has a *telos*. To use an analogy from the arts, a block of marble is in its own way perfect, but in the hands of a sculptor, it is also perfectible.

The topic of this essay is the eschatological destiny of one part of the created order, the personal. Are human beings made to go somewhere – and if so, how do we get there? More elegantly, do we have a destiny, and how is it to be realised? To pursue our enquiry, we need to look at the one (particular!) human person who is what he was created to be. What makes Jesus the particular person that he is? The answer is to be found in his relation to Israel and Israel's God realised through the Spirit. That is the point of the Gospel stories of his birth: as the eternal Son of God he becomes the son of this particular mother by the Spirit's recreating act; as this particular Israelite he is driven by the Spirit into the wilderness to test his messianic calling against other possibilities, and, by virtue of his obedient choice empowered by that Spirit to tell the truth, drive out the demons and in general re-establish God's rule; and raised from the dead as the first born of many brothers and sisters who become the Church. Some words of that great theologian of the humanity of Christ, the author to the Hebrews, make the point: 'he learned obedience from what he suffered' (5.8), a reference surely not to the cross alone, but to his whole life as it so culminated. We might gloss: he learned obedience through what happened to him, through what he experienced, went through. It was thus that he was 'made perfect' – Mary's child perfected through life and death and resurrection – something we must surely construe by reference to the eschatological perfecting of the Holy Spirit. Despite the paucity of direct references to the Spirit's activity – because of the essential self-effacingness of the Spirit's action, his activity has often to be read between the lines of Scripture – this letter has sometimes been argued to originate as a pentecostal address. At a crucial stage there is explicit pneumatology, and it comes in connection with Jesus' perfecting: 'who through the eternal Spirit offered himself unblemished to God ...' (9.14). If it is indeed the case that the Father sends him, as is the overall message of the New Testament, it is equally the case that his painfully achieved sinlessness derives from the Holy Spirit's maintaining him in relation to his Father. The perfection of Jesus' life as a whole consists in its conforming, realised by his relation to the Father through the Spirit, to that which he was created to be, to his particular *telos*. What we make of that, however, is somewhat complicated, and requires a little more analysis of our terms.

Human Virtue in a Fallen World

So far one concept in particular has been considered, that of perfection, and particularly the characteristic action of the Holy Spirit in realising it. We now approach a second: that of virtue. In relating virtue and perfection, I want to take a risky and speculative step, combining Aristotle with some hints from Karl Barth, who, it may be remembered, resisted talk of God's attributes, preferring rather to speak of his perfections.[8] Perfections are the ways God both is and acts, both in his triune eternity and in relation to the world. God's grace and mercy, justice and holiness are God in action, and so are, we might say, the divine virtues in the exercise of which God is himself and not another. It is almost as if Barth were speaking of God's perfections as his virtues according to Aristotle's definition of virtue as a *hexis proairetike*: (a settled disposition in exercising choice?).[9] God's 'virtues' are God in the perfect coincidence

---

[8] Karl Barth, *Church Dogmatics*, trans. and ed. Geoffrey Bromiley and T. F. Torrance (Edinburgh: T&T Clark, 1957), II/1, section 29.
[9] Aristotle, *Ethics* 1106b36. Indeed, *proairesis* might well be a way of characterising both election and providence according to Barth's scheme of things.

of being and act. This, we might say, is God's character, the settled shape of what he is and does.

May such an Aristotelian notion be applied by analogy to the human sphere? Can we speak in all this of the formation of Jesus' 'character', of his exercising 'virtues'? Luke certainly thinks so, for according to him the young Jesus was subject to his parents and 'grew in wisdom and stature, and in favour with God and men' (Luke 2.52). He would certainly appear to exercise what we would call virtues, even if not always in Aristotelian form: courage, truthfulness and love, if not impassibility, were Jesus' settled disposition, as the narrative depicts them. We can then understand human virtues, and certainly Jesus' virtues, as human perfections. His life as a whole is offered to God perfect because his *hexis*, his settled disposition, is determined by his relation to God the Father through the perfecting Spirit. How easily can this pattern be applied to our situation?

Here we reach the first difficulty we must surmount if we are to root what we say in the life of the Church. Human virtues are habits of the heart, in the sense that they are dispositions rooted in the fundamental orientation of the human agent. In our liberal culture we tend to think of acts as the undetermined effects of individual acts of will, forgetting that there is no act of will which does not arise out of a history – including a history of habitual behaviour. Let me illustrate with an extreme but illuminating case. In the second decade of the nineteenth century, Samuel Taylor Coleridge performed two acts whose meanings are inseparable. He professed orthodox trinitarian belief and made confession of his addiction to opium, a drug he had taken originally for medical reasons. His addiction – his enslaving habit – gave him insights into the universal human condition which represent a modern republication of Augustine's anti-Pelagian arguments:

> By the long Habit of the accursed poison my Volition (by which I mean the faculty instrumental to the Will, and by which alone the Will can realise itself – its

Hand, Legs, & Feet, as it were) was completely deranged ... and became an independent faculty.[10]

The distinction between the will and acts of volition is important: between that which we would do, and that which, as Coleridge shows, we actually do in acts of volition. Our will and our acts of willing have to be distinguished, because to be fallen is to act in a way that one essentially – that is to say, eschatologically – is not. 'For I have the desire to do what is good, but I cannot carry it out. For what I do is not the good I want to do; no, the evil I do not want to do – this I keep on doing' (Romans 7.18b–19). What we call acts of will take shape in the heart, the settled disposition of the personal agent. Disable that, and the acts of volition become not only misdirected, as Coleridge realises in what is in effect a rehearsal of the argument of Romans 7, but actively work against the wishes of the heart.

In sum: an ethic of virtue is good in that it makes possible a criticism of the anthropology of pure will that underlies so many modern characterisations of the person, and its accompanying view of acts as merely punctiliar, single acts without relation to past and present. Actions flow from and manifest being. But in so far as that being can be badly formed, and, indeed, according to the doctrine of sin, is badly formed, an ethic of virtue cannot be sufficient apart from a theology of redemption. Apart from redemption, action does not correspond to eschatological destiny, but negates it. If, then, autonomy refers to the law of our being, that law must be understood eschatologically, with reference to what we are created to become, to the perfection to which we are called. This is an Irenaean theme: Adam and Eve's childlike nature implies a growth to maturity; but our fallenness, our turning backwards, requires the incarnation, death and resurrection of the

---

[10] Cited by Richard Holmes from S. T. Coleridge, *Letters* III 498–90, in *Coleridge, Darker Reflections* (London: HarperCollins 1998), 356f. Coleridge continues 'I used to think St James' text, "He who offended in one point of the Law, offended in all", was very harsh; but my own sad experience has taught me its awful, dreadful Truth.'

eternal Son of God if a way forward is to be found. Does Stanley Hauerwas fail to emphasise satisfactorily this aspect of the matter, or is he in danger of an exemplarism of the cross, an implicit Pelagianism which lays upon human agents a burden too great for them to bear? I leave it as a question, and am, I think, not alone in doing so.

Remaking the Human

Professor Charry has rightly criticised those who oppose the being and the act of God, advocating as they do 'a modern understanding of personhood that embraces growth and change and views personhood as constituted by action, not character'.[11] Of course it is a mistake to read into God's eternity categories taken from a temporal and fallen world. But a developmental view of created persons is inescapable. The three-personed God creates persons who are not eternal, but are made to have their being in time, as Stanley Hauerwas reminds us. They are finite and, as created, both mortal and directed to an end which exceeds their beginning, as the mature adult exceeds the child. 'Person' is an eschatological concept, so an eschato-logically-oriented conception of the human involves training in virtue – in human perfections.

Further, human characters need change because we are fallen beings. This means that our character – our settled disposition – is such that our acts flow as much from vices as from virtues, sometimes more. Character and act belong inseparably together: the slavery at the heart of our being determines the wrongness of our acts, and can be broken only by redemption. The enemy is not action versus character, but the modern view that life is constituted more by decision than through character; or rather that our decisions come somehow out of the blue, unrelated to the kind of people that we are. There Hauerwas is absolutely right. To give centrality to decision is to make two mistakes: it is to treat life as a series of points; and it is to

---

[11] Charry, *By the Renewing of Your Minds*, 125.

throw too great a weight on a certain conception of human autonomy at the expense of grace. In this respect, we cannot evade the fact that apart from redemption, our virtues will be but shadows of what they should be. That means, however, that we need not accept a disjunction between a more Reformation-oriented dialectic of *simul justus et peccator* and a more Methodist ethic of virtue.[12] Renewal of character is based in God's reconciling act in Christ, so that, as Calvin knew, we need to find room in our theology for both sanctification and justification.[13]

That takes us back to the doctrine of the Trinity. To gain as clear as possible a view of all the elements which must be held in proper relative weight, we must retain in careful juxtaposition the way we relate being and act in God and in human agents. We have seen that, for Barth, God's perfections constitute the utter consistency of his being and act. We turn now to the way in which God's act, rooted in his being, serves to redirect human being to its proper end. Here Irenaeus, as always in these matters, helps us, especially in one remarkable chapter:

> [God's] only-begotten Word, who is always present with the human race, united to and mingled with His own creation, according to the Father's pleasure, and who became flesh, is Himself Jesus Christ our Lord, who did also suffer for us, and arose again on our behalf, and who will come again in the glory of His Father, to raise up all flesh. ... There is therefore ... one God the Father, and one Christ Jesus, who came by means of the whole dispensational [economic?] arrangements ... and gathered together all things in Himself. ... [S]o that as in super-celestial, spiritual and invisible things, the Word of God is supreme, so also in things visible and corporeal He might possess

---

[12] For a careful account of his position, see the new introduction to Stanley Hauerwas, *Character and the Christian Life; A Study in Theological Ethics* (San Antonio, TX: Trinity University Press, 1985), xxixf.

[13] Colin Gunton, 'Aspects of Salvation: Some Unscholastic Themes from Calvin's *Institutes*', *International Journal of Systematic Theology* 1 (1999), 253–65.

supremacy, and, taking to Himself the pre-eminence, as well as constituting Himself Head of the Church, He might draw all things to Himself at the proper time.[14]

For Irenaeus, the overall consistency of God's actions in the economy is rooted in his triune being; we might say, his acts flow from his eternal character. For our purposes, the crucial consistency is found in the linking of creation, incarnation, cross and eschatology. The one through whom the world is created is the one through whom it was, is being and will be redeemed. The Word 'mingled with His own creation ... suffered for us ...' and 'will come again in the glory of His Father, to raise up all flesh. ...' Let us explore some of the rich possibilities of this remarkable passage.

1. 'Mingled with his own creation'. Once again, we find that it is Christology which provides an essential basis for a theology of character and virtue. The modern notion that to be human is to be a series of actions, decisions, choices – the ideology of the consumer society – is to take people out of the created matrix in which they are embedded. As the incarnation shows, this matrix has two aspects, the material and the social. The eternal Son of God became flesh – whole, embodied, human being; and he became flesh as one tied up with the social and political being of Israel, his people. Correspondingly, (a) Coleridge's moral slavery was also a bodily slavery to opium. This is but an extreme example of what we all are. As our willed actions become habitual, they correspond to tracks formed in the brain's nervous system, because our bodies embed what we are.[15] The incarnation of the eternal Son of God in Jesus of Nazareth establishes the necessity and possibility of the reorientation of the whole person; the development of

---

[14] Irenaeus, *Against the Heresies* 3.16.6. This ought surely to dispel all the nonsense that Irenaeus' is only an economic trinitarianism, and that the evil of ontology came in only with Nicene theology.
[15] That is not, of course, to adopt a crude mind–brain identity theory and conclude that brain states are identical with their actions, but to suppose that we are what we are in and as the particular bodies that we are.

proper perfections, virtues, correspondingly a renewal of the whole person, body, mind and spirit, a retraining of body as well as soul. (b) The social dimension involves similar claims. My disinclination to certain types of action and my tendency to perform others are functions of the way I was brought up and am still formed in both family and church, the way I was and am taught, the books I read and the way – to cite but one 'secular' example – the ubiquitous pressures of the modern media reinforce some and alter others of my genetically-inherited tendencies to act. All in all, to be a created human being is to be part of a material and social dynamic, and, because under the conditions of fallenness that dynamic is at once progressive and regressive, ecclesial formation exists to reorient us to the eschatological promise of perfection in Christ; but it does so in a context which continues to resist it – hence 'at once justified and a sinner'. Therefore, every action makes for life or makes for death, and it is so not just for individual agents, but for the whole context, material and social in which we live.[16]

2. 'Suffered for us'. At this stage, we return to Ellen Charry's thesis: that good theology is aretegenic, productive of virtue. In certain respects, this is a variation on Karl Barth's belief that dogmatics is ethics and ethics is dogmatics, but by specifically tuning into the recent rediscovery of the ethic of virtue, she enables the thesis to become more concrete than it sometimes appears to be in Barth. We have seen, however, that an ethic of virtue is not enough because character formation takes place in a dynamic of death as well as of life, so that vices need more than a process of retraining. Apart from redemption; in other words, apart from a radical redirection of the created order through Christ, death will have the last word. The Fathers are insistent that it is the corruption of the image of God in the human creature that is the source of the creation's subjection to vanity, to that nothingness which is the subversion of the creator's purpose. Accordingly, the

---

[16] In sum: the modern understanding of autonomy cannot encompass a satisfactory account of created being, let alone of sin.

Church cannot become a school of virtue unless it is first a community that lives and proclaims the forgiveness of sins achieved by the life and particularly the death of Jesus Christ her Lord as the sole basis of the reconstitution of the disabled human will. In traditional terms, justification is the precondition of sanctification. We cannot set out on the Hauerwasian journey without being turned about from the way we were going.[17] Anything else simply fails to do justice to the seriousness of the Fall in which all participate apart from redemption. There has to be a re-forming before there can be a forming. Things being what they are, characters are deformed: their settled disposition works against their eschatological perfecting rather than for it. In sum, we cannot use Jesus' formation in virtue simply as an analogy for ours. For, though he was like us in all things sin apart, that 'sin apart' presents a disanalogy so great that another, intermediate, step must be taken to supplement the weaknesses of a too Aristotelian anthropology.

With respect to the more explicitly churchly dimensions of our subject, we must say that a theology of virtue must be grounded in a theology of baptism. Here the efforts of the self-consciously Anabaptist end of the Free Church spectrum, encouraged as its representatives are by Barth's theology of baptism, can militate against an ethic of grace. Joining, or being joined to, the Church is not an ethical act but one whose stress is on that which is received: the turning round of the old Adam symbolised by the water which drowns. The strengths of the traditions of infant baptism are that they stress that the path of virtue is one on which we have to be set, by others, as they place us in a community oriented to the death of Christ, a death which was, though finally chosen and after much struggle, imposed upon him by his Father. Only after going through that strait and narrow gate may we borrow – and therefore radically transform – the terminology of the worthy Aristotle.

3. We now come to the third feature of the passage from

---

[17] As much of Hauerwas' theology makes clear. At issue is a matter of weighting: where the stresses are put.

Irenaeus: 'will come again in the glory of His Father, to raise up all flesh ...'; to which should be prefaced the conclusion of the cited passage: that, 'as well as constituting Himself Head of the Church, He might draw all things to Himself at the proper time'. Irenaeus generates an eschatological ecclesiology, without which we shall not find the anthropology we are seeking. As 'Head of the Church' Christ draws all things to himself, 'at the proper time'. Any theology of virtue must take shape within the fields of ecclesiology and eschatology. As the community of the last days living before the last days, the community of God's people exists to receive, through the action of the Spirit, a forward orientation, away from the realm of sin and death. The following few remarks will not attempt a comprehensive account, but offer, I hope, at least a possibility for further thought about this complex matter.

In Aristotle, as is often pointed out, there is a tension between two conceptions of the purpose of virtue. First of all, it is needed for the life of the polis; in that respect, clearly social. But, second, human virtues exist to serve individual well-being, *eudaemonia*, so that their ethical end is the pure contemplation of thought thinking itself. They are thus secondary to a theological end, individualistically conceived. Ethics in the sense of a concern for the goodness and badness of human action are not autonomous(!) but instrumental, a means to the end that is contemplation of the timeless self-thinking thought that is God. For Christian theology, ethics are similarly provisional, but not, I think, in so radical a sense as for Aristotle. We are, according to the Letter to the Ephesians (2.10), created in Jesus Christ for good works, and the incarnation necessarily means that those things done in the body are of more ultimate importance than they could be for either Plato or Aristotle. The end, the purpose of it all, which Irenaeus has picked up at least in part from this same letter, is that God in Christ may reconcile all things to himself. The end is not contemplation of the timeless but God's eschatological purposes for the whole project of creation. One of the central means to that end, signalled by the doctrine of the image of God, is the 'good works' for which we are both created and redeemed. What is the place of the virtues in all this? How central do we make them?

The Church as a Community of Virtue?

A recent writer has argued that the weakness of an ethic of virtue is that, unless its Aristotelianism is transcended, it contains a danger of ethical narcissism inasmuch as the subject's intentionality is directed towards itself and its own self-realisation.[18] Unless virtues come unnoticed and unremarked, they are not truly describable as virtues. It is in this light that the author brings to bear some criticisms by Luther of the Aristotelianism of both Aristotle and Aquinas as involving, in its tendency to narcissism, a problematic anthropology. It sees the human being too much as looking inwards, too little as oriented without. Against this, Professor Asheim shows that Luther's anthropology is *exzentrisch, enklitisch und responsorisch*.[19] In other words, virtue is received before it is exercised and takes shape in relation to what, with a radical change of meaning, we may call significant others.

There are two focuses for the exocentricity we need. First, the outward centredness has to be understood christologically and trinitarianly, moving from Jesus' human formation to that of others. Jesus' formation as the particular human being that he was is characterisable as a triune act: the incarnation – the sharing by God the Son in the human condition – can, as the work of the Son, only be understood as at once also the work of Father and Spirit. According to Hebrews the shape of this life was also fully human, for Jesus was 'tempted in every way, just as we are – yet was without sin' (4.15), and that can surely serve as a summary of one side of the whole New Testament portrayal of the saviour. Hebrews is emphatic: 'for this reason he

---

[18] Ivar Asheim, 'Lutherische Tugendethik', *Neue Zeitschrift für Systematische Theologie und Religionsphilosophie* 40 (1998), 239–60. As has often been pointed out, narcissism is another way of characterising the slavery in which modern Western society is bound.

[19] Asheim, 'Lutherische Tugendethik', 245f.

had to be made like his brothers in every way, in order that he might become a merciful and faithful high priest. ... Because he himself suffered when he was tempted, he is able to help those who are being tempted' (2.17–18).

That latter reference to those who are tempted enables us to move by analogy to the condition of those for whom Jesus is the primary significant other. That members of the Church are forgiven sinners means that they enter the community, by baptism, with a common inheritance, that of fallen humankind. In genetics-speak, our genes encode bad information, which each embodies differently. Whatever some theologies of justification and some charismatic accounts of conversion may sometimes suggest, this bad information cannot be simply wiped from the slate. That would represent an over-realised eschatology. Although the 'bond which stood against us is cancelled' (Colossians 2.14), God no longer counting our sins against us (2 Corinthians 5.19), it is clear that the work of re-formation has only just begun. Whatever it may mean to say that 'you have been raised with Christ', the injunction, to 'seek the things that are above' (Colossians 3.1) makes it clear that there is an end to be striven for. Paul's image of athletic training likewise indicates that the end in view has both to be worked at and is eschatological in character (1 Corinthians 9.24–7).[20]

We can put this in the language we took from the Letter to the Hebrews. If Christ's perfect sacrifice offered to God through the eternal Spirit is the way for others to enter the sanctuary cleansed of their stain, then, to transfer to a combination of modish and Pauline language, training in virtue is part of the process consequent upon that sacrifice. But it is only a part. Romans 12.1–2, which flows from a theology of justification and election, combines liturgical and ethical language: 'offer your bodies as a living sacrifice'. The end – end as aim, *telos* – is not moral perfection, which is too narrow a concept, but virtues, human perfections, in

---

[20] Thus we become virtuous not by imitating God – though there is an element of imitation – but by being brought into a particular relation to God the Father through the Son and by the Spirit.

the service of holiness, which is the offering of the whole person to God. Human virtue provides one of the central ways by which God the Spirit may enable anticipations of the end to be realised in course of the human journey, because it refers to the way settled dispositions to 'good works' are shaped. The 'fruits of the Spirit' in the Apostle's list include forms of human being and action that are recognisably virtues: 'love, joy, peace, patience, kindness, goodness, faithfulness ...' (Galatians 5.22–3). These do overlap with the virtues of the Aristotelian philosopher, as forms of being human which enable a belonging with the other, but take significantly different shape because they serve to make human being truly an image of the being of the triune God.[21] In sum, it is the christological orientation which turns the moral agent outwards, away from self-development, to being conformed to the image of God which is Jesus Christ.

Christology is, then, the determinative motor of the exocentricity which take us from an Aristotelian to a biblical focus. There are two aspects. The first is that what can be called the channel of an exocentric theology of virtue is the worship and praise of God, grounded in faith. The heart of worship, and consequently also of training in virtue, is the actualisation of a relation to God the Father, mediated through God the Son by God the Holy Spirit. Worship is like the virtues in being a human practice learned from others, and only over a long process of time. It can serve the cause of virtue, but it is not itself the exercise of virtue, and is the primary activity of the Christian Church to which all other practices should be ordered. It is also a communal form of activity, however individualistically it is sometimes understood. Like the moral goodness with which we are concerned, it can come only as a gift, a gift which is an anticipation of the worship of the last times. Yet it is, as Paul's ever-illuminating

---

[21] The contrast with Aristotle and his successors is also shown by the fact that we are here concerned not with the flight of the alone to the alone, but with the orientation of the community of faith to the promised Kingdom of God.

discussion of the Lord's Supper in 1 Corinthians 11 demonstrates, bound up with the moral shaping of the community. Those who respect economic and social divisions fail to recognise and practise the reality of the Supper; correlatively, the proper practice of worship bears fruit in transformed human relations. This, says Asheim, is Luther's view of the matter also. Those who are conformed to Christ's image are ground and pressed along with the wine and bread into a common form: the body of Christ, a fellowship of service which nourishes the world with its love, the blessing of the Supper carrying over into an ethic.[22]

And that brings us to the second aspect of exocentricity, that virtues are not for self-realisation, but for the sake of the world. The Fourth Gospel teaches that the love within the community is to serve – its ulterior motive – the divine purpose of bringing all nations into the fold. This Gospel's interest is primarily in the relation of the believing community to its Lord, but in view of the fact that other New Testament writings, and indeed John himself, teach that the one who became incarnate is the mediator of all creation, Irenaeus was not wrong to see in the use of bread and wine a promise of the participation of all created beings in the recapitulation achieved by Christ. A theology of ecological virtue can, with care, also be elicited from all this, but it would be wrong to make it anything but secondary to the primary values of human community. The whole world is represented in the bread and wine, but they are primarily a focus for the relation of human beings to their creator. The Holy Spirit's eschatological work is first of all focused on the personal, the renewed human community.

Conclusion

Finally, a return to the question of freedom with which the essay began. First of all, we have learned, to be free is to be set free, and that is the point of the references to the crucifixion and baptism. They are free whom the Son liberates, as John 8.32–6 claims emphatically and repeatedly. But

---

[22] Asheim, 'Lutherische Tugendethik', 251.

Christianity is not a fatalism or determinism which leaves things there, even though it has sometimes been made to appear like that. Freedom may need to be given, but it is given to be exercised, and can be defined even in individual terms as what we make of our human particularity. That of it which we receive as inheritance we are not free to change, in the sense that we are at any time that which we have become. The gospel of forgiveness is rather that which gives resources – resources of the Spirit who perfects – for the movement of what we have been and are towards that which we shall be, when we are presented in Christ *teleios* before the throne of grace. They are free who are freed by the Spirit to praise God in both liturgy and life.

This orienting of freedom to the vertical realm, to God's action, has implications for the horizontal realm also. The freedom we must exercise is, on the one hand, what we receive from the others who contribute to the constitution of our persons; on the other, it is what we likewise give to others. That of course is why the families and other institutions intermediate between the individual and the state to which we belong are so important, and why their decline is so depressing a feature of the modern world. What, distinctively, of the Church? If we are not to make historically and morally implausible claims about the Church as a community of character and focus for training in virtue, we must define the Church exocentrically also, after Calvin, by reference to the primacy of the Word and sacraments. No moralistic criterion will do, because of the place of the incarnation, cross and resurrection. The Church is distinctively the institution that it is by virtue of its orientation to the Word and sacraments, the two constitutive features of its worship. According to the ecclesiology of the Fourth Gospel, the Spirit is the one who enables believers to share Jesus' relation to his Father, by incorporating us into it. That relation should not be understood, as it often is, experientially or individualistically – that is, as if individuals in some way replicated Jesus' relationship – but in terms of reconciled personal relations mediated within the structures of a community. These relations begin – anti-autonomously, we might say – by the acknowledgement of a headship ('we are not our own'); but lead to a form of autonomy, according to which the created *telos* of the human being – created for community with God and with others – comes to be, in anticipation of the community of the last days, from time to time realised. The virtues, therefore, are prominent, but not supreme, among the vehicles of human perfecting, and are not to be despised wherever and in whomsoever they are found. To grow in grace is to develop virtues, provisional perfections, and those settled dispositions are the matrixes for forms of human action which enable us to be that which we were created to be.[23]

---

[23] Particular kinds of persons tend to perform particular kinds of actions. Which comes first, the person or the act? If we are created for good works, then it would seem that the act is in the centre. Yet we both learn to be particular kinds of persons by doing particular kinds of acts, and in turn express what we have learned in further acts. That is the nature of the human person, somewhere between creation and perfection – or reprobation, as must, humanly, remain a possibility. The question is how we are to move between the one and the other, and the Christian account of the matter is that we are, by the converting and sanctifying Spirit, related first to God through Christ and then, at the same time, related to one another. I am grateful to members of the Research Institute in Systematic Theology, and in this case especially Brian Brock, for helping me to work through these questions.

11
On Abortion: Some Feminist and Theological Reflections

Ann Loades

It is no easy matter to address the issue of abortion as a theologian at the beginning of the twenty-first century, let alone as someone with feminist sympathies. By 'feminist' I mean someone committed to seeking greater justice for women, and I take it that men as well as women may be feminist and that Stanley Hauerwas is as much a feminist as I am. I also assume that since we are constituted as human persons by and through our interactions with others, we need a wide range of conversation partners to discern who we are, as free as possible from distortion and self-delusion. I think that women need to talk with men about abortion, and that theologians need to listen to non-theologians, not least where any matter that relates to the lives of women is concerned. Whilst not all women give birth to children, or nurture them, and not all of them experience abortion, the child-bearing capacity of women, and therefore the refusal (for whatever reason) of that capacity by abortion has considerable significance for all of us. In this essay, therefore, I shall endeavour to explain how I see that significance at this time. It must be obvious that I cannot discuss every possible issue about abortion in an essay, though I hope by my selection of issues to offer some fresh reflections on the topic, at once I hope both feminist and theologically constructive, whilst not being prepared to rule out abortion in absolutely every circumstance.

Until the last third of the twentieth century in very privileged societies, sexuality for women was a life and death matter, that is, if women engaged in sexual intercourse, they were unable reliably to prevent conception, and there was a strong possibility that they would die as a result of pregnancy or childbirth. Too many of us forget that without anaesthetics, surgery and blood transfusion, only Caesarean section prevents the loss of children, and until very recently Caesarean section cost women their lives. In some parts of the world, pregnancy and childbirth still costs the life of one woman in sixteen – a reminder to privileged women, and to the men who father children, of just how inherently dangerous women's life-giving capacity may be to women themselves. In the 'developed' world, one woman may die out of one thousand four hundred in giving birth, but even this figure reminds us that childbearing may take a woman to the very threshold of death. In addition, too many of us assume that if a woman gives birth to a child she will have access to or be readily given sufficient personal and social support to rear the child. Unfortunately in precisely those privileged societies where women may most safely give birth, the financial resources needed to see a child through to adulthood may be beyond parental reach. It is and will remain the case that women will opt for abortion rather than give birth to a child they do not believe that they will be able to rear, for whatever reason or combination of reasons. Yet for the last two centuries, developing straight out of the periods of 'revolution' and the advocacy of 'rights' associated with the American as well as European revolutions, legislators have attempted to stamp out or control abortion, and the very existence of such legislation indicates abortion's significance.

Nineteenth-century legislation casts a very long shadow in this area, beginning with the British Ellenborough Act of 1803, which became of much significance as a model for legislation elsewhere. There had, of course, been criminal sanctions for abortion after 'quickening', but now 'prequickening' abortions were criminalised, and condemned were not only those who had attempted to procure abortion, but those aiding and abetting them. For abortion after quickening the penalty was death, and among the penalties available if a woman was not 'quick', or not proven to be, were fines, imprisonment, whipping, being put on a pillory, and transportation. In other words, long before women had a vote (crucial to acknowledgement that they had minds, wills and consciences of their own) legislation to regulate central aspects of their lives was introduced.

Although today's legislation is likely to differ significantly from that of the early nineteenth century, it remains the case that movements for the total repeal of state regulation of abortion are few and far between long after women have achieved the vote in many countries. Even when it is no longer 'criminalised', abortion remains a fiercely contentious issue. We deem actions to be 'criminal' either if they result in serious harm to others, which is at least arguably the case in late-stage abortions, or if they seriously damage respect for certain principles which it is good to hold. Taking account of the fact that in many parts of the world abortion has been decriminalised, whether or not its widespread practice does indeed damage respect for values and principles which it is good to hold may require careful discernment over a long period of time.

The Ellenborough Act of 1803 looks like the sort of legislation which one might expect in a culture attempting to take some of its moral and political clues from Scripture, as in Exodus 21.22–23. I assume for the sake of argument that the moral and political should be inextricably connected, but the extent to which this particular text, or any others from Scripture, can be of assistance in providing those clues needs some careful thought. My own position is that Scripture does indeed have something to offer as part of a lively and developing Christian tradition, but that not much is to be gained by attending exclusively to this particular text from the book of Exodus, as I shall explain. Before turning to my own biblically-related reflections, however, I offer some preliminary comments. I hold the view that abortion is a form of killing, and that it is not analogous to having even a vital organ such as a kidney removed. 'Killing' may seem to some to be too strong a word to use, but I think that we have to acknowledge that what is being dealt with is the presence within a woman's own body of a nascent human life which will, if brought to term, have a life of his or her own, and a life in relation to his or her father, as well as his or her mother. This is one way of making the point that the capacity of women to give birth to children is significant of women's centrality to the lives of their families and networks of kin. We could of course say much about the significance of children in human societies, about the role of male parents in child-care and rearing, and the possibility that children may be nurtured and reared most happily in households where all the adults are women, or all the adults are men. There seems to me to be ample evidence from the past as well as the present that children may come to flourish in almost any context where there is sufficient stability and care for them, whatever the age-range or sex or gender-orientation of the adults concerned. Whatever one says about the lives of children once born, however, the fact is that only women can give birth to them, and that abortion kills the very possibility of birth. From these preliminary comments I turn first to some biblically-related reflections.

So far as the biblical world is concerned, in common with most cultures until very recent times what was involved in the conception and gestation of a child was largely unknown, in marked contrast to what presently counts as knowledge as a result of scientific and techno-logical developments, and the relationship of power over others this knowledge necessarily entails. Human fertility was valued and deemed to be a divine blessing (Isaiah 54.1–3) not least in contexts where poor food, scarce resources, untreatable and untreated infections and mediocre health in both sexes affect fertility. Males begat children, women were fertile or barren; polygamy and concubinage might ensure progeny – important in a society in which few children might survive beyond the age of ten, and the rate of women's death in childbirth might be between one in fifteen and one in fifty, as in so much of the 'developing' world in our own time. We have no way of knowing how many women in the past suffered morbidity even if they survived a fourth pregnancy (a critical threshold) but have no reason to suppose that the statistics were significantly different from those pertaining today. And if a woman died in childbirth, the survival of her newborn would depend entirely on the ability and willingness of another woman's being able to breast-feed and rear it.

Notwithstanding the risks inherent in pregnancy, biblical texts display the anguish of childless women (however much loved) praying directly to God in their affliction (e.g. 1 Samuel 1). Independently of their husbands, women could be the recipients of angelic visitation as a means of conveying news of the divine blessing of pregnancy for them (Judges 13; Luke 1.26–38) especially when deemed to be barren. To be 'virginal' was unenviable if interpreted as 'unblessed by children'. Like Eve as the 'mother of all living', women wanted to give birth to male children, specially valued as those whose 'seed' God blessed (Ruth 4.13–17). When resources were under stress, female newborns might be abandoned (Ezekiel 16.1–5) a matter of horror to the compassionate, but clearly observed in at least this instance. A female child might represent too big a drain on resources, depending on social arrangements about inheritance, property and maintenance, all of which are alterable, but only over time. In our preoccupation with abortion, it is easy to forget that the practice of exposing or even killing some newborns is widespread in human cultures, as is their abandonment, which both avoids their direct killing whilst making it possible for babies to be acquired by others, if only as possible slaves if not as heirs. Seeing what one has before disposing of it must seem sensible in principle, and any obviously 'deficient' will be the first to be abandoned or killed, even though God could be held responsible, as it were, for those born dumb, deaf or blind or otherwise handicapped (Exodus 4.11; John 9.2) and who might of course otherwise survive childhood. God might also bring a child's life to an end, as in the destruction of the first-born of Egypt, or the first child born to David and Bathsheba. A child might also be offered back to God not merely as Hannah placed Samuel with Eli, or even Jephthah sacrificed his daughter, his only child. The complex traditions of the interpretation of the divine command to Abraham to sacrifice Isaac in Judaism alone exhibit just how problematic could be the conviction that God was the immediate creator of life who could demand the return of that life.

In the interests of being constructive, however, and to arrive at some sense of a theologically-grounded conviction about the importance of nascent human life, it is important to notice the texts which associate divine creativity with nascent human life in the womb. Job 10.10, for instance, reflects some knowledge of the stages of the development of the pre-born, perhaps as a result of observation of miscarriages. From being 'poured out like milk and curdled like cheese' there was a stage of being 'knit together with bones and sinews'. Again, Psalm 139.13–16 refers to the intricacy of the human frame being made where only God could see its being formed. Miscarriages might arise as the result of injury, treks for food and water and heaving both home, and there would be naturally occurring miscarriages of at least some children whose bodies were not developing properly. Analogies from animal husbandry presumably also helped. Being safely born, able to breathe and suck, being given to one's mother to feed and nurture is a natural experience of deep trust which is appropriate in relation to finding metaphors for relationship to God (Psalm 22.10; 71.6; Isaiah 46.3–4). Even giving birth itself as well as nurture through life become metaphors for redemption (Isaiah 42.14; 66.7–13) and divine compassion (Jeremiah 31.15–22). The mystery of a child's coming-to-be (its genesis) and its birth and life manifest in breathing depict the new life to be associated with Jesus (John 3.4–8; 16.21; 20.22). Even though present-day understanding of the genesis of a child is far different from that of the biblical world, it may be important in a theological evaluation of abortion to sustain the sense of wonder at the process, if we want to foster the conviction of the divine protection and shelter of the new life beginning. Surviving the peril of birth for a woman, a child's being able to breathe, its mother's recovery from blood-loss and pain and being able to breast-feed and nurture the child into life, are readily appreciable metaphors for life beyond sorrow. Confidence in the divine creativity which breathes life into dust, and into bone and flesh built into sexual difference in human beings, yields also the hope of resurrection (2 Maccabees 7.22–23), forged in the agonies of persecution rather than of childbirth, and perhaps inevitably associated with women's care of human bodies, especially on the boundary of life and death (John 20).

To make the point differently, I redeploy a concept developed in the course of Christian discussion, and suggest that to be 'ensouled' is, in the first instance, to be one into whom divine breath has been blown (to use the biblical metaphor), that is, to have lungs, to be able to breathe, to be capable of being nurtured from birth onwards. More than that, however, in the Christian scheme of things, to be ensouled is to become someone to whom God may give resurrection.[1] Or, as Helen Oppenheimer also puts it, 'soul' is the whole of us as spiritual, loving and lovable to ourselves, to others and to God who 'consecrates' this developing body to be 'me', and who gives to human persons a surprisingly large part in that consecration. Filter out such love, and we filter out 'sacredness'.[2] This perspective helps us to see why appeals to the 'sanctity' of life (nascent human life rather than a mother's life) detached from such explicit theological moorings seem so thin and unconvincing even when given such eloquent defence as in Ronald Dworkin's 1993 *Life's Dominion*. From a theological point of view, the notion of the 'sacredness' of human life and its inviolability, which must begin from thinking of a woman's life, and not just of the nascent human life within her, needs to be thickened out in terms of the relationship between law, grace and forgiveness on the one hand, and love and the promise of resurrection on the other. Detached from such a theological

[1] Helen Oppenheimer, 'Abortion: A Sketch for a Christian View', *Studies in Christian Ethics* 5 (1992) 46–60, at 47.
[2] Helen Oppenheimer, 'Ourselves, Our Souls and Bodies', *Studies in Christian Ethics* 4 (1991), 1–20, at 9.

perspective, to refer to human life as sacred is to indicate
the legacy of religious conviction rather than its substance.
We need not assume, however, that such a theological
perspective will rule out abortion in all circumstances, or
that it will mean much to women who associate their
religious tradition with devaluation of their dignity and
worth. Much reconstruction of the tradition needs to be
done, assuming that to be possible.

The loss of a possible birth was and remains a serious
matter, and so was the risk of death to a woman who might
not survive pregnancy and birth in any case, but who did
not need in addition to contend with the hazards of
accident whilst pregnant. In discussions of abortion,
appeal to Exodus 21.22–23 is common enough in some
Christian discussions, but taken in context, it is far from
obvious that it is helpful, given the number of problematic examples to which it is connected. These include
the management of slaves, still relevant well into the
nineteenth century, and including the sale of a daughter as
a slave; the circumstances in which someone might be put
to death (including striking or cursing one's parents); the
loss of an eye or tooth of a slave resulting in the slave's
freedom – all these lead on to penalties which arise in
connection with the management of an ox which may gore
another beast or human being. It is in this context that
attention is given to accidental hurt to a woman caught up
in conflict between men. The relevant part of this text is
commonly translated 'so that there is a miscarriage' but
this is an interpretation of the Hebrew, which may be
rendered so that 'the child comes forth' with the qualification 'yet no harm follows'.[3] That is to say it may be
referring to the premature birth of a child who survives, as
does its mother. In other words, an accident may precipitate the birth of what would nowadays be described as a
'viable' baby, that is, one capable of being born alive, able
to breathe, to suck and survive. If a prematurely born child
were to die, a 'life for life' penalty would require judicial
sentencing by analogy with an 'eye for an eye and a tooth

---

[3] D. W. T. Brattson, 'Abortion in the Bible', *Churchman* 108 (1994) 353–6.

for a tooth', that is, limited but appropriate damages. More severe punishment would have to be agreed if harm followed to the woman concerned, apart from the birth or miscarriage of the child.[4]

The text presumably served as a reminder to keep conflicts between men well clear of a woman to whom one or other of them may be related, so that a woman intervenes. Harm to her was a serious matter, and perhaps not just because of her relationship to the father of the child, for if she died, as I have already noted, the survival of her newborn, or of other children, would depend upon another woman's being willing and able to breast-feed it and rear its siblings, assuming that she was herself sufficiently well-nourished to be able to do so. It is unsurprising that the image of the breast-feeding mother is found in many cultures as a centrally important image of charity, with eye-to-eye contact between the child being fed and the one feeding him or her developing from birth the child's capacity for interrelationship and intimacy with others. Whether in Hebrew or in its Septuagint translation, however, the Exodus text by itself can hardly be used in any simple or straightforward way as a prohibition of abortion. That the well-being of a pregnant woman was important, however, seems an acceptable inference from this and other texts.

For instance, Aquinas' use of Exodus 21 in his discussion of homicide arguably remains of some interest (*Summa Theologiae* 2a 2ae 64 a 8). If striking a pregnant woman is wrong, which it clearly is, in that physical conflict must be resolved without risking either her death or the death of the unborn, the implications for at least unskilled abortion which may result in a woman's death seem clear enough. In the case of striking her, it could not be excusable on the grounds that homicide was not directly intended, since death may indeed result from such a blow. By extension, the death of a woman from abortion in some circumstances might well result in and would be homicide, even if that were the last thing intended by those who aided her in her

---

[4] Rabbi Ishmael, trans. J. Z. Lauterbach, *Mekilta de Rabbi Ishmael* 3 (Philadelphia: Jewish Publication Society of America, 1935), 62–7.

determination to secure one, rather than risk death in childbirth, or give birth to a child she does not believe she can rear.

Concern for a woman's well-being might also, however, dislodge the most unfortunate conviction which has been expressed in some Christian quarters that integral to motherhood must be a woman's willingness to forfeit her own life rather than seek rescue from death by having someone aid her in killing the child she bears. If her well-being is as important as it seems to be, where both lives are threatened it has seemed to other Christians far too harsh to argue that either she should die or that both should die rather than risk having the 'homicide' of a child on one's conscience, when her life or both their lives will be lost if that appears to be the only available option. Rather, to lose both, or to lose her, may well seem to be a major failure of conscience. Only saving her life could possibly justify the death of a child if that tragedy cannot be avoided, and it is the only way of avoiding the even greater evil of her death. A woman may well want to sustain her pregnancy as long as she possibly can even if she suffers from a life-threatening condition, but at the time of birth her responsibility is transferred to others, and her trust is placed in them to see her through it, though she and they need to have explored what range of harm may and must be avoidable in advance. Whilst neither she nor those she trusts can intend the death of a child to preserve her own, either when giving birth or at any other time (since the loss of one's own life is no greater or lesser an evil than the loss of another's life), in this situation it may well be felt that it is her life that has priority. Assault on the child's body must be the very last resort in a tragic situation where otherwise the mother will die, with perhaps disastrous consequences for other members of her family, and not only its youngest members. As Helen Oppenheimer has written, 'Where two lives are threatened and cannot both be saved, the doctrine of the sacredness of life can say only that we must do our best. To be "pro-life" should not mean sacrificing the grown woman, loving and beloved, for a new human being incapable of knowing or caring what is going on. The actual/potential distinction does have relevance here.'[5] In other words, its relevance has to do with the tragic circumstance of 'therapeutic abortion' in extremity. If women's well-being is a biblical value, therefore, it needs expression in terms of putting determined effort and the necessary resources into ensuring safe pregnancy and childbirth, in the clear recognition that low mortality rates are indeed achievable. That said, the balance of probability will sometimes tip in favour of the justification of abortion, since pregnancy and giving birth are potentially life-threatening in some circumstances.

As in most societies, knowledge of pregnancy was based on women's experiences of it, transmitted intergenerationally by mothers and by midwives. Externally visible changes to a woman's body, and her own experiences of 'quickening', that is, of the movement of the child or children within her body (e.g. Luke 1.41–44) were likely to have been especially significant. The meeting of Mary with Elizabeth was in medieval art shown with clear representation of miniature fully-formed (quickened) male children contained in each of their bodies. Despite such representation, there is no evidence from the biblical period of any stage in the life of the unborn being particularly associated with bearing the divine 'image'. The genesis of a child was understood to be a process, and miscarriages would reveal only how 'somewhat human' a non-viable child might be. In Jewish tradition, only if a child's head and the greater part of its body were born, and it was able to breathe, be nourished and loved and protected into human relationship, would it come to bear that 'image'. Born children were too obviously fragile in their early days of life to have such significance, and image-bearing seems to have to do with the making of one's own kind, or of God's kind, one might say, which is neither a simple nor an instantaneous matter. Precisely because fertility and the making of God's kind was known to be problematic, it is unsurprising to find that in the Greco-Roman period 'conception' has a primarily 'active' meaning, that is to say

5 Oppenheimer, 'Abortion', 49.

that whatever human or divine creativity is involved, the word itself means that the woman has to 'take to herself', 'take in and hold', 'collect and gather' the promised child, which in present-day terms is recognised to be the stage of implantation. Thus 'being with child' is an entirely appropriate way of referring to a pregnant woman,[6] for she brings the child to life, at one level an ordinary, at another level a quite extraordinary achievement. Thus, how to think about women's unique role in pro-creativity is hardly new, and it would be surprising if it were. So, for instance, some rabbis of the biblical era thought carefully about the role of the father beyond the original causing of the pregnancy, and suggested that both human parents contributed to the very substance of the child. It was thought that the father supplies the 'white substance' out of which the child's bones, sinews, nails, brains and the white of the eye were formed. Out of the mother's 'red substance' were developed skin, flesh, hair, blood and the pupil of the eye, and her breast-milk. Some of these rabbis were profoundly humane and compassionate, for contraception was known and permitted especially to those women who suffered greatly in pregnancy and in giving birth. Abortion by dismembering a child impacted in a woman's pelvis in labour was also known as a last-ditch measure to save a woman's life. Bewilderment and anguish over still-births and the birth of children with 'defects', and even the birth of daughters were, however, unfortunately sometimes thought of in punitive terms, as indeed were pain and death in childbirth.[7]

Moving from biblically-based reflection to some Christian feminist reflection requires honest recognition that the Christian tradition has hardly unambiguously advocated a 'woman-centred' ethic for the sorts of reasons with which we are already familiar. Rare indeed are such reflections as those by Janet Martin Soskice who addresses

---

[6] Norman Ford, *When Did I Begin? Conception of the Human Individual in History, Philosophy and Science* (Cambridge: Cambridge University Press, 1991), 182, 8.

[7] Tal Ilan, *Jewish Women in Greco-Roman Palestine: An Inquiry Into Image and Status* (Peabody, MA: Hendrickson, 1996).

the theological significance of 'mothering', the realm of the ordinary and the necessary in which mothers and attentive fathers find something 'inchoately graced' in their dealings with their children, attention to whom yields clues to divine creativity, for, like a child, God's creation bears all the marks of its making.[8] The reasons for neglect of the theological significance of 'mothering' are explicable, given Christian views of women's secondary status and subordination, derived from and supported by some biblical texts, and the determined dissociation of what it is to be female and feminine from the godlike and the divine. Whether women can be convinced that the Christian tradition represents a life-giving rather than a harmful resource for them and their children and for their relationships with the fathers of those children remains at present an open and perhaps undecidable issue. As a result of reflection so far, though, we might hope that it may be possible to foster a new woman-centred ethic of pro-creativity, or (with a marital or quasi-marital commitment) of co-procreativity with divine life-giving and blessing. For freed from lingering subordination to a male 'other' (and God is not 'male'), and aptly associated with Mary the mother of Jesus of Nazareth, such co-procreativity could manifest a grace which by definition cannot be in any way coerced. Helen Oppenheimer writes perceptively that human grace of course is not to be totally trusted, that it is apt to fail. Even here, as she points out, sometimes law can 'stand in' for grace, and give it time to grow. We might think that ensuring women have had time and space to think about whether abortion is the best course of action, or whether it is better to continue with a pregnancy, would illustrate her point. And grace can overflow from others so that expectant mothers can be supported and babies be adopted. 'But sometimes in human affairs the absence of grace must simply be allowed whether in desperation or in cool self-understanding. A mother may make it plain that

---

[8] Janet Martin Soskice, 'Love and Attention', in Michael McGhee (ed.) *Philosophy, Religion and the Spiritual Life* (Cambridge: Cambridge University Press), 1992, 59–72.

she has not the resources, physical or moral or both, to be the "grace-giver" to support the life of the growing human being."[9]

I would make three further suggestions. One is that the grace of consent to pregnancy (Luke 1.34–38) must presuppose a prior grace, the grace of consent to penetrative sexual intercourse, free of seduction or coercion. At this point, a 'right to choose' makes sense, as the choice to ensure that conception does not occur. Prime importance needs to be given at the earliest stage of a possible sexual relationship to the freedom of the actions that begin a new life, and to the desire of both partners to continue their lives with one another. That said, it is no use having a punitive attitude to a woman's pregnancy, whatever one makes of the causal responsibility of both genetic parents for a woman's pregnancy. The second is that if pregnancy does occur, the range of choice must include the possibility of single parenthood, even without being entirely clear about where financial or other resources are to come from. This could not be deemed to be thoroughly irresponsible in the kinds of Christian communities envisaged by Stanley Hauerwas. My third suggestion is that there may be a grace of deliberate refusal (rather than simply a failure or absence of grace) which would result in a decision for abortion, taking everything into consideration.

Graced consent and generosity at all stages are important because so much is demanded of a woman's gift of herself, as another life grows within her own in a unique relationship of which other forms of human interdependence and altruism are mere analogues. We need here to beware of sentimentality, however, for no forms of such interdependence or altruism need be supposed to be free of ambiguity and excruciating difficulty at times, which is why some might prefer to avoid parenthood in the first place. That said, however accidental the pregnancy, and however unconscious or involuntary its progress, the capacity to give one's life to another, and even for another,

---

[9] Oppenheimer, 'Abortion', 59.

is displayed in women's procreativity, a significant and generous realm of achievement. Such a grace as may be manifested in her commitment to pregnancy equally cannot compel from others the support needed to see her safely through the pregnancy and birth. On the other hand, to be left in isolation and indignity and vulnerable to threats whilst pregnant is intolerable, and the grace of support from the rest of the human community needs to be manifest. So does support through the years of child-rearing, which is far from being a woman's sole responsibility, and which could be seen to be the grace of the consent of others to a woman's pregnancy and well-being, and to the gift of new life being entrusted to the human community. Then a woman's decision to carry a child to term commits its parents and the rest of us to referring to a 'future child' and to a particular woman as his or her mother. Such a child could then be acknowledged as a 'child of God', even as 'God with us', and a matter of gratitude and praise to its mother from the rest of us.

Within this frame of reference all argument against abortion must be backed with unambiguous guarantees of constructive long-term support, and it must be obvious too that societies with very high infant mortality rates are hardly able to occupy the moral high ground in respect of abortion.

> Outside this Christian frame of reference it is hard to say anything to a woman who repudiates her potential child with really open eyes but, 'You are the person through whom this human life must come, or not come'. If she refuses, Christians may think that she has refused an annunciation, that she has declined to say, 'Be it unto me according to thy will': but her acceptance could hardly be praised unless her refusal were a possibility'.[10]

We do not, of course, want to foster the possibility of such

[10] Oppenheimer, 'Abortion', 60.

refusal by giving motherhood too much of a theological 'overload', and impossible or idealised expectations of what parenting may involve. Associating pregnancy, childbirth and child-rearing with divine blessing and procreativity needs rather to be connected firmly with the 'good-enough' as with the conviction of present grace and future resource, and not with a state of being which is beyond realistic human possibilities. Nor do we want to obscure the importance of a male parent. Whereas the biblical world may have taken the demands of being a male parent for granted, in circumstances where it cannot be so taken for granted it may require particular care to foster in men as well as women the generosity beyond calculation which being a parent necessitates. We might think that shared covenant-commitment may be appropriately associated with the figure of Joseph in the Gospels, as Roman Catholic piety has sometimes fostered.[11] Advocacy of the integrity of heterosexual monogamy and procreation which has been characteristic of most forms of Christianity should not be allowed to obscure the point that irregularity and even illegality are not far absent from the circumstances surrounding the birth of Jesus. References to the Tamar of Genesis 38, to Rahab, Ruth and 'the wife of Uriah' in the Matthean genealogy mark the irregularity, but the 'God with us' character of the promise associated with a future child or children overrides it. It might also be said that if it is possible to become a 'child of God' by 'adoption and grace', the practice of human forms of such hospitality might be appropriate from some who could be parents to a child born to others. The 'others' might even be married, but with too many children of their own to rear; the social 'parents' of the children could in principle be anyone capable of such hospitality. If killing nascent human life by abortion is a serious matter, some unusual family forms could well sustain the lives of the children who may be

---

[11] Rosemary Drage Hale, 'Joseph as Mother: Adaptation and Appropriation in the Construction of Male Virtue', in John Carmi Parsons and Bonnie Wheeler (eds), *Medieval Mothering* (New York: Garland, 1996), 101–16.

born, where abortion is regarded as the worst of the available alternatives. This would require a major change in attitudes, however, for whereas in the past various modes of adoption were widespread, both official and unofficial, and simply practised as part of normal social arrangements, in the 1990s, if a woman decides against abortion, she may well have decided to keep her child, and to hope for the arrival of a 'social parent' in her life, if a child's genetic father departs from her and from his child. Abortion may well be one way of pre-empting the emotional pain of giving up a child to others for adoption and may seem too much to endure, though there are in some countries meetings between birth mother and prospective adoptive parents, and some limited news of the child's well-being communicated back to the birth mother, which may ease some of her distress. Her pain might be less acute in the first place if there were greater social acceptance of family 'blending', expressive of affirmation and praise for stand-in social parenting, as well as for a child's mother.

So far, it seems to me that pregnancy profoundly symbolises human interdependency as a new life grows within a woman's life, and also the interdependence of human life with divine life-giving. To jeopardise that interdependency has far-reaching significance. To endanger either the new life growing within a woman's life, or her own life, irrespective of her relationship to that new life, given her relationship to other born children, and to those already parents, destabilises and helps to disintegrate many of the ways human beings relate to one another from the minute they begin to draw breath. Discussion of abortion (and contraception) in the Christian tradition cannot, however, rest on discussion of biblical or non-biblical tradition without reference to the development of medicine and of law, given the interconnection of the Christian tradition with these two realms of human practice, from the Ellenborough Act and subsequent legislation onwards, and the development of medicine as a profession in the ensuing period.

It is certainly difficult to be sure that when theologians,

lawyers and medical practitioners (overwhelmingly male until very recently) have responded to the phenomenon of abortion, or in the latter case, have been directly involved in bringing abortions about, that they have deemed women's decisions to abort their pregnancies as rational, and as right in the circumstances as other forms of killing for which justification has certainly been advanced, such as 'just war' and capital punishment. Notoriously, being pro- or anti-abortion does not necessarily connect with attitudes to other forms of killing, though in Stanley Hauerwas' case, his position as a pacifist and his disquiet about abortion is exemplary among contemporary theologians.[12] On the other hand, it should not be too readily assumed without evidence that men have lacked compassion for women in respect of pregnancy, childbirth and childrearing, a compassion which has involved some of them in helping women to secure abortions. We cannot in the space of this essay attend to the intricacies of debates and legislation during the course of the last two centuries about these matters, but it is worth remembering that whilst the dangers of pregnancy and birth to women have long been known, the dangers to women's lives of many forms of contraception and abortion as two closely connected practices were in the past enough to account for their condemnation. In addition, the capacity to distinguish with some precision between a drug to regulate menstruation and a drug to precipitate an abortion is a very recent development from the end of the nineteenth century, depending on levels of laboratory sophistication even now not universally available. And only in the latter half of the twentieth century did it become common knowledge that missed menstruation signifies that some cells of a fertilised zygote

---

[12] Stanley Hauerwas, 'Why Abortion is a Religious Issue' and 'Abortion: Why the Arguments Fail', in his *A Community of Character: Toward a Constructive Christian Social Ethic* (Notre Dame, IN: University of Notre Dame Press, 1981), 196–229; 'Abortion, Theologically Understood', in Paul T. Stallsworth (ed.), *The Church and Abortion: In Search of New Ground for Response,* Nashville, TN: Abingdon Press, 1993), 44–66, and in Nancey Murphy, Brad. J. Kallenberg and Mark Thiessen Nation (eds), *Virtues and Practices in the Christian Tradition: Christian Ethics After MacIntyre* (Harrisburg, PA: Trinity Press International, 1997), 221–38.

have become placental cells, that one or more stabilised embryos have implanted, each with its initial 'primitive streak' body axis in place. This is one of the few points at which women's experiential knowledge of themselves and research-based knowledge on women coincide. In addition, pregnancy before implantation can be confirmed if present without waiting for missed menstruation by a blood or urine test, administered about a week after fertil- isation may have taken place. This knowledge in turn makes possible 'medical termination' of pregnancy, that is, relatively non-invasive forms of abortion as compared even with vacuum aspiration. Where the danger of death is clearly past, it is not surprising to find in the twentieth century that legislation has been focused on the regulation rather than the prohibition of abortion, not least to protect medical practitioners from prosecution as a result of their actions. And legality, after all, makes it possible to acquire the skills needed to perform abortions, and much to the benefit of women, the availability of antibiotics curbs both deaths from uncontrollable sepsis following birth or abortion whether legal or illegal, and infections consequent on either which may result in infertility.

The USA is a particularly interesting example of how difficulties and differences about the significance of abortion have been exacerbated rather than eased with changes in legislation, though some of the difficulties have to do with the relationship between the courts and the Constitution (which takes families and child-rearing for granted without mentioning them). The American example is especially interesting since the USA developed from the 'revolutionary' era with many splendid ideals, compro- mised for years by its accommodation of slavery and the public denial of bodily integrity to some human beings which slavery represents. This indeed it shared with many European societies, as well as the disenfranchisement of women, and legislation about marriage and abortion influ- enced by Britain at least for part of the nineteenth century. The role of the USA's Supreme Court and the impact of its deliberations on state legislatures is the key to develop- ments there, since it has the last say in interpreting the

Constitution modified as it has been by a series of Amendments which themselves are open to interpretation. To cut a long story very short, the situation in the USA by the mid-1990s was that whilst it has been conceded that a woman has a constitutionally protected 'right' to abortion in the first trimester of pregnancy, abortions need not be funded at the taxpayer's expense except to save a woman's life. The USA is the only 'developed' country to hold to this position. Abortion in early pregnancy is relatively inexpensive, but is available only in cases of rape, incest, serious foetal deformity or direct danger to a woman's life (probably less than five per cent of pregnancies). Just as no one can occupy the moral high ground in respect of abortion in a society with high infant mortality rates (scandalously true in parts of the USA), nor can anyone occupy that ground in a society unprepared to provide resources for the lifelong support of those born with such physical or mental abnormalities as to be seriously handicapped – and their care is another cause dear to Stanley Hauerwas' heart. In the USA a nasty twist in the story is that sterilisation which is expensive is available on public funding, and the relation between this practice and abortion for some population groups should be controversial, even if it is not at the present, since at least for some women sterilisation is a mutilation or a maiming, and a woman may want to terminate a particular pregnancy without wanting to be permanently sterile.

To stay with the problem of abortion, however, just as the Christian tradition has operated with a disastrous split between 'personal' and 'social' ethics which has left some women floundering without resources, so we find that governments, including that of the USA, may think they have no positive duty to intervene in respect of provision for women's conditions of life and their poverty, conditions which profoundly affect the meaning of whichever 'choices' they make in respect of pregnancy. Strategies to ensure that women are sufficiently well-informed to know what they are doing, whether they continue with a pregnancy or have an abortion, have very different impacts on the lives of women of different races and social position, and what may not count as an 'undue burden' for one may be very burdensome for another. It seems that only a fifth of US counties have medical practitioners willing to perform abortions, which represents major restrictions on women's access to abortion, unless and until nurses and midwives and physicians' assistants are trained and licensed to perform at least early abortions. Abortion as early as possible in a pregnancy is certainly the safest stage at which to have one, and is a minor procedure by comparison with what some women will undergo in their attempts to conceive and give birth to children.

The present position in the USA is the result of the controversies precipitated by changes in legislation, changes in women's self-perception and their determination to secure control over their own fertility, and major shifts in justification for abortion, from literally life-threatening circumstances to women's health, very broadly construed. The USA is not the only country where it has been necessary to pass legislation making it a criminal offence to interfere with clinics (whether free-standing from hospitals or not) where abortions are carried out, given the unprecedented alliance in the USA of normally a-political religious groups and a politically activist 'right' over abortion. Some might want to congratulate themselves on the absence of controversy about abortion in their own societies, but such congratulation may be misplaced. In England, for instance, the 'market' for National Health Service hospital income from abortions is likely to be three-quarters of all abortions in England, yet there is no agreement about the extent of responsibility for participation in abortion procedures, let alone the possibility of questioning whether it is right that hospital income should be generated by abortion. It is of course cheaper and easier to have abortion available than to tackle the social and political circumstances which make it seem the most appropriate option for women.

In our brash new era of technological development in matters related to human fertility it remains entirely unclear how these can or should impinge on women's perceptions of what may be at stake in abortion, and it is also unclear how far women's perceptions might influence technological development. The very fact that the new verbal coinage of 'pre-embryo' is now common currency in referring to a fertilised but unimplanted embryo, astonishingly discontinuous from the gametes from which it has developed, discussion of the possibility of the collection of eggs from aborted foetuses, and disposal or use of aborted embryos, and foetal tissue use – all these reveal public interest in what in my view has to be seen as the 'commodification' of women's body 'products': and there may be considerable interest in keeping abortion rates up so as to make these 'products' available. Whilst the implantation of an embryo in a woman desperately trying to achieve fertility and bring a child to term, together with our knowledge of early embryonic development might push in the direction of restriction of abortion except in extreme circumstances, so much else of what goes on, allied to the experience of menstruation and of spontaneous abortion, may incline women to think that at least very early abortion is morally trivial. Other new developments may also encourage that view. For instance there is now the possibility of 'reduction of pregnancy' in the multiple pregnancies brought about in fertility clinics. Where a woman has undergone 'treatment' by gonodotrophic hormones, a disastrous multiple pregnancy sometimes results, hazardous to her, and likely to produce fragile and dying babies even if they come to term. A technique for the reduction of pregnancy has been developed which involves injecting potassium chloride into the 'heart' of the most accessible 'surplus' embryos, then reabsorbed into the mother's body. This also means that a technique is available for the 'reduction' of a twin to a singleton pregnancy conceived in the normal way. And there are now post-coital and abortifacient drugs available in 'emergency' (such as contraceptive failure) to ensure that if fertilisation has taken place, implantation cannot occur, even in advance of testing for a pregnancy, with or without the insertion of an intra-uterine device.

It is not impossible that women will evaluate these

laboratory-produced drugs as the modern equivalent of the 'natural product' drugs used in the past and in the present in some societies to 'regulate' or 'restore' menstruation, and be deeply grateful for the human enterprise, initiative and ingenuity which has produced them. Whatever proves finally to be the case, women will need to evaluate the new technologies very carefully indeed, and everyone needs to evaluate various methods of abortion. In addition, until there is widespread acceptance by men of shared responsibility for reliable contraception, and support for the children for whom they are responsible, whether genetically related to them or not, and public and institutional support for mothers and their children, it seems likely that some women will continue to abort their pregnancies by one means or another.

Likewise, unless Christian communities can persuasively foster women's full human dignity, whether or not women are mothers, it seems unlikely that women will inevitably want to appropriate the 'grace' of pregnancy and childbirth, as a biblically-based but Christian theologically-developed ethic might propose. In the absence of unambiguous Christian affirmation of women, still in remarkably short supply in some quarters, it will be difficult to advocate the view that abortion (except in the most extreme difficulties) is ultimately destructive of female self-worth and hopelessly subverts the possibility of developing a woman-centred ethic of procreativity with divine life-giving and blessing which I have suggested we might seek. We should, I think, be deeply grateful that we have had these problems kept on the agenda by Stanley Hauerwas, and his insistence that the Church should demonstrably become and be the community into which children are welcomed. He is, after all, one of the very few theologians from any tradition to have reflected on the theological importance of children in Christian communities.

12
Looking:
The Ethics of Seeing in Church and Cinema

Gerard Loughlin

Hauerwas' Theft

When reading some Christian ethicists, one can wonder if they are living on the same planet as oneself, so arcane and abstract are their arguments, so removed from the concerns and commerce of the world.[1] Not so, with Stanley Hauerwas. He is a robust and worldly ethicist. Though he writes of a church that is seeking to live *out* of the world – from resources other than those offered by the world, and for a world other than that which most of us inhabit – he also writes for a church so seeking *in* the world: for finally there is only the one world that God creates. To characterise Stanley Hauerwas as worldly may seem odd to anyone convinced that if nothing else, Hauerwas writes of a church *against* the world – as indeed he does.[2] But the Church of and for which he writes lives in the midst of the world, with people who are always having to learn again how to see the world differently, striving daily to see it as in faith and hope they pray it will be.

---

[1] An earlier and shorter version of this essay was read to the Annual Conference of the Society for the Study of Christian Ethics, Oxford, England, September 1999. I am grateful to Stephen Barton for the invitation to do so, as also to those who on that occasion commented on the paper, and to Tina Beattie, Gavin D'Costa and Linda Woodhead for their comments on a subsequent draft.

[2] See for example, Stanley Hauerwas, 'No Enemy, No Christianity: Preaching Between "Worlds"', in *Sanctify Them in the Truth: Holiness Exemplified* (Edinburgh: T&T Clark, 1998), 191–200. 'God knows what God is doing to us in this strange time between "worlds", but hopefully God is inviting us again to engage the enemy through the godly weapons of preaching and sacrament' (9).

Hauerwas' worldliness shows in his writing on Christianity as culture, and in particular the culture of his *local* church, Aldersgate United Methodist Church in Chapel Hill, North Carolina.[3] It is, he thinks, a 'good church' with a 'warm heart', where you would not expect to find 'resident aliens'.[4] It is 'largely white', largely Protestant (celebrating the Eucharist only once a month), and it has a softball team, composed of men and women. It also has 'prominent gay members' who can pass as straight, valued because they too play softball and 'are "just like us"' – no visible aliens at Aldersgate.[5] Hauerwas is well aware that his church does not escape the comfortable and somewhat self-satisfied culture of 'middle-class' America. Nor does it escape the culture of consumer capitalism. 'No matter what its peculiar attractions may be, it is finally part of a capitalist economy that means my involvement at Aldersgate is but another consumer choice. Therefore, in my own ecclesial life I reproduce the kind of church shopping I otherwise wish to defeat.'[6] Like many of us, Hauerwas worships in a church that is not only in, but *of* the world. 'Most of us at best remain about half-Christian, possessed as we are by practices that give us the illusion we are in control of our lives.'[7]

Another aspect of Hauerwas' worldliness is his willingness to engage with texts other than treatises on

---

[3] Stanley Hauerwas, 'In Defence of Cultural Christianity: Reflections on Going to Church', in *Sanctify Them in the Truth*, 157–73. My italics indicate one of the many ironies in which Hauerwas delights, since his church is not at all local, but at some distance from where he lives, found after shopping around for a church with sufficiently rich liturgies and sound sermons (160–1).

[4] Hauerwas 'In Defence of Cultural Christianity', 163. Though if anyone is an alien in the Church it is Hauerwas, since he teaches at Duke University, and Chapel Hill is home to the University of North Carolina. Consequently he and his wife 'have to endure a good deal of friendly abuse' (p. 161 n. 10). On why and how Christians should seek to live as aliens, see Stanley Hauerwas and William Willimon, *Resident Aliens: Life in the Christian Colony* (Nashville: Abingdon Press, 1989) and Stanley Hauerwas and William Willimon, *Where Resident Aliens Live: Exercises for Christian Practice* (Nashville, TN: Abingdon Press, 1996).

[5] Hauerwas, 'In Defence of Cultural Christianity', 162.

[6] Hauerwas, 'In Defence of Cultural Christianity', 163.

[7] Hauerwas, 'In Defence of Cultural Christianity', 173.

theology and ethics, written by people who are other than Christian. One such, is Iris Murdoch, whose novels are so worldly, so concerned with the love of death, that Hauerwas wonders if Christians should read them at all, so powerfully can they possess their readers' imaginations.[8] The Christian reader of Murdoch's fictions may forget that the world is not meaningless contingency, requiring fortitude, but created gift, inviting celebration.[9] Yet despite this danger, Hauerwas is a reader of Murdoch's novels and philosophy, and admits to wondering if he has ever said anything of importance that was not stolen from her. In particular, he admits to stealing her teaching that in order to see the world as it is, with a 'clear vision', we must be schooled in seeing through the exercise of our 'moral imagination'. It is not so much at what we look, as how we look at it, that matters. Through the work of continuous 'attention' our vision ceases to be mere 'looking' and becomes 'just and loving'. Then we can see what 'really is'.[10]

Murdoch's fundamental insight – from which Hauerwas extravagantly claims to have 'made a career' – is that 'looking' can be either virtuous or vicious, attentive or inattentive, and that it is something we learn how to do through schooling in literature.[11] That Hauerwas has come to recognise a fundamental difference between Murdoch's

---

[8] Stanley Hauerwas, 'Murdochian Muddles: Can We Get through Them if God Does not Exist?', *Wilderness Wanderings: Probing Twentieth Century Theology and Philosophy* (Boulder, Co: Westview Press, 1997), 155–70.

[9] This is undoubtedly too crude a description of the difference between Murdoch's vision and that of the Church, too careless of what George Steiner describes as her 'ideal of immanent transcendence, of down-to-earth "rapture" or illumination' (Foreword to Iris Murdoch, *Existentialists and Mystics: Writings on Philosophy and Literature* ed. by Peter Conradi, Harmondsworth: Penguin Books, [1997] 1999, xv). But while Murdoch's work is germane to much in this essay, it is not its subject. See further, Fergus Kerr, 'Back to Plato with Iris Murdoch', *Immortal Longings: Versions of Transcending Humanity* (London: SPCK, 1997), ch. 4, 68–88.

[10] Iris Murdoch, *The Sovereignty of Good* (London: Routledge & Kegan Paul, 1970, 37). Murdoch takes the idea of loving attention from Simone Weil (34).

[11] '[T]he most essential and fundamental aspect of culture is the study of literature, since this is an education in how to picture and understand human situations' (Murdoch, *The Sovereignty of Good*, 34).

school of vision and that of the Church, does not take away from her insight, but raises the question as to how far those schooled in the Church can risk entering the schools of others. 'Murdoch ... offers, through her novels, a reimagining of our existence that powerfully reflects "the way we live now" '. Her novels, even more than her philosophy, become a temptation for us, since being trained through them we lose our ability to imagine any other world'. If novels, such as Murdoch's, offer alternative and powerful schools for looking, how much more so does cinema, an all pervasive reflection on 'the way we live now'.[12] And if Hauerwas is right in thinking that the Church lacks the 'imaginative power' to combat Murdoch's stoic nihilism, how much more does it lack the power to combat Hollywood.[13]

This essay is concerned with the cinema and the Church as two schools of looking. It is an exercise in worldly theology, attending to Hauerwas' theft. Its dominant image is that of the cave, which is explored in three forms: the pagan temple, home to demons and images; the cinema, which repeats the temple in modern form; and finally the Church, which like temple and cinema also projects images whose power resides in the context of their viewing.

Into the Cave

If at first we walked in a garden, of grasses, herbs and fruit trees,[14] and rested beneath their boughs, we later sought

---

[12] It is unlikely that Iris Murdoch – who erroneously refers to 'dull photography' as 'simple reduplication' (*The Fire and the Sun: Why Plato Banished the Artists* (Oxford: Oxford University Press, 1977, 7) – would have recognised cinema as being as educative as the novel.
[13] Of course there have been and are those who think that the Church should and can educate its members in looking at cinema, both responsibly and critically. For a variety of approaches see James M. Wall, *Church and Cinema: A Way of Viewing Film* (Grand Rapids, MI: William B. Eerdmans, 1971); Margaret R. Miles, *Seeing and Believing: Religion and Values in the Movies* (Boston: Beacon Press, 1996) and Clive Marsh and Gaye Ortiz (eds), *Exploration in Theology and Film: Movies and Meaning* (Oxford: Blackwell, 1997).
[14] Genesis 1.11. King James Version.

darker refuge in the safety of the cave. We were become like the apes, the early hominids, who, at the beginning of Stanley Kubrick's *2001: A Space Odyssey* (1968), shelter beneath rock, fearful of the night and its savageries. While Kubrick's film tells the story of our ascent from the cave, from the earth on which we walk to the stars above our heads, it is still told in the cavern of the cinema, a techno-logical marvel that mimics the ancient practice of telling stories in the shelter of the night, when the sun has set and it can no longer dazzle our eyes, blinding us to other imagined worlds, other ways of being human.

Plato's parable of the cave locates the truth of the world outside and above the cave, amongst the stars. Yet it would seem that the cave is the womb of our imagination, the place in which we can see the truth of the real. Rather than escaping the cave, we must go within in order to see what is without. This trope is the burden of my essay, a reversal of Plato – and thus in some sense still platonic – that is repeated in thinking about church and cinema. I shall suggest that in both cinematic and ecclesial caverns, the real is suspended, bracketed, and that this is not its destruction but its mobilisation. This suspension of the real is necessary for faithful living, for being able to see and live by the light that burns in the dark.

However, this necessity is not without its dangers, and it is with the fear of images, of shadows and illusions, that I begin. In the first instance, these are the images of ancient religion, and in the second, those of modern cinema. To look upon either is to participate in phantom, alien dreams, the imaginings of others. Entering the darkened chamber of temple or cinema permits a reciprocal entry, through the eye, of alien spectres. The danger is that of demon possession.

Demons

From the earliest days of cinema, the perceived power of film to possess its viewers impelled the desire to control the content and distribution of films. While those concerned to resist censorship asserted film's ineffectuality or neutrality, propagandists of all persuasions have seen in cinema a tool for social transformation. For in writing its images on the silver screen, the cinema writes them on the retina of the eye, and thus on the mind of the viewer. The light of the image strikes from screen to screen, from the cinematic to the retinal, the first reflecting, the second altogether more permeable, allowing the image to penetrate to that final screen which is the play of consciousness itself. As Freud mused, the mind is like a 'photographic apparatus, or something of the kind', forming conscious images at an ideal, intangible point within the apparatus.[15] If today scientists are proposing a prosthetic cinema, a machine that writes moving images directly on the retina of the eye,[16] they are only intensifying what has long been feared from before the birth of the cinema: that to look upon an image is to be looked at, and thus possessed, the image taking up residence within the mind and body of the viewer.

Such was the fear of the second-century Christian apologists who sought immunity from the hostility of neighbours and local authorities. They wrote their tracts in order to gain freedom for themselves and their co-religionists to profess the name of Christian without persecution.[17] For the most part, their texts flatter and entreat their addressees, defend the author and his fellow Christians and revile their enemies. To the latter are ascribed all manner of foolishness, including the worship of images. In their attack on Greek religious art, the Christian apologists sought to show the congruence of

[15] Sigmund Freud, *The Interpretation of Dreams*, in the *Penguin Freud Library*, Vol. 4, trans. James Strachy, eds James Strachy, Alan Tyson and Angela Richards (Harmondsworth: Penguin Books, 1976), 684–85.
[16] 'It may sound like science fiction, but the technology is almost with us now. Virtual Retinal Display scans images directly onto the retina, without the intervention of anything so crude or conventional as a TV screen, computer monitor or even the latest active matrix LCD panel.' Jason Thomas, 'One in the Eye', *The Guardian* (Online), 29 July 1999, 8.
[17] On the second-century apologists see Paul Corby Finney, *The Invisible God: The Earliest Christians on Art* (New York: Oxford University Press, 1994, chs 2 and 3).

Hebrew prophecy with Greek philosophy, indeed drawing upon an older tradition of Hellenistic-Jewish apology, and like it, asserting the dependency of the philosophers on the prophets. The ancient wisdom of both Greek and Hebrew supported the Christians' denunciation of contemporary religious art, and in this they flattered their addressees' contempt for popular and superstitious forms of religiosity.

Christians did not participate in the worship of the temples, nor publicise their own cultic practices. This led to the charge of atheism, to which the apologists responded with a Stoic disdain for cult objects and rituals. The temples, divine images and sacrifices were at best allegories of where the invisible God is to be truly found and worshipped: in the human person and in a virtuous life. The truly spiritual, God-filled person has no need of imagery. Moreover, in rejecting religious imagery, the Christians were seeking to repeat that earlier, more primitive time, when, as many pagans believed, society was simpler and purer, and people worshipped without images.[18]

Clement of Alexandria alone among the apologists used the platonic topography of two worlds, upper and lower, noetic and phenomenal, to denounce religious art as illusion and deceit. Mimetic artistry produces only shadows of the things it would portray, and this is especially so in seeking to picture the divine, since what are reproduced – human and animal forms – are themselves merely shadows, phenomenal objects of which we have opinion but no true knowledge. The dangers inherent in the making and use of such objects are evident in the story of Pygmalion, whose love for the simulacrum of his own making can never be returned. The realism and beauty of the statue is deathly. Thus Christians, in refusing the allure of the mimetic arts, refuse the enthralment of shadows and are able to worship the invisible God.[19]

The deceit and impropriety of representing the invisible

[18] Finney, *The Invisible God*, 46–7.
[19] See Clement, *Protreptikos*, Bk 4; Finney, *The Invisible God*, 42–3.

God was further supported by appeal to the ancient Greek tradition of anti-anthropomorphism in religion, which mocked the idea that in a human form one can see the God who is like no one.[20] Clement's pagan contemporary Celsus could press this even further, in claiming against Genesis, that man was not made in the image of God because God has no form whatsoever.[21] The apologists, in addition to accusing the pagan Greeks of anthropomorphism, chided them for being hylotheists, worshippers of matter (*hyle*). Ignoring the symbolic interpretation of cult figures, the apologists mocked those who worshipped sticks and stones, mistaking them for the non-material divine.[22]

Notwithstanding their scorn for those who imbued insensible matter with divinity, the apologists contended that demonic powers had taken up residence in cult statues. They made this accusation in defending Christians against the charge of superstition, turning the accusation against their accusers, while insisting upon the calm, rational and inward nature of Christian piety. The apologists attributed the foolishness of pagan idol worship to the power of the demons who, in animating the otherwise senseless cult images, took possession of their acolytes. These demons were in a sense material, having bodies that needed to be fed on the blood and scraps of the cult sacrifices. 'It is these demons [*daimones*]', Athenagoras tells us, 'who drag men to images', and 'give birth to illusions which bring with them a mad passion for idols'.

> When the soul is weak and docile, ignorant and unacquainted with sound teachings, unable to contemplate the truth, ... the demons associated with matter, because they are greedy for the savour of fat and the blood of sacrifices, and because their business is to delude humans, take hold of these deceitful movements in the soul of many, and by invading their

---

[20] Antisthenes the Cynic cited by Clement, *Stromateis*, 5.14.108, 4.
[21] Origen, *Contra Celsum*, Bk 6.63; Finney, *The Invisible God*, 45.
[22] Finney, *The Invisible God*, 47–53.

thoughts flood them with illusory images which seem
to come from the idols and statues.[23]

For Athenagoras and other apologists, idol worship is
ethically debilitating, leading to moral and mental collapse.
The degeneration attendant upon cult worship is nowhere
more evident than in the sexual licence sanctioned by
stories of divine debauchery, the sexual misdemeanours of
the gods, whose material images were foolishly, dangerously worshipped in the temples. In this way the
apologists again turned an accusation – that of sexual
immorality – against their accusers. It was not Christians,
but pagans who flouted common decency through their
worship of immoral divinities. The behaviour of Christians
was altogether seemly, and their complaint against pagan
perversity was one already made of Homer and Hesiod by
Greek moralists, such as Plato.

There are, of course, instabilities in the apologists'
ridicule of their opponents. On the one hand they mocked
the idea that senseless matter could be imbued with
spiritual presence through consecration, yet on the other
hand, they allowed in some cases the effectiveness of such
invocations, albeit to conjure malign forces. More
generally, they practised their own Christian cult, which
involved the use of material objects, and which was
premised on the belief that God had taken human form in
Christ and took form again in the eucharistic elements.
Thus the attack on Greek religious art has to be understood
as a particular polemic, responding in kind to specific
accusations. Pagans, and not Christians, fail to worship
true divinity, mistaking matter for spirit; pagans and not
Christians are given to superstition and sexual licence, and
the focus and (imbued) agent of these failings is the cult
image; a mere shadow of a shadow, flickering in the

---

[23] Athenagoras, *Legatio*, 26.1 and 27.2 in *Legatio* and *De Resurrectione*, ed.
and trans. by Wiliam R. Schoedel (Oxford: Clarendon Press, 1972), 65–7;
slightly adapted after Finney, *The Invisible God*, 54. The Christian
contention that the pagan deities were really demons persisted in
Christian polemic. See Augustine, *The City of God*, Bk II.

fire-light of the temple, wreathed in the smoke and stench of slaughtered animals.

The second-century apologists are not therefore anomalous with regard to the later development of Christian art, as it came to adorn the underground burial chambers of third-century Christians. Nor anomalous with regard to the possible use by Christians, already in the second century, of generic figures, such as shepherds and fishermen, for pietistic purposes.[24] Neither do the apologetic texts rule out the later use, from the fourth century onwards, of images in the Christian cult; pictures and effigies of Christ, his mother and the other saints. Later Christians could always avoid the gross errors that the apologists attributed to pagan imagery, by deploying a symbolist theory, a distinction between signifier and signified: the very move advanced by astute pagans, but tactically ignored by the apologists. Nevertheless, the second-century apologists exemplify a recurring distrust of representation in general, and of religious imagery in particular, especially where it encroaches upon divine invisibility. Moreover, they ethicised the making and use of images, as leading to vicious rather than virtuous behaviour. Though often dormant, this concern has never died in Greco-Western and Christian traditions, and has attended the cinema throughout its life.

At the end of 1973, just after Christmas, William Friedkin's film of William Peter Blatty's *The Exorcist* was released in North America. The effect that the film and its publicity had on audiences in America and elsewhere, make it a perfect metaphor for the power of film. Its story of demon possession so possessed audiences that many thought the film itself possessed. The Christian evangelist Billy Graham reputedly asserted that there was an evil 'embodied' or 'buried' within 'the celluloid of the film itself'.[25]

---

[24] Finney, *The Invisible God*, ch. 5.
[25] Reported by William Peter Blatty to Mark Kermode in 1990 and 1998. See Mark Kermode, *The Exorcist*, second edition, BFI Modern Classics (London: British Film Institute, 1998), 110 and 112 n. 2.

Set in the suburbs of Washington DC, the film tells the story of the young Regan McNeil's (Linda Blair) possession by an ancient, pre-Christian force, the demon Pazuzu, and its eventual exorcism by Father Damien Karras SJ (Jason Miller). In the interests of 'verisimilitude,' Friedkin insisted that the special effects should, for the most part, be produced on set, mechanically, rather than optically,[26] and any creakiness in the stage machinery was disguised through skilful editing and pacing of the material, and the manipulative use of sound effects. The publicity for the film prepared audiences to expect something more than mere trickery, something that was perhaps truly demonic.

Thus the film's production was believed to have been cursed, with a number of deaths attributed to its malignancy. The actor Jack MacGowran died shortly after completing his scenes in the film. Linda Blair's grandfather died, as did the brother of Max von Sydow, who was playing the part of Father Merrin SJ. There were various injuries and mishaps during filming, and eventually the studio set burnt down, and on a Sunday. Friedkin was not averse to spreading these stories, blaming delays in the production of the film on the interference of devils.[27] He also suggested that there was something fiendish about the special effects, inventing bogus explanations, such as the use of electro-magnetism for the levitation of Linda Blair, and asserting of her head's bone-breaking 360 degree turn, that 'any way you think I did it is not the way we did it'.[28]

While the combination of skilful acting, inventive effects and cinematic craft, with astute publicity, produced a commercial success, it also produced devilish effects in its audiences. Reportedly, people vomited and fainted, had heart attacks and miscarriages, all of which furthered interest in the film, for as one woman said, 'I want to see what everybody is throwing up about.'[29] Four women in Toronto were in need of psychiatric care after seeing the

[26] Kermode, *The Exorcist*, 68.
[27] Kermode, *The Exorcist*, 76–7.
[28] Kermode, *The Exorcist*, 72.
[29] Quoted in Pauline Kael, *Reeling* (London: Marion Boyars, [1976] 1977), 320.

film. In Europe there were reports of people so possessed by the film, that they were led to criminal and suicidal behaviour. There were calls for the film to be banned in West Germany when a teenager shot himself after seeing the film, and in England people made the obvious connection when a sixteen-year-old boy died from an epileptic attack, a day after seeing *The Exorcist*. In 1974, the murderer of a nineteen-year-old girl pleaded that he had felt something take possession of him when seeing the film. 'It was not really me that did it. There was something inside me.'[30] It is little wonder then that the Christian 'Festival of Light' in Britain picketed showings of the film, warning against demonic powers; though in 1975 the film was banned in Tunisia for being Christian propaganda.[31]

William Friedkin's film is exemplary of cinema's power to affect an audience, because, at least in popular folklore, its audiences, or some members of them, became possessed in the way that its central character is possessed. Like her, they underwent physical changes, fainting and vomiting, and in more extreme cases, causing harm to themselves and others. The film itself became the possessing agent, the demon; its celluloid became demonic. Moreover, within the film, the demon is itself metaphoric of cinema, since it possesses the girl in order to be seen and cause terror in those who witness her possession. As Mark Kermode notes in his analysis of the film, various characters – Regan's mother, the doctors and priests – on hearing the demonic noises within Regan's bedroom, rush toward it and the camera rushes with them and enters the room with them.[32] But before we are shown what is within, we are shown the revulsion and terror on

---

[30] Kermode, *The Exorcist*, 85.

[31] Kermode, *The Exorcist*, 86–7. Pauline Kael – who did not like the film – noted that 'the movie may be in the worst imaginable taste – that is, an utterly unfeeling movie about miracles – but it's also the biggest recruiting poster the Catholic Church has had since the sunnier days of *Going My Way* and *The Bells of St Mary's*'. Pauline Kael, 'Back to the Ouija Board', in *Reeling*, 247–51 at 249.

[32] Kermode, *The Exorcist*, 43–4.

their faces, as they stand in the doorway, looking in, spectators of the film's horror. We see in them what is about to happen to us, as we too are caught in the gaze of the cinematic demon.

As in the second century so in the twentieth, people fear possession by the images on which they like to look. They fear that they or others, usually others, will be corrupted by showings in the dark, by powers that at the same time they know to be illusions: senseless matter and shadows on the wall. And as in the second century so in the twentieth, Plato's parable of the cave proves to be an enduring picture of our relationship to images, as much in the picture palace as in the temple. For uncannily, at the dawn of philosophy, Plato imagined the cinema: the projection of moving pictures in the dark, a trick of light and shade taken for reality.[33]

Plato's Cinema

Imagine the condition of men living in a sort of cavernous chamber underground, with an entrance open to the light and a long passage all down the cave. Here they have been from childhood, chained by the leg and also by the neck, so that they cannot move and can see only what is in front of them, because the chains will not let them turn their heads. At some distance higher up is the light of a fire burning behind them; and between the prisoners and the fire is a track with a parapet along it, like the screen at a puppet show, which hides the performers while they show their puppets over the top. ... Now behind this parapet imagine persons carrying along various artificial objects, including figures of men and animals in wood or stone or other materials, which project above the parapet. Naturally, some of these persons will be talking, others silent. ... prisoners so confined would have seen nothing of themselves or one

33 Plato, *The Republic*, Pt VII, Bk VII.

another, except the shadows thrown by the fire-light on the wall of the Cave facing them. ... And they would have seen as little of the objects carried past. ... Now, if they could talk to one another, would they not suppose that their words referred only to those passing shadows which they saw? ... And suppose their prison had an echo from the wall facing them? When one of the people crossing behind them spoke, they could only suppose that the sounds came from the shadow passing before their eyes. ... In every way, then, such prisoners would recognise as reality nothing but the shadows of those artificial objects.[34]

Since the invention of cinema, its affinity with Plato's cave has often been remarked. F. M. Cornford, in his 1941 translation and commentary on *The Republic*, noted that a 'modern Plato would compare his cave to an underground cinema, where the audience watch the play of shadows thrown by the film passing before a light at their backs. For the film Plato has to substitute the clumsier apparatus of a procession of artificial objects carried on their heads by persons who are merely part of the machinery, providing for the movement of the objects and the sounds whose echo the prisoners hear.'[35] The puppeteers or mechanicals, who are merely part of the cave's machinery, answer to that other chamber which precedes the projector and the screen, namely the mechanical eye, the *camera obscura* that produces the celluloid image, the puppet or effigy whose shadow is cast on the wall of the cave. Like cinematic screen images, Plato's shadows are double simulations, the ghosts of ghosts.

Plato, and the Christian apologists after him, would have us shun these phantoms, especially when the product of the poetic imagination, since as phantoms they are insubstantial deceits; doubly deceitful not only in the

[34] Plato, *The Republic*, trans. with introduction and notes by F. M. Cornford (Oxford: Oxford University Press, 1941), 227–9 (l.514–515).
[35] Cornford, *The Republic of Plato*, 228 n. 2. See further Ian Jarvie, *The Philosophy of Film: Epistemology, Ontology, Aesthetics* (New York: Routledge & Kegan Paul, 1987), 44–55.

structure of their production, being twice removed from source, but also in their deceiving. They not only pass themselves off as realities, but offer corrupted images of the Good, presenting the degenerate as edifying. They are treacherous, both ontologically and ethically (epistemologically).[36] Thus Socrates objects to 'Homer and Hesiod and the poets' for telling stories about gods who commit horrible crimes, punish fathers unmercifully and make war among themselves.[37] The children of the state should not be told such tales, but rather stories that 'aim at encouraging the highest excellence of character', by showing only excellent characters.[38] In the modern world it is not only Homer and Hesiod we must shun, but the fictions that play in our contemporary cave, the cinema, which is also one of our cherished temples, where the screen deities enthral and excite our devotions.

When in May 1967, Michael Cooper and Terry Southern submitted a screenplay of Anthony Burgess' novel *A Clockwork Orange* (1962) to the British Board of Film Censors, they were told that it was unacceptable, that it would not get even an X certificate. While Audrey Field, in her censor's report, noted that the script contained a moral message indicting a 'world in which violence is the only law and human beings are programmed like computers', she felt that the Board could not countenance the showing of 'vicious violence and hooliganism by teenagers' to teenagers.[39] Nothing came of the Cooper–Southern script, which the producer Sandy Lieberson wanted to film with Mick Jagger and the other Rolling Stones, nor of Ken Russell's interest in the novel.[40] Instead it was filmed by Stanley Kubrick, with Malcolm McDowell in the lead role,

[36] For Plato, knowledge is an ethical category.
[37] Plato, *Republic*, 131–2.
[38] Plato, *Republic*, 133.
[39] Quoted in James C. Robertson, *The Hidden Cinema: British Film Censorship in Action, 1913–1972* (London: Routledge, 1989), 143–4.
[40] Vincent LoBrutto, *Stanley Kubrick* (London: Faber and Faber, [1997] 1998), 337. Lieberson went on to produce Nicholas Roeg and Donald Cammell's *Performance* (UK 1970), starring Mick Jagger; and Russell turned his attention to filming Aldous Huxley's *The Devils* (UK 1971) with Oliver Reed and Vanessa Redgrave.

the film being released at the end of 1971 in North America, and at the beginning of 1972 in Britain, with an X certificate.

Kubrick's film answers to the problematic of Plato's cave, not only because it is illusory like all films, a play of shadows, and not only because it seemed – in the eyes of some – to laud the deplorable, inviting the audience to exult with its protagonists in scenes of brutality and rape, but because it thematises the seductive power and social effects of cinema. The narrator of both book and film, whose narration beguiles reader and viewer, is Alex DeLarge,[41] a mere youth of 15 in the book, though significantly older in the film – Malcolm McDowell being nearly 28 when he played the character. Alex still lives with his parents and nominally attends school, but spends most of his time with his droogs [friends], speaking their Russian-cockney slang or nadsat, drinking at the Korova milkbar, where the milkshakes are laced with more than fruit-flavours, real 'horrorshow' [good], and indulging in acts of violence: beating up tramps, fighting other gangs, and making surprise visits on such as the author of *A Clockwork Orange*, 'making his litso [face] all purple and dripping away like some very special sort of juicy fruit', and gang-raping his wife.[42] Alex and his droogs also go to the sinny [cinema], though 'only for a yell or a razrez [cut, rip, tear]

---

[41] This is the name Alex gives in the film, but not in the novel. As Kevin Jackson notes ('Real Horrorshow: A Short Lexicon of Nadsat', *Sight and Sound* 9/9 (September 1999), 24–7), Alex's self-appellation derives from the passage in the book where 'two young ptitsas' have to 'submit to the strange and weird desires of Alexander the Large' (Burgess, *A Clockwork Orange*, 39). Later in the film, however, newspaper articles give his name as Alex Burgess. This inconsistency need not be either 'Kubrick letting his attention wander' or a 'half-hidden dig about Burgess' identification with his terrible hero', as Jackson suggests (27), since the identification of author and hero is already established in the book through Alex's namesake, victim and nemesis, F. Alexander, who is identified as the author of *A Clockwork Orange* (Burgess, *A Clockwork Orange*, 124). Burgess wrote of his terrible hero's violence that 'I was sickened by my own excitement at setting it down, and I saw that Auden was right in saying that the novelist must be filthy with the filthy.' Anthony Burgess, *You've Had Your Time* (London: Heinemann, 1990), 61.

[42] Anthony Burgess, *A Clockwork Orange*, introduction by Blake Morrison (Harmondsworth: Penguin Books, [1962] 1996), 22.

or a bit of in-and-out in the dark'.[43] But that is the 'filthy old Filmdrome, peeling and dropping to bits'. Later in the story Alex enters a somewhat different cinema, a modern version of Plato's cave.

Plato's picturegoers are held in their seats and made to look at the screen, at the flickering shadows on the back wall of the cave, and listen to the reflected sounds of the puppeteers, which they take to be made by the shadows. The inhabitants of the cave are like those people who sit in the front row of the cinema, so as to avoid all distractions and lose themselves in the world of the film; like the philosopher Wittgenstein, who would sit 'as far to the front as he could get', leaning forward in his seat so as to be 'utterly absorbed by the film'.[44] But Plato's movie-watchers have no choice in the matter, they are more like Alex in Kubrick's film, as he undergoes the Ludovico technique, a 'very simple but very drastic' behavioural therapy.[45] The technique is intended to cure Alex of his desire for 'ultra-violence', and at first seems to involve nothing more than going to the pictures and being shown some films. But Alex is strapped into his seat, his head clamped and his eyes held open, so that he cannot shut his 'glazzies' but must watch the film, which turns out to be not so much 'horrorshow', as 'a real show of horrors'.[46]

Alex is shown scenes of extreme violence – a man being beaten, a woman being raped – as well as war footage of Nazi troops and aerial bombardments. Alex is impressed.

> So far the first film was a very good professional piece of sinny, like it was made in Hollywood. The sounds were real horrorshow. You could slooshy the screams and moans, very realistic, and you could even get the

[43] Burgess, *A Clockwork Orange*, 18.
[44] John King, 'Recollections of Wittgenstein', in *Recollections of Wittgenstein*, ed. Rush Rees (Oxford and New York: Oxford University Press, 1984), 68–75, at 71.
[45] Burgess, *A Clockwork Orange*, 67.
[46] Burgess, *A Clockwork Orange*, 81. 'Horrorshow' is formed after the neuter form of the Russian for 'good', *kharashó*, and used in the same way as 'wicked' in 1990s English slang. Blake Morrison, 'Introduction' to Burgess, *A Clockwork Orange*, vii–xxiv, at ix.

heavy breathing and panting of the tolchocking malchicks, at the same time. And then what do you know. Soon our dear old friend the red red vino on tap, the same in all places like it is put out by the same big firm, began to flow. It was beautiful. It's funny how the colours of the real world only seem really real when you viddy them on the screen.[47]

However, as Alex continues to watch, unable to take his gaze from the screen, he begins to realise that he is 'not feeling all that well'.[48] The scenes that would have once excited him, now take on new associations as the drug with which he has been dosed begins to take effect, causing violent nausea. After nearly two weeks of this treatment the drug is no longer needed, the mere thought, let alone sight, of aggressive behaviour induces sickness. Even in sleep, in dreams – which Alex thinks are 'really only like a film inside your gulliver [head]'[49] – the treatment has its effect, and he awakes retching. In this way Alex is cured, and he is returned to the community.[50]

Alex is not affected by the horror films in themselves,

[47] See Burgess, A Clockwork Orange, 81–2 for the passage on which this piece of the screenplay is based.
[48] Burgess, A Clockwork Orange, 82. Alex is forced to endure images that are considerably more sadistic and horrifying in Burgess' novel than the stylised, almost pantomimic renditions in Kubrick's film. Kubrick sought a balletic quality in the film's violent scenes, answering to Burgess' invented slang, its seventeenth-century rhythms derived from the King James Bible, and intended to act 'as a kind of mist half-hiding the mayhem and protecting the reader from his own baser instincts' (Burgess, You've Had Your Time, 38). See LoBrutto, Stanley Kubrick, 338. If the film, because visual, is more horrifying than the book, it is yet less violent, and Burgess' protestations at its 'highly coloured aggression' can seem disingenuous. See Burgess, You've Had Your Time, 244–5. For Burgess' reaction to Kubrick's film and his part in its promotion, see also Anthony Burgess, The Clockwork Testament or Enderby's End (London: Hart Davies, MacGibbon, 1974).
[49] Burgess, A Clockwork Orange, 88.
[50] For Burgess, the central burden of his story is that Alex is perhaps more sinned against than sinning in having his free will destroyed through the Ludovico technique, making him a moral automaton, a clockwork orange. In the novel this concern is expressed by the prison 'charlie' [chaplain], who protests that Alex has ceased to be both a wrongdoer and a 'creature capable of moral choice' (Burgess, A Clockwork Orange, 99). At the end of the novel, Alex regains his moral freedom, and

but by the drug that attends them, administered by the cinema's technicians. To have an effect, the film images must first be augmented by the drug, the *pharmakon* that saves by making ill. It is not the images as such, but the context of their viewing that affects Alex. The peaceable Alex is produced by infusing the images with the power to incite, not emulation, but fear and distress. Dr Brodsky and his assistants are like the puppeteers in Plato's cave. In the novel, Alex first sees them as 'shadows' moving behind a wall of 'frosted glass' beneath the 'projection holes' in the

---

in the last chapter begins to abandon his former life, becoming increasingly interested in settling down and fathering a child. He freely becomes what 'society' would wish him to be. However, this last chapter was omitted from the American edition of the book, and it was this edition that Kubrick filmed, so that in the movie Alex's regained moral choice remains a choice for self-indulgence and violence. As a consequence, the film can seem more concerned with the good of choosing than with that which is chosen. Yet the film's undoubted irony may be more subtle than Burgess' own reworking of this theme in his musical-play version of *A Clockwork Orange* which ends with the chorus: 'Do not be a clockwork orange,/ Freedom has a lovely voice./ Here is good, and there is evil –/ Look on both, then take your choice./ Sweet in juice and hue and aroma,/ Let's not be changed to fruit machines./ Choice is free but seldom easy –/ That's what human freedom means!' (Anthony Burgess, *A Clockwork Orange: A Play with Music* (London: Methuen, [1987] 1998, 51). In this – which was written as a protest against the ending of Kubrick's film, the chorus being immediately preceded by the stage direction: 'A man bearded like Stanley Kubrick comes on playing, in exquisite counterpoint, "Singin' in the Rain" on a trumpet. He is kicked off the stage' – Burgess so emphasises choice for choice's sake, that one forgets that Alex's change of interests is not simply a matter of choice but of the company he keeps and the passage of time – he has just turned 18 at the end of the novel. Ethics is not just a matter of 'will', but of bodies and their social contexts, of their schooling in moral imagination. New images have come to dominate Alex's life.

> Walking the dark chill bastards of winter streets ... I kept viddying like visions, like these cartoons in gazettas. There was Your Humble Narrator Alex coming home from work to a good hot plate of dinner, and there was this ptitsa all welcoming and greeting like loving. ... I had this sudden very strong idea that if I walked into the room next to this room where the fire was burning away and my hot dinner laid on the table, there I should find what I really wanted, ... for in that other room in a cot was laying gurgling goo goo goo my son. Yes yes yes, brothers, my son. And now I felt this bolshy big hollow inside my plott, feeling very surprised too at myself. I knew what was happening, O my brothers. I was like growing up. (Burgess, *A Clockwork Orange*, 1.47)

back wall of the cinema.[51] Like Plato's mechanicals, they produce the images on the screen, but they also produce associated feelings in Alex. In this, they are less like the mechanicals and more like the demons in the temples, who 'drag men to images', and 'by invading their thoughts flood them with illusory images which seem to come from the idols and statues'. It is not the images, but the demons by which people are possessed, and in Alex's case the demons are Dr Brodsky and his assistants.

Neither the book nor the film excuses Alex's behaviour, but in both, moral depravity is shown to afflict all sections of society. This is especially evident in the film, where victims as well as assailants inhabit a pornographic culture, that relentlessly codes women as sexual objects, ever ready to comply with heterosexual male fantasies. Most famously, the Korova milkbar, in which the film opens, is furnished with naked female mannequins, legs apart and breasts thrust forward.[52] As well as Alex and his droogs, the Korova also attracts 'sophistos from the TV studios around the corner'. Later in the film, one of the droogs' bourgeois victims is killed with a 'very important work of art', a large ceramic phallus.[53] The demons are everywhere, as are the images they inhabit.

Yet both Plato and the apologists imagined that it is possible to escape the illusory and deceitful and find a way out of the cave, to the real, the true and the good. The apologists in particular invoked a Christian worship free from the dangers in the temples. But in Plato matters are not so certain, and we must now consider the paradox of Plato's parable, before turning to consider why the Church can no more escape the cave than it can the cinema, but must ceaselessly venture the difference between shadows, between demon and Spirit.

[51] Burgess, *A Clockwork Orange*, 80.
[52] These were made by Liz Moore, and based on furniture-sculptures by the London artist Allen Jones. See John Baxter, *Stanley Kubrick: A Biography* (London: HarperCollins, 1997), 249.
[53] This sculpture, together with that of four naked dancing Christs, was made by the Dutch artists Herman and Cornelius Makkink. Baxter, *Stanley Kubrick*, 255.

Socrates' Magic

Plato's parable of the cave supposes that we can see the distinction between shadow and reality, interior and exterior. Plato's Socrates adopts an omniscient perspective that can see both sides of the parapet wall, both the puppets and the shadows they cast. Yet at the same time, Socrates insists that both he and his interlocutor, Glaucon, are inside the cave, on the inner side of the parapet wall. For 'the prison dwelling corresponds to the region revealed to us through the sense of sight, and the fire-light within it to the power of the Sun'.[54] It is a moment of Platonic irony. For if the parable of the cave is true, if we and Socrates mistake shadows for reality, then Socrates' parable is itself but an appearance, a flickering shadow on the wall of the cave, an illusion; and more generally, what we take to be real, is really shadow.

This paradox often goes unremarked, or if noted then disarmed. Thus Desmond Lee cautions against taking Plato 'too solemnly'. Plato only means that 'the ordinary man is often very uncritical in his beliefs', and we are to suppose that neither Socrates nor Glaucon, or ourselves, are ordinary men.[55] But Plato's analogy in this regard is quite specific: the sun is the fire, and we are the prisoners, and as such see only shadows. This is why Glaucon has already been warned that Socrates' account might be a forgery. The three related similes of sun, line and cave are all meant to suggest what the Good is like, but they are only shadows, children (copies) rather than parents (originals), interest on a loan but not the loan itself. 'You must see to it', Socrates warns, that 'I do not inadvertently cheat you with false coin.'[56] Thus while Socrates is 'caught in his own game',[57]

---

[54] Plato, *The Republic*, l.517, 231.
[55] Plato, *The Republic*, trans. with an introduction by Desmond Lee, second revised edition (Harmondsworth: Penguin Books, 1987), 317 n. 1.
[56] Plato, *The Republic*, l.507a 305. There is a play on the Greek *tokos*, meaning both 'offspring' and 'interest'.
[57] Luce Irigaray, 'The Analysis of that Projection Will Never Take (or Have Taken) Place', *Speculum of the Other Woman*, trans. Gillian C. Gill (Ithaca, NY: Cornell University Press, [1974] 1985), 310.

as Luce Irigaray puts it, and forgetful of the screen upon which the Good is projected, this necessary subterfuge is yet slyly remarked by Socrates. Philosophers are magicians also.

To live in Plato's cave, not as one of the prisoners, but as Socrates or Glaucon, would be to live like John Murdoch in Alex Proyas' *Dark City* (1997). In the time before the story of the film opens, Murdoch (Rufus Sewell) is like most of the city's other inhabitants, prisoners who do not know they are prisoners in a city that is the projection of the 'strangers', aliens who come among them as animated corpses, demons in dead matter. Each night, at midnight, the city stops. Its machinery halts, and everyone sleeps. It is then that the strangers transform the city through their collective and mechanically augmented will-power, raising and lowering city blocks, rearranging roads and rail tracks, and changing the memories of the city's inhabitants. No one has knowledge of these nocturnal transformations, which occur both within and without their minds; no one knows that they – and not the aliens – are really strangers to themselves, their bodies occupied by multiple characters. No one realises that it is always night in the city, and that no one has been outside its limits, which anyway can never be found, because the roads are never quite as remembered. Anyone searching for the exit loses the way. The story of the film is the escape of the 'prisoner' Murdoch from the cave of the city.

Murdoch's escape is at first accidental, in that the drugs administered to change his memories don't take, and he awakens as the city sleeps, having gained some of the strangers' telekinetic powers. Later, his journey out of the city-cave is assisted by Dr Schreber (Kiefer Sutherland), who is reluctantly working for the strangers, producing the memory cocktails that are nightly administered to the city's sleeping inhabitants. Schreber inducts Murdoch into the mechanism of the dream-city. Like Socrates to Glaucon, Schreber carefully explains to Murdoch the means by which the shadows are cast. In order to learn the secret of the city, Murdoch does not ascend above it, but is led beneath it, into its bowels. Nor is he simply the prisoner become Glaucon, he is a Glaucon who comes to realise that Socrates' tale of an upper, more real world, is itself a shadow, a forgery.

Throughout the film, Murdoch is searching for the city's exterior, impelled by childhood memories of a visit to a seaside resort, Shell Beach, of which he has a memorial postcard. They are memories of golden sand, blue sea and bright sunlight, and they are all the product of one of Dr Schreber's cocktails. By insisting on the veracity of this memory, Murdoch is led to a door through which both he and we the audience, momentarily catch a glimpse of sea and sky, before realising that it is only an electrically lit hoarding, advertising the pleasures of Shell Beach. Refusing to admit that his memory is but an illusion, and convinced that he has reached the edge of the city, Murdoch tears down the poster, and begins to smash the wall behind it, until he breaks through, revealing that outside the city there is nothing, save the limitless depths of outer-space. The city is a machine between worlds, producing its reality out of the dreams and memories of its human inhabitants, as these are cut and pasted by the strangers. The view of the city in the void is an impossible one, seen with dead eyes, apparently those of Inspector Bumstead (William Hurt), as he is swept through the hole in the wall, and out, not into an upper world of dazzling light, but into the darkness of the void, punctured only by distant stars.

Proyas' interpretation of Plato's parable takes seriously Socrates' warning to Glaucon as to its veracity, the fact that Socrates tells his tale from within the cave, imagining an exterior that can be only a shadowy projection. At the end of Proyas' film, Murdoch defeats the strangers, and takes control of the city's cinematic apparatus, remaking the world after his own desires and memories. He surrounds the city with a sea, and makes the sun to rise, before walking off with his beloved, toward Shell Beach. In this way the film has a conventional 'happy ending', that is nevertheless disturbing, since John Murdoch's newly enlightened world exists only as he wills it, based on childhood memories that are themselves illusions, without originals within the city-cave. Plato offers no reason for the apparatus of his cave-world, for why the mechanicals run it as they do.[58] Proyas' puppeteers – the strangers – are aliens who have perhaps abducted their prisoners from the earth, in order to study the nature of humanity, but the original of the city is off-stage, unknown and unknowable. Its reality is suspended or bracketed.

Reality is equally suspended in Plato, since it is located outside that which can alone be known. Plato ventures that the story of the cave is a shadow of this outside, but it is only a venture. Can we trust the mechanical, the philosopher-magician who shows us the shadow? In Proyas' retelling of the story, Murdoch takes control of the cave, and from then on he will conjure the shadows, and the inhabitants of the once dark city must trust his judgement. Murdoch answers to a certain contemporary nihilism, since unlike Plato, he is disabused of any hope of an outside. For him, there is now only the cave, and he is its Demiurge.

How do matters fare in the Church, which is also a kind of cave, a kind of cinema?

Christ's Cave

When Camille Paglia first saw Walt Disney's *Snow White and the Seven Dwarfs* (1937), she was transfixed by the Wicked Queen, a 'temperamental diva bitch', who didn't have to be charitable and didn't have to be nice. The Wicked Queen was totally unlike the Virgin Mary, the ideal of womanhood that Catholicism presented to the young Camille. 'OK? Mary, this silent mother; and here was the witch queen who has this weird dialogue in the mirror and it didn't have to be charitable and it didn't have to be nice. I thought she was fabulous.'[59] There was simply no competition. The contest between the Wicked Queen

[58] Irigaray, 'The Analysis of that Projection', 287.
[59] Camille Paglia quoted in E. Jane Dickson, 'The Wicked Queen', *The Independent* (Monday Review, 7 June 1999) 1.

and the Queen of Heaven may seem frivolous, but Paglia contends that cinema is the 'the single biggest cultural threat to the Christian church since Islam in the medieval period'.[60]

In the Wicked Queen, Paglia sees not only the projection of negativity toward the real mother, but also the return of a 'pre-Christian form of the malevolent nature mother', a 'persona lying utterly outside the moral universe of Christianity'.[61] This answers to Paglia's more general contention, that in cinema – and especially the cinema of Hollywood – we see the return of repressed but never finally vanquished pagan powers. 'The twentieth century is not the Age of Anxiety but the Age of Hollywood. The pagan cult of personality has reawakened and dominates all art, all thought. It is morally empty but ritually profound. We worship it by the power of the western eye. Movie screen and television screen are its sacred precincts.'[62] Once more the demons drag people to images and intoxicate their minds with illusions.

Camille Paglia is not the first to have suggested a fundamental contest between church and cinema. A rather more suburban staging of the conflict was offered by David Lodge in his first novel *The Picturegoers* (1960), which considers the impact of the local cinema on the Catholic community of Brickley, and the fruitless attempts of Father Kipling to win back his flock from the temptations of what Alex and his droogs will come to know as the 'sinny'. Fr Kipling is convinced that the Saturday night flicks are an occasion of sin, and in a desperate bid to offer a rival attraction, moves the Thursday Benediction to Saturday evening, which results in empty pews.[63]

As the character Mark Underwood notes, Father Kipling is 'fighting a losing battle'.[64] Cinema has already become a

---

[60] Dickson, 'The Wicked Queen', 1.
[61] Camille Paglia, *Sexual Personae: Art and Decadence from Nefertiti to Emily Dickinson* (Harmondsworth: Penguin Books, [1990] 1992), 346.
[62] Paglia, *Sexual Personae*, 32.
[63] David Lodge, *The Picturegoers* (Harmondsworth: Penguin Books, [1960] 1993), 125. A thematically related novel is Walker Percy, *The Moviegoer* (New York: Alfred A. Knopf, 1961), also a first novel.
[64] Lodge, *The Picturegoers*, 106–7.

substitute for religion, and Mark fears that it will become a substitute for life. But as a substitute for religion, cinema parodies the Church, so that the Church in its worship becomes a less interesting, less seductive parody of the cinema. Mark muses that 'going to church was like going to the cinema: you sat in rows, the notices were like trailers, the supporting sermon was changed weekly. And people went because they always went. You paid at the plate instead of at the box-office, and sometimes they played the organ. There was only one big difference: the main feature was always the same.'[65] Yet this recurring 'feature' is not without its effect, offering an education in 'looking' that by the end of the novel, has led Mark to lose his atheistic faith and resolve on life as a Dominican.

Cinema can be viewed as a quasi-religious practice. It is this not only in its use of religious symbols and themes, but in and through its social practice, which congregates people in the dark for visions of desire. Like church, cinema creates social bonds through the projection of other forms of life that exceed the mundane, through the production of visions or dreams that can be sustained only through their repeated attendance. Of course, one might want to say that cinema as religion is an impoverished substitution for what the Church offers, even if it is as close as many people now come to the latter. One might also want to question the longevity of such a socio-religious practice much beyond the twentieth century, for it is possible that we are now living in the last days of cinema, since technological developments promise new media, which will intensify what is increasingly for many their only social bond, the consumption of infinitely commodified pleasures. Nevertheless, movie-going has enjoyed a rebirth in recent years, with the advent of video and pay-TV enhancing rather than diminishing the communal viewing of film.[66] It is as if the video of the film, usually

---

[65] Lodge, *The Picturegoers*, 108–9.
[66] In both North America and Britain film-going was at its height in 1946, with 1,635 million cinema admissions in Britain alone. Cinema attendance declined markedly in the 1950s with the growth of TV ownership, and continued to decline throughout the 1960s and 1970s, reaching a low point

only available sometime after the release of the picture in the movie house, were become part of household devotion, not supplanting but supplementing communal worship. It is like the candle blessed in the church, taken home and used for apotropaic effect, which in the case of the video is to avert tedium and constitute a socio-sacral memory of the film through repetitious viewing of it in whole or in part, alone or with partners and friends.

That it is possible to read church and cinema as parodies of one another, suggests the intensity of their potential rivalry, since both are cinemas, places where dreams are projected, and both are churches, 'inside' places where images of an 'outside', other than that from which the viewers have come, are shown. When the lights go down, one can see other imagined worlds, other ways of being human. This is to repeat the identity and distinction already drawn between Christian and pagan in the ancient world. In all three places, temple, church and cinema, we can detect the shadow of the cave, which establishes the distinction between the illusory and the real. As I have tried to suggest through my discussion of Proyas' *Dark City*, that distinction is itself shadowy, suspending the real and constituting its identification a venture of the imagination.

At the same time, what makes any particular image compelling, inviting trust, is not the image alone, but the power with which it is invested by others. By demons, the apologists claim of pagan statuary; by medical technicians, Burgess and Kubrick claim of Alex's 'show of horrors'; by society, we might say, of the films that at any one time grip the public imagination; and by the Holy Spirit, we might further say, of the images proffered in the Church, as when Lodge's Mark Underwood comes to see the 'real presence' through the eucharistic practice of the 'drab, smug, self-righteous people' of Brickley, 'who coolly

in 1984 with only 54 million British admissions. However, since then there has been a steady increase in cinema admissions, with 123 million in 1996 (UK). See *BFI Film and Television Handbook 1998*, ed. Eddie Dyja (London: British Film Institute, 1997), 42.

lined up to snap their dentures on the living Christ'.[67] It is thus a matter of discerning the context in which an image can nourish its viewers, feeding their imaginations and ethos.[68]

Churches remain caves for the projection of dreams, of other ways of being human and social. Like Plato's cinema-cave, they marshal their inhabitants for the viewing of images, scenes of sacrifice and fellowship, in which they also participate. A distinction between reality and representation is maintained, yet overcome, because invisible. The Church acts in memory of its Lord, yet the past that is remembered, and the future that is invoked, as if they were absent, are really present, in the tokens and actions of the memorial. What appears as deconstructive irony in Plato, is positively embraced in the Christian cave, where it is held that knowledge of the exterior can be gained only inside the cave. The dazzling light of the real is to be seen by fire-light.

The Church is Plato's cave turned inside-out, since what he refuses to acknowledge for the sake of the game, is openly avowed in the Church, or at least avowed in certain of its symbolics and practices. Which is to say that the Church reflects itself as itself, as the cave in which life is made and formed. From the first Christian theology has thought the cave the womb of life, human and divine, the space for the imagining of a different reality, so that Freud was only repeating a series of theological symbolic displacements when he related the womb with the dream symbols of 'pits, cavities and hollows', 'churches and chapels'.[69] In the Freudian context, an appropriate example would be Leonardo da Vinci's Madonna of the Rocks, in which the mother of the child is pictured in a kind of grotto, viewed perhaps from the deeper interior of the

[67] Lodge, *The Picturegoers*, 110. The worshipping community is the 'screen' on which God appears, and worship is to be a daily undertaking.
[68] Thus censorship is not so much about denying people the right to view images, as judging the context of their showing. This is why film censorship is always a judgement on audiences, rather than films; and why what is deemed passable changes with time. Censorship also assumes that there is at least one audience with clear vision, the censors; and it is their implied judgement on the rest of us that causes affront.
[69] Sigmund Freud, *Introductory Lectures on Psychoanalysis* (1915–17), in *The Penguin Freud Library* Vol. 1, trans. James Strachy, ed. by James Strachy and Angela Richards (Harmondsworth: Penguin Books, 1973), 89–190.

cave, looking toward the entrance. We are again reminded
that unlike Plato's story, the Christian tale locates the Good
not beyond but within the cave.

Christ is traditionally pictured as born in a cave and in
the resurrection reborn from one. Thus the new life offered
by Christ, individual and communal, comes forth not only
from the actual womb of the virgin, but also from the cave-
womb of the tomb, that ancient underground cinema in
which the dream of another life, another way of living –
beyond death – is projected. Freud's equation of womb,
cave and chapel repeats a set of substitutory identifications
already at play in the Christian imaginary and issuing in
the complex symbolics of Leonardo's painting, or indeed,
in the more humble Christmas crib that uses crumpled
brown paper to represent the rocky enclosure of the divine
nativity. Fundamentally, the Christian cave projects that
which is alone truly desirable, the projected image enticing
the gaze of the congregation by whom it is projected,
caught up in the power of the Spirit. As in my discussion of
The Exorcist, to see is to be seen and possessed, and indeed
to see the crucified Christ might be to react with an equal
horror and terror; but to see the crucified become the risen
Christ, is to have terror give way to wonder; and to see
Christ present in the Eucharist, in the bread and the wine
and the gathered community, is to have wonder transfused
with joy and the hope of once more walking in the garden.

Then we are like the picturegoer who has become like a
little child, enamoured of the screen, unable to tell shadow
from flickering shadow. It is to become like the most
saintly character in *The Picturegoers*, who is envied for the
'primitive intensity of her dramatic experience' when at
the pictures. Clare Mallory is a devout Catholic, who in
church or cinema, is a happy inhabitant of the cave. 'Any
dramatic or cinematic performance, however crudely
executed, seemed to draw from her the same rapt,
child-like attention. To her, as to a child, what she saw on
the screen was real.'[70] Only such a gaze can believe the
beatitudes.

[70] Lodge, *The Picturegoers*, 54.

13
Prophecy or Politics?
The Role of the Churches in Society

Enda McDonagh

Some of Stanley Hauerwas' most provocative and illuminating work has focused on the public role of the Church,
on the Ekklesia and Polis – or Ekklesia *as* Polis, to adapt a
title of one of his recent books. Much of my own work has
dealt with similar problems, reaching back to my doctoral
dissertation of 1960 on Church and state in the
Constitution of Ireland. With different ecclesiological
backgrounds (Methodist and Catholic), different political
contexts and challenges (primarily the United States and
Ireland) and different theological personae we have
followed quite different paths and arrived at quite
different if provisional perspectives. Yet I continue to read
Stanley with considerable sympathy and profit while
finding that I have to struggle with my own problems in
my own context. This essay is not then a critical evaluation
of the Hauerwas contribution to the American and wider
debate on Church and society, or however he might phrase
it. I do not feel equal to that. It is something much less
ambitious, an effort to discover for myself first of all where
I stand on the role of the churches in society (my phrase)
after forty years of struggle in practice as well as in theory.
It is the best way I know to pay tribute to more than twenty
years of personal friendship and theological enrichment.

Catholic Theology and Social Engagement

Without attempting an analysis of 'One Hundred Years of
Catholic Social Teaching', as it is sometimes called, still less

any serious reflection on the much longer and more tangled tradition of the relation between Christian/ Catholic faith and social justice, the concern here is with certain developments in this relationship which have occurred in the working life of this theologian. The justification for this is twofold; the significance of the shifts that have occurred in theory (theology) and practice (engagement) in the relationship during this period, and the theologian's own experience of them in theory and practice.

The 1950s were not particularly exciting years for the student of Catholic theology in Ireland. The post-war European fermentation already bubbling did not really affect undergraduate theology. This was heavily neo-scholastic but not exclusively so. It did in hindsight correspond rather closely to the non-historical orthodoxy attributed in the 1960s to the Roman schools of theology by Michael Novak. More relevantly here academic theology was sharply separated from practice – understood in a rather narrow pastoral and sacramental sense. Even moral theology, professedly the most practical of theological disciplines, was largely concerned with categorising personal sins for confessional purposes. Personal moral development was discussed, but social justice issues were for an entirely separate, and by definition non-theological, course in Catholic Social Teaching. In some significant sense theology – in the language used by John-Baptist Metz and other 'political theologians' later in the 1960s – had been privatised.

Ireland and Maynooth, however, were not so easily pigeonholed. The Catholic Church in Ireland, lay and clerical, had a long history of social involvement. The struggles for democratic participation led by Daniel O'Connell, a layman, depended for its effective organis-ation on church leaders, especially priests in their parishes. This combination of a Catholic laity and clergy in promotion of democracy in the early nineteenth century in Ireland was greatly admired by people like Lacordaire. Subsequent struggles throughout the nineteenth century for educational, social and economic development continued in varying forms and degrees this alliance between politicians and clergy as community leaders. Although the bulk of the clergy and perhaps all the bishops rejected the armed struggle as a legitimate means of political and social change, it had its clerical and theological defenders, at least post-factum. While this was dominantly a Nationalist–Catholic alliance, clergy and laity from the Reformed Churches in Ireland, Presbyterian, Church of Ireland and Methodist, played key roles in the nationalist political, cultural and economic enterprise. This bore fruit in the relatively tolerant laws and constitutions of the new state despite some serious counter-examples in law and social practice.

The partition of Ireland, with the six north-eastern counties retaining political union with Great Britain, had political roots and consequences which influenced considerably the relationships of all the churches with the two political entities – the Republic of Ireland and Northern Ireland as they are now usually called. Within Northern Ireland, Protestants were overwhelmingly unionist; Catholics were overwhelmingly nationalist. The coincidence of political and religious affiliation on both sides made for a very troubled relationship which erupted in the violent troubles of the last thirty years in Northern Ireland. In the South or the Republic the tension and trouble were much less, partly because of the tiny proportion of Protestants, and partly because, after independence, 'bread and butter' politics gradually replaced republican and unionist ideals or ideologies. In the Republic, points of tension remained, sometimes inflamed by events, North and South, such as Bloody Sunday in Derry (Northern Ireland) 1972, or the Fethard-on-Sea boycott of Protestants in 1957 (the Republic).

These scraps of Irish history may help in understanding why and how some Irish students of theology even in the 1950s were prompted to stray beyond the confines of 'pure' theology and engage theologically with the social and political situation. In that spirit this theologian undertook a doctoral dissertation on early Anglican theology in the theology faculty at Maynooth, and followed it up with one on Church–state relations in the canon law faculty at the University of Munich. With the acumen with which some church and even university administrators sometimes operate, the end-result of all this was a teaching post in moral theology in the faculty at Maynooth. Earlier engagements were not neglected, as a series of articles on Church–state relations in the 1960s and as two books on *Roman Catholics and Unity* (London, 1962) and *Religious Liberty* (London, 1967) can attest.

The intersection of the Catholic theological tradition and the Irish political tradition influenced how Irish theologians related Catholic theology and social engagement. It influenced but it did not initiate it. Indeed the divisions in Catholicism on this matter were already evident in public debate in Ireland. Since the introduction in 1937 of the new Constitution of Ireland, which refused to establish the Catholic Church as the official state church – or as the 'one true Church', in the phrase of some advocates – there had been a campaign to have this amended, and the Catholic Church duly recognised. In theological lecture hall and journal this became a disputed point also. For the proponents of 'establishment', the manuals of Public Ecclesiastic Law of Cardinal Alfredo Ottaviani, Head of the Holy Office, as it was then called, and sundry nineteenth-century predecessors, were source and authority. For their opponents, the new situation of democracy, the experience of churches free of involvement with the state, and the reflections of Jacques Maritain, John Courtney Murray and others suggested new relationships between Church and state, new ways of being Church in the world, and fresh insights into theology's social engagement.

In a semi-autobiographical essay the chronology of personal concern and involvement may provide the easier and indeed clearer line of argument. The case for recognition of the Catholic Church as the one true Church as advanced by Ottaviani and others in Europe and by J. C. Fenton and others in the USA had surfaced in Ireland but was rejected by Eamon de Valera for the Constitution adopted by the people of Ireland in 1937. The debate rumbled on into the 1950s. The very terms involved for Church and state were looking increasingly unreal, each a perfect society in its own sphere with its own end and the means to that end. The one supernatural and the other natural, each had independent responsibility in its own sphere. As they served the same people they ought to co-operate; in case of conflict the supernatural as superior ought to prevail. There were softer expressions of the theory but the essentials remained the same. In practice all kinds of accommodation were made, *faute de mieux*.

Early attempts to refute this position were partly inspired by the conviction that it was inapplicable in the Republic of Ireland, despite its 95 per cent Catholic majority, and partly by what appeared to be double standards in claiming religious freedom for Catholics when in a minority, while refusing it or at least restricting it for others when Catholics were in a majority and the Catholic Church became 'established'. The re-reading of the work of Leo XIII by John Courtney Murray, tortuous as it appeared at times, enabled a more robust magisterial defence of the separation of Church and state and of religious freedom than seemed possible when the debate was first aired in the halls of Maynooth by Jeremiah Newman, later Bishop of Limerick. Much gratitude is due to Newman for introducing students so quickly to that debate and for his continuing friendship despite deep and lasting disagreement about the issues.

Murray was naturally influenced by the American experience, in which the Catholic Church thrived on freedom rather than privilege. The state, he argued, was incompetent in religious matters and so could not determine which was the one true Church in order to establish it. The Church best exercised its influence through its members who were citizens and legislators, not through formal recognition or legally-binding agreements like concordats. Murray endorsed religious freedom as a citizen's right in relation to the state to profess and practise any religion or none within the limits of public order. This is the heart of Vatican II's document on religious liberty, of which Murray was the chief draftsman. For all his regard for certain aspects of the liberal tradition and for human rights in general, Murray was no defender of a simple liberal individualism or of rights language as a comprehensive political language. He recognised the state's obligation to the good of the whole community – as expressed, for example, in public order. The moral values which the state should protect would, in his thinking, correspond to the central values of the natural law tradition. This is a feature exemplified in much recent papal and episcopal teaching.

Religious freedom defined and defended along the Murray lines had further implications for understanding Church, state and their relationships. Some of these were already anticipated in the work of Jacques Maritain on Christian faith, democracy and human rights. Maritain was even less of an ideological liberal than Murray, but he had a genuine sense of the value of democracy and of personal human rights, which owed much to his reading of St Thomas and the natural law tradition. In particular he alerted one to the limits of the state – not by the Church in itself but by the Church's role as the servant of society or wider community. The distinction between society and state and the priority of society as the people in its overlapping structures and relationships was widely accepted in Western democratic theory, if not always in practice. Its relation to the original Christian claim for freedom to worship its own God while asserting its loyalty to empire and emperor was not always given due credit by defenders of democracy, Christian or non-Christian. In the further development of Christian understanding of the role of the churches in society the distinction between society and state beyond any Constantinian accommodation was bound to be crucial. (The Irish version of this may have escaped Stanley in his romantic recall of Confirmation day in Sneem, County Kerry.)

The distinction between society and state, with its implications for the defence of human rights, personal and social, was, whatever its remote origins, now a political and secular reality. A church shaped by a Constantinian polity did not necessarily fit. Understanding of the Church was also changing. For Catholic theology Vatican II was crucial to this. And for the purposes of this essay perhaps the more crucial was the *Pastoral Constitution on the Church in the Modern World*, rather than the *Dogmatic Constitution on the Church*. The recovery of the image of the Church as the pilgrim people of God cleared the way for a possible alternative and prophetic vision of its role in society as distinct from the persisting Constantinian model, however diluted.

The diluted Constantinian model could be discerned in both the theology and practice of Church–state relations after, as well as before, Vatican II. It still survives in more attenuated forms where civil governments and church leaders have formal or informal arrangements on issues like education or church taxes, on social welfare or health, on particular offices like chaplaincies to Parliament or to the army, or on laws restricting specific 'immoral' activities as crimes. Some of these provisions may still be justifiable but all will need re-examining in the context of Church, state and society undergoing constant change.

The *Declaration on Religious Freedom* defended against any state coercion the right of the individual citizen and community to freedom of faith and its public expression within the limits of public order and morality. This both resolved a problem and displaced it from the religious to the moral arena. Christianity's inextricable link with morality and the understanding by the Catholic Church and by Catholic theology of natural law as applicable to all human beings combined with that Church's claim to be the authoritative interpreter of natural law, ensured many sharp disputes in the Western world between state legislators and church leaders, in particular on issues such as divorce, contraception, abortion and homosexuality. Justice and peace issues, such as poverty, racism, militarism and discrimination against women were sometimes the sources of church criticism of state authorities, but seldom with the same intensity and persistence, or above all with the same widespread support, from the church membership. In the Irish debates which came later than those in the rest of the Western world neither side learned much from what had happened elsewhere in Europe and North America. By now the debate was shifting geographically and theologically.

Praxis and Theory: Theology's Uncertainty Principle

The recent sharp theological debate on the relation between praxis and theory, prompted in particular by the development of liberation theology in Latin America, and undoubtedly influenced by earlier Marxist ideas, had its own latent Christian origins and tradition. Faith in Jesus Christ meant discipleship, a way of life, a praxis. Understanding at this basic level of acceptance of his claims simultaneously involved acceptance of his lifestyle. Theory or intellectual recognition was inextricably linked with praxis. Even within the Gospels themselves and among his closest and most avid disciples there were failures in faith and following. The ambition of the Sons of Thunder to sit at his right hand and left when he should come into his kingdom, or Peter's denial at the trial so soon after his boast of loyalty, might be interpreted as failure in either faith or following, or more plausibly in both. However the distinction between moral failure and loss of faith was an early part of the way of discipleship and provided a basis for what might be called a distinction between theory and praxis. In contemporary terms Irish playwright Brendan Behan's remark that he had 'the honour to be a bad Catholic' is in that tradition of distinguishing faith from morality. To deny the distinction leads to a puritanical and unforgiving church far from the koinonia of love envisaged in the New Testament. To separate faith and morality leads to corrupt Christians and a corrupt church which have surfaced too frequently in history and is no less unfaithful to the promise of the New Testament. Like faith and morality, Christian theory and praxis belong together, although it is never easy to determine at a particular juncture which, if either, has priority in what might be described as a communion of sinners struggling to be a communion of saints.

Although faith/morality are close correlates of theory/praxis in Christian discourse, the theory/praxis distinction in current usage has tended to operate at a more self-consciously intellectual or at least analytic level. At this level they remain also inextricably bound together, while the question of which gets prior attention also depends on the particular situation. Indeed to focus on the one affects understanding of the other in a way that may be said to be crudely analagous to how concentration on the speed of a subatomic particle interferes with the exact observation of its location. To speak of theology's uncertainty principle on such an analogy is indeed crude. It has the merit of drawing attention not only to the mutual influence of Christian theology (usually presented as theory) and Christian living (sometimes described as praxis). It also exposes the difficulties of providing both a settled theology and practice, as the dimensions of the one change, and so influence, the other.

For the first Christian communities the acceptance of Gentile converts free of regular Jewish obligations or the debates about eating meat sacrificed to idols offered classic instances of the interaction of theology and Christian practice. What began as debated practice ended in changing the theological understanding. And so it was that the early Christians made their way uncertainly in the world of the frequently hostile Roman empire. The development of the second plank of salvation, as Tertullian called it, with the practice of the sacrament of penance not only confirmed the distinction and relationship between faith and morality but promoted a deeper understanding of the teaching and practice of Jesus' saving and forgiving mission. Later developments from public to private penance illustrated further the changing relationship between theory and praxis which continued to characterise the life of the Christian community. Not all of these interactions were faith-enhancing or life-giving to the community – as the many corrupt historical practices and attempts at their theological justification demonstrated.

The Reformation divisions over indulgences involved a notable example of how corrupt practice can corrupt faith.

Even four hundred years later there has not been an entirely satisfactory solution to the problems posed earlier by the practice and theory of indulgences. However, the decline of the practice among the Catholic faithful has prompted neglect by theologians of the traditional forms of explanation and near silence among preachers and bishops of this once trumpeted way of development in the Christian life. Practice and theology move in parallel here as indeed they do in the near dormant state which the Catholic Church is experiencing in regard to the practice and theology of the sacrament of private penance. These are the developments primarily of particular times and places, the late twentieth century in the Western world. Their future here is as unpredictable as the retention of some of the older understanding and practice is in other parts of the Catholic world. What is significant is the mutual influence for change of Catholic theology and practice in diverse social and cultural situations. That is the certainty and the uncertainty which Church and theology must always expect to experience on their pilgrim ways.

Although they were influenced by their social and cultural situations and had their own social and cultural impact in turn, the examples examined of the interaction between theory and praxis in Christian tradition were primarily internal to the Church and only indirectly related to the political arena. This would need much further explication and qualification as one recalls the unconditional acceptance of non-Jews and its impact on the Roman Empire and on the public continuation of Judaism. Inherently religious as the development of the sacrament of penance might appear, the order of public penitents and the summons of the Emperor to Canossa had profound political implications. It was the formal entry of the Church into the public life of the Roman Empire in the fourth century which made the social engagement and praxis of the Church so significant for its self-understanding, its theory or theology. Indeed as indicated earlier the remnants of this development were evident in the theory and praxis of Church–state relations well into this century and have not yet entirely disappeared.

The most striking instance of change in church theory and practice prompted by the change in Church–Empire relations was the development of the just war theory and practice. During its first centuries the Church maintained a basically pacifist stance. This was in fidelity to the teaching and practice of Jesus, but also influenced by the Roman army's confession of Caesar as divine. With Christians taking on responsibilities for administration of the Empire and the Emperor himself becoming Christian, many Christian leaders began to reconsider this purely pacifist role which had begun to be eroded in practice on the margins of the Empire even earlier. Ambrose and Augustine were notable early leaders in justifying the use of arms at least in defence. The detailed development of just war theory through the centuries and by such outstanding thinkers as Aquinas and Victoria were at least as much attempts to restrain the practice as to justify it. The practice it must be said outran the theory and the theological criteria were readily distorted or ignored. Right into our own decade theology has limped behind practice in the initiation and conduct of war by political leaders who would consider themselves Christian. It has been on rare occasions that church leaders have had the courage to criticise the war-making of their own state, despite the formal and informal separations of Church and state.

The Search for a New Paradigm

In personal terms the inadequacies of just war theory in face of the actuality of war and the repeated tendencies of churches to justify their own side raised serious questions not only about any form, however diluted, of traditional Church–state relations, but about the terms in which the whole debate and actual relationships were cast. These questions were not easily formulated or answered. Some critical experiences at home in Ireland and abroad, particularly in Africa, suggested serious adaptation of older models and then rapidly exposed the weakness of the new.

(a) The Irish Experience

Over the last thirty years Irish experiences, North and South, however different they might be, contributed to the rethinking of the relations between Church and state in ways which may be relevant well beyond the island. Partition, introduced by the British in 1921, resulted in what many people perceived as two confessional, if not sectarian, states; Northern Ireland, with its own parliament and government within the United Kingdom and subject to the British monarch in parliament at Westminster; and what was eventually declared in 1949 to be the Republic of Ireland, a fully autonomous state with its parliament in Dublin. The religious influence on the legislation and administration of the two states may still be sharply debated, but undoubtedly the near Protestant homogeneity of the Unionist majority in the North and the near Catholic homogeneity of the Nationalist majority in the South ensured very close relations between the respective church and state leaders which inevitably created difficulties for, and between, the churches and the states.

In the South, or more properly the Republic, the difficulties focused on law and morality issues, particularly issues of sexual morality. Much of the Republic's law in this area had been inherited from the British regime, although the Constitution of 1937 had introduced a new element by banning the passing of a law permitting divorce. Debates on these issues began in the 1960s, and dragged on until the passing of the referendum allowing divorce in 1995. Catholic church leaders opposed these changes, although not primarily on religious grounds but on those of natural law or of damage to society or the public good. Protestant church leaders for the most part endorsed the changes, again not on religious grounds but on those of individual human rights or of the lesser damage to the public good. The arguments advanced on both sides had their merits but there was clearly a too-easy coincidence between the moral positions of the different churches and their attitudes to legal change. Of course church leaders were not the only ones in these debates who might be accused of adopting self-interested positions. Politicians and citizens, conservative and liberal, were often pursuing interests other than human rights or the public good. This kind of ambiguity is inevitable in such debates. To call attention to it is not to impugn the good faith of any side but to encourage a more tolerant attitude to difference and to discourage the kind of self-righteousness which is sadly seldom avoided in these situations. It was not avoided in Ireland.

The political nature and the frequently hostile and self-righteous tone of the debates exposed the Catholic Church in particular to the accusations of being simply another self-interested and power-seeking social force. However justified such an accusation – and it could be contested – the image of the Church as herald of the Good News of salvation and healer of a broken humanity was badly damaged. The clerical sexual scandals, including paedophilia, which became a feature of the 1990s, added the accusation of hypocrisy to a church leadership which had taken such a hard line on sexual morality and legal change in this area. The humbler Church which many clerics and church members called for would have to find a new and radically changed role in society to replace the once cosy relationship with the state.

The developments through Maritain and Murray, documents such as John XXIII's *Pacem in Terris* and those on Religious Freedom and on the *Church in the Modern World*, had, without offering a blue-print, opened up again the distinction between society and state and at least pointed to the proper role of the Church as operating freely in society, rather than seeking power-agreements with the state. Indeed it became increasingly clear that the defence of personal freedoms and the defining and seeking of the public good depended on seeing the state and its institutions as the servants rather than the masters of society – where society was understood as the totality of the people within the territory in which the state was recognised with all that people's complexity of culture, religion and voluntary organisation. In such a society the Church could claim freedom to preach, to worship and to organise on the same basis as other religious traditions without claiming in state-law any privileges for itself.

Any further role of the Church in society would depend on the traditions of that society. A symbolic role might be appropriate on certain national occasions; or the Church might offer educational and social services endorsed by the people. The state might and perhaps should be neutral religiously but the society would reflect the plurality and social values of the religions of its people. As servant of society the state would respect its people's traditions as long as they did not violate the human rights of others and the good of the society as a whole.

Of course in practice in Ireland, as in so many other countries, such an approach was bound to leave many loose ends – for example the precise definition and reach of a particular human right and how it differed, if it did, from a civil right. Some people argued in the Irish debate that divorce was a civil right due under the law here and now, but not necessarily a human right deriving from the nature of the human person and under any civil law, anytime, anywhere. More complex issues arise with claims of personal rights over one's own body and the translation of this into a right to abortion, an issue still unsettled in Irish law. Similar difficulties emerge in any discussion of the public good – although the new batch of Irish controversies over corruption in politics and business, and over the provisions for the indigenous deprived and the newly arriving immigrants and asylum-seekers, may allow for more objective and fruitful debates than former heated sexual ones did.

Theologically the theologians and documents cited did not entirely escape the shadow of Constantinianism. This was more an achievement of the 1970s and later. In particular the humbler role of the Church which it was being forced to recognise in Ireland could appear to be no more than a political tactic without a fuller theological understanding of what that humble role of servant might mean. For this a return to the theology of the Reign of God as originally preached by Jesus was necessary. This did occur to some extent in Ireland but more in the context of the 'Troubles' in Northern Ireland and the inter-church problems which they involved.

Protestant and Catholic divisions in Northern Ireland were closely intertwined with the political divisions so that the Civil Rights marches by Nationalists/Catholics began in the late 1960s in protest at the discrimination against them by the Unionist/Protestant government.

Ordinary Catholic Church members composed the bulk of the protesters, with at least tacit support from many of the clergy. Opponents of the protests, both police and citizens, were dominantly Unionist/Protestant, with very loud support from some of the more extreme Protestant clergy. As protest and counter-protest eventually degenerated into violent campaigns by both sides which have only recently ended, church members and leaders faced more difficult decisions. The majority, lay and clerical, disowned and increasingly denounced the violence, but their credibility to the other side was damaged by their apparent support for the objectives of the men of violence – United Kingdom v United Ireland. Many individual clerics and lay Christians sought to promote inter-church relations as a way of distancing the churches from the disputes and so of removing one source of the tension. This had some impact but very little hard thinking or self-sacrificial practice followed. The churches remained for the most part captive to their own peoples, chaplains to their own tribes in a form of post-Constantinianism.

An attempt was made by some Catholic commentators to apply Latin American liberation theology to the Northern Ireland situation. Religious division and its presence among the poorest and most oppressed made it very difficult if not impossible to claim Jesus as liberator for just one side. The actual violence on both sides obscured such Christian claims also. Recourse was had to the theory of just war by Republican supporters – even after Pope John Paul II's powerful plea for a peaceful search for justice. As the relations between the churches continued to exacerbate the differences, some theological relativising of the churches seemed imperative. The role of the churches in society had to be properly subordinated to the Reign of God preached and inaugurated by Jesus. In the service of that Reign they were called to work together in society without necessarily betraying their own identities. The churches would not then relate primarily to state or tribe but to the Reign of God as it sought to emerge through peace and justice in society. Such theology and its implementation did not develop to any great degree in Ireland, North or South.

(b) The African Experience

In the late 1960s the Catholic Church in South Africa established a series of winter schools in theology to help bring the theology of Vatican II to its clergy and people. In 1970 Bishop Christopher Butler and myself were invited to offer together a week's course in each of six centres. As the moral theologian on the team I was faced with responding to the moral dilemmas confronting the South African Church. As this was my first visit and my first exposure to the apartheid system I saw it as South Africa's primary moral challenge. So did many of the participants in the various schools we attended. Yet its public discussion was muted compared with that of a number of sexual and marital issues like divorce and particularly contraception. Two years after *Humanae Vitae*, bishops, clergy and laity were still animatedly discussing how far contraceptives might be used by married couples in particular situations. In trying to help the South African Church with these two moral difficulties, some clarity emerged about the different attitudes involved and the divided approaches adopted. For the majority of the bishops and clergy, opposition to apartheid was real but muted, and outweighed by the more prudent and effective way of protecting the African peoples against its worst excesses and promoting gradual change in its theory and practice. There were of course significant exceptions to this approach at the different levels of the Church, which advocated a more radical and vocal opposition to a great injustice. In regard to *Humanae Vitae* the (perhaps smaller) majority adopted the radical and uncompromising line of no exceptions, while a large minority favoured a softer line of approval of contraceptives in exceptional circumstances. Generally speaking, those who favoured the more muted approach on apartheid were the uncompromising on contraception, while the radical opponents of apartheid tended to be more lenient on contraception. The divisions within the South African Church on such issues were not peculiar to it. In reflecting subsequently on the different reactions, the more radical, whether in opposition to apartheid or contraception, had the ring of the prophetic tradition of Israel and the Church, while the more lenient and accommodating to immediate circumstances belonged rather to the Wisdom tradition of Israel and Church. All this would require much more analysis and qualification to which further African experiences would contribute.

In the 1970s there came an invitation from the Catholic Institute of International Relations in London to work with the Justice and Peace Commission of the Church in Rhodesia, as it then was, on moral aspects of the war between the Smith regime which had seized power in 1965 and the guerrillas fighting for an independent Zimbabwe, as it was to be called. Over a three-year period involving a number of extensive visits to the country I prepared a report on the war and eventually a book on the relations between Church and society.

In studying the moral legitimacy of the origins and conduct of the war I encountered very deep divisions among church leaders and members. My own conclusion that on the application of just war criteria the war of independence could be termed a just war was qualified by my reservation about war being an appropriate way for Christians to deal with these matters. It was perhaps another example of the distinction between the Wisdom tradition accepting war as justified in extreme circumstances and the prophetic call to seek alternatives.

The Rhodesian situation, with neither of the warring groups able to claim international recognition as state, emphasised more deeply the distinction between state and society. The Church, however, had its difficult role to fulfil in preaching and promoting justice and peace, the message and substance of the Reign of God in society. In this context the four distinct elements in theological social analysis and engagement were more clearly discernible – Church as *community of disciples*, in *service* of *the coming Reign of God*, within a society which would be served by a newly *legitimised state*. When the new state of Zimbabwe emerged the Church still had the task of preaching and promoting the Reign of God. The behaviour of the new state did not always make that easy but it did make it more necessary. How far the Zimbabwean Church fulfilled its task in a spirit of wisdom as the new state sought to establish itself and in a spirit of prophecy if fresh injustices appeared I am not in a position to judge.

The Church's call to preach and promote the Reign of God as preached by Jesus was being developed more radically during this time, first of all by Latin American theologians in what came to be known as liberation theology. Their emphasis on doing theology from the perspective of the poor and oppressed, and their insistence on the primacy of praxis – engagement in the struggle for liberation as the starting point for theology – began to influence theology throughout the Church. In other third world countries in Africa and Asia, as well as among oppressed communities in the first world such as women and African-Americans and Hispanic-Americans, liberation theology in different forms offered the most profound challenge so far to the lingering elements of Constantinian relations between Church and state. In the new world of liberal capitalism and its version of globalisation, liberation theology became the instrument of the poor in prodding the Church into opposing the economic oppressions of the powerful nations and corporations. The Catholic Church always had a global role in service of the universal Reign of God. That would have to assume a particular prophetic form in the vision of liberation theologians and in the light of the dominantly economic shape which globalisation is assuming. My latest round of African experiences over the last decade may shed some further light on that prophetic role.

As a member of the Caritas Internationalis Task Force on HIV-Aids I have been working as theological and ethical adviser with educational programmes for Aids carers and educators, for community leaders including church leaders in third world countries, mainly in Africa, throughout the 1990s. The theological-ethical problems are multiple and complex. The two mentioned here relate to issues discussed earlier and help illustrate once more the role of the Church in an entirely new context, the Aids-ravaged situation of Sub-Saharan Africa.

The concern and commitment of the Church in these African countries in the fight against HIV-Aids can be impressive in its education, prevention and caring programmes, particularly given its puny resources and the other massive health, education and poverty problems these countries face. However one typical ethical difficulty recurs – that is, the use of condoms as a means of prevention, and the co-operation with public health programmes which promote their use. Many bishops and other Catholics oppose their use as violating the teaching of *Humanae Vitae*, as likely to increase promiscuity and so the spread of HIV-Aids, and as unreliable in any event. Faithfulness in marriage and abstinence outside it is the only secure moral way. This last prophetic message needs to be preached and repeated but it will not halt or much diminish the spread of the infection in the cultural and social circumstances of many current African situations. Meantime the prudent promotion and use of condoms in Uganda, for example, has helped at least to stabilise the spread. From a theological point of view the use of condoms in Aids prevention programmes is far removed from the spirit and the letter of *Humanae Vitae*. The latter deals with the prevention of life-giving, the former with the prevention of death-dealing. In the older Wisdom theology of choosing the lesser evil where evil is going to occur in any event, condoms could be advised to reduce the risk of infection. They are not entirely safe but they are safer if of good quality and properly used. This is the Wisdom message which the Church also needs to articulate.

The condoms issue is a significant, but still minor, one in

the overall ethical and theological discussion of HIV-Aids in Africa. On a quite different plane it is becoming gradually clearer that the greatest obstacle to fighting and overcoming the pandemic in these countries is poverty. HIV-Aids is becoming increasingly a disease of the poor – and not only in the third world, as the figures for African-Americans and Hispanic-Americans confirm. The areas and groups listed in recent UN Reports on Human Development as most deprived under a wide range of headings coincide to a great extent with the areas and groups listed by UNAIDS and other reports as most affected by HIV-Aids. Without major and sustainable development the poor countries will fail to serve or even preserve their people in face of this and other disasters, human and natural. In a globalising world the neighbour is all humankind and the reach of charity and justice is world-wide. In Christian and prophetic terms justice is the call of the poor to the wealthy. It is a call become the more urgent in the midst of HIV-Aids, as the Caritas Task Force in its various activities seeks to make clear.

The Priestly, Prophetic and Wisdom Roles of the Church

In theology, as in life, the complex roles of the Church in the world do not yield to any easy or complete categori-sation. The role of the Church as herald, servant, embodiment and promoter of the Reign of God at once liberates and binds it. It liberates it from an enslaving relationship with the earthly powers, political or economic, while binding it to the creating, healing and liberating God of Jesus Christ. This is the God who makes freedom possible in the first place and transforms through history the waywardness of initial human freedom into the love commitment of the one who laid down his life for his friends – and enemies. In charting some recent particular involvements of the Church in society as it seeks to serve the Reign of God, recourse was had to terms and categories drawn from the traditions of Israel, the New Testament and the later Church. The prophetic and wisdom dimensions of Church and its activities are firmly rooted in these traditions but they would be grossly incomplete without that critical third dimension, the priestly.

The priestly is probably the oldest element in the traditions of Israel and in many ways the central one. It is certainly central to the tradition of the New Testament, to the person and activity of Jesus Christ, and to the community of disciples, the priestly people. Without getting drawn into the complexities posed by particular scriptural texts or by the later Christian designation of ordained ministers as priests, we may focus on the role of priest and priestly people as guardians of the Holy of Holies, as protectors of the explicit presence of God amongst us, as immediate servants of the sacred and of the transcendent. These overlapping descriptions fit the continuing role of the Church in the world. To ensure the survival and the authenticity of the Church as priestly it needs, as Israel needed and as Jesus embodied, the challenge of the prophetic and the caring prudence of wisdom.

In history the priestly castes of Israel and of the Church have tended to mistake themselves for the whole community and to assume a worldly style of power on their own. From imperial popes to prince-bishops to power-hungry pastors (to speak only of the Catholic tradition) the priestly role of the Church was often secularised in power to the neglect of its sacred trust, of the sacred entrusted to it. Prophetic voices (male and female) were frequently raised against the exercise of such power and the adoption of its trappings. As the true divinity revealed in Jesus was obscured by this earthly power-seeking, so was the true humanity revealed in Jesus. In the vision of Amos, ritual and sacrifice were vacuous because the poor were oppressed. In Judaism and Christianity reverence for God, for the sacred, and respect for humanity, particularly the poor and the powerless are inextricably bound together. The priestly and the prophetic belong to each other.

The prophet and the prophetic in the Church are no more

immune from temptation and failure than the priest and the priestly. They may well be intimidated by the overt power of the priestly. Prophetic voices may fall silent in face of priestly authority. Historically, prophets have been rejected by those most in need of their message, and some of course have suffered Jesus' own fate by being put to death. Much insight and energy may thus be lost to the revitalisation of the Church, although the witness of the martyred or even silenced prophets has, by the power of the Spirit, had its revitalising effects which a later priestly authority may have the wisdom to recognise and even canonise.

The prophetic temptation may not always be to uncourageous silence but to destructive exaggeration which may be at least subconsciously a self-centred search for attention and power. How to distinguish such false prophetic voices from the true is a continuous challenge to the Church community and can require a lot of time and effort. It certainly requires the prayerful attention to the sacred of the priestly and the wisdom with its tolerance and patience which the Spirit has also bestowed on the Church. Without the openness to such wisdom the prophet, his supporters and opponents may damage rather than assist the Church in its role of preaching and promoting the reign of God in society.

Despite its Judaic and Christian credentials, wisdom in the Church may also decline into a mere worldly wisdom of compromise. Abandoning the Spirit of Jesus with its cruciform wisdom, church leaders or members could surrender to a self-preserving or self-promoting involvement with the powers of this world. Without the challenge and corrective of the priestly and prophetic the gift and guidance of the wisdom of the Spirit may be and has been lost to the Church at various times.

A catholic church in a global society

After such a long excursus in theological autobiography and analysis a summary conclusion may seem unsatisfactory. Yet it could have the merit of locating the present point of arrival even though it be no more than a new point of departure for this as well as other theologians. The conclusion's title is deliberately lower-case and low key, to get away from the inflated pretensions which catholic in combination with church and global in combination with society are prone to. In that deflationary mode a catholic church visualises a worldwide network of local churches whose diversity in unity will seek to preach and promote the reign of God in ecumenical alliances. These alliances within and between different church traditions will draw on the priestly, prophetic and wisdom resources of one another in discerning and entering into the coming of God's reign.

The context of this work will be first of all global. Christians form a global or catholic Church in a new sense and they share a new global responsibility. Particular local experiences such as the Irish or African as recounted here have an increasing global dimension. It is not possible to be an authentic catholic Christian without recognising and accepting this global context and responsibility. At the same time Bangkok is not Belmullet or the Bronx. The priestly, prophetic and wisdom roles of the Church will have to develop their particular local strengths in praxis and theory which will no doubt enrich the wider Church in their turn. But it will be in terms of priestly, prophetic and wisdom service to the inbreaking Reign of God that the emerging catholic Church with its international, intercultural and interchurch dimensions will fulfil its role in the emerging global society and not in any Constantinian set of power relations however developed or diminished. For an Irish theologian, then, the African experience is more illuminating of the Church's new situation than the disintegrating Irish one and more promising of a renewed church in its task of global evangelisation as well as in its internal structures.

CONTINUING THE
CONVERSATION

14
Where Would I Be Without Friends?

Stanley Hauerwas

Does Being Taken Seriously Mean I Should Take Myself Seriously?

'Jesus, I must be dead.' That was my first thought when I first got wind of this book. As Wells notes, I will soon be sixty. Which means I am beginning to realise that death is not just a theoretical possibility – even for me. Yet my friends tell me that today, meaning 'our time', sixty is not all that old. Moreover, I do not feel 'all that old', but then how would I know what it means to 'feel old' one way or the other. I do not trust accounts of 'consciousness', or as some put it, self-awareness, that presume we can know what or how we feel on our own. Thus my oft-made claim that we only know who we are by being told who we are. Does this book mean, whether I know it or not, that I have reached, at least intellectually, the end of the road?

Of course there is no way to know the answer to that question because it is not clear that the work I have been doing constitutes anything so grand as a 'road'. My beginning may have been a dead end. Which means I am particularly grateful to Sam Wells and Mark Nation, not only for claiming me as a friend but for the way they have conceived this book. As Sam puts it, the book is not meant to be a 'funeral address' but rather a 'serious questioning, combative engagement, and robust conversation' not so much about my work but more importantly about what my work has been about. Though I cannot pretend to do justice to the many questions raised by each of the essayists who have contributed to this book, I hope at the very least this response indicates how deeply I appreciate the gift those questions represent.

To suggest that criticism is a gift may sound odd, but I think that is not the case if you consider the alternative. To be criticised at least suggests I am not dead. The gift of criticism, however, is a gift that at once delights and frightens me. I am frightened because it is frightening to be taken seriously. Of course, as I just indicated, it is not so much that I am being taken seriously but rather what I have tried to be about is being taken seriously. Yet to distance myself from what I have done can be self-deceptive just to the extent that what I have been about makes the distinction between what we are and what we do problematic. I have always assumed that my 'position' is really very simple just to the extent I have tried to do no more than display the life Christian convictions entail, given Aristotle's understanding of practical reason and Wittgenstein's arguments against private language. But that means I cannot try – even in the spirit of gesturing appropriate humility about myself and my work – to distance myself from what I have written. I should want to be taken seriously, which means I should want lives like Sam Wells and Mark Nation to exist.

For what Wells' and Nation's essays in this book exemplify is that reading my work, and perhaps as importantly the work that has made my work possible, has changed their lives. And, of course, that is exactly the result I want. I want Wells to see the work he is doing at St Elizabeth's (a work that may seem frustratingly insignificant) to be at once in tension with the humanism of the New Deal initiative and yet also necessary for the best hopes the New Deal represents. I want Mark Nation to be able to see his commitment to nonviolence comes from a formation in a church that was not able to see the nonviolence inherent in the practice of footwashing. Those are exactly the results I at once want and fear.

I fear such results because I realise that I am (as we say in Texas) 'messing with people's lives'. I have never tried to write theology in a manner to be just another academic alternative. I have wanted to be taken seriously and yet I have feared being taken with the kind of seriousness Wells and Nation exemplify. I have feared being taken so seriously because I, perhaps more than anyone, sense the incompleteness as well as fragility of my work. Most of the time I feel like I am flying by the seat of my pants, more clearly knowing what I am sure is mistaken than knowing how to go on. Yet I go on attempting to help myself and others rediscover the power of Christian convictions for helping us live well in a world that no longer believes it is in fact God's world.

That I go on trying to mess with as well as mess up people's lives and that I do so by (I am sure from the perspective of many) going on and on is the result of my conviction that the task of theology is not to develop accounts of the meaning or truth of the gospel allegedly more fundamental than the gospel itself. In other words, if what I have written has messed up Wells' and Nation's lives, I hope it has done so only to the extent they discovered through reading me the implication of the language they in fact use in prayer and worship. In other words, I think of theology as an attempt to assemble the grammatical reminders that point to the significance of what we say for helping us live truthful lives, that is, lives that witness to the fact that all that is is God's good creation. Theology as grammar, of course, does not presume all forms of prayer and worship are created equal or even whether we can distinguish between prayer and worship. Of course we should be able to distinguish between better and less good forms of worship, and surely one of the ministerial tasks of theology is to help us locate those differences. But any theological judgements about such matters gain their intelligibility by recourse to forms of prayer and worship.

I recognise, of course, that one of the reasons some find it difficult to take what I do seriously is because I write so much and in so many different voices and venues. That I write so much is partly the result of the fact that I cannot say no to people that want me to speak at this or that conference or to write for this or that journal issue. I usually assume that I am supposed to do what I am asked to do. However, I do not try to do – as John Howard Yoder always tried to do – exactly what I am asked to do. There is a limit to some servant ministries. I am not the least embarrassed to write or speak in a manner in which I try to show that the question I was supposed to address is wrongly put. Moreover, I often try to use requests to continue to investigate issues that I think, given what I am trying to do, should be investigated. The books I put together are not as haphazard as they may appear or even as I sometimes pretend they are, even though they are collections of essays I have written for various occasions.

The main reason I write so much, however, is because I do not believe that any theory can be, or should be, developed that is more determinative for understanding the truth of what we believe as Christians than the language we actually use as Christians. If you are assembling grammatical reminders, the task is never ending. As soon as you get something right, it can become wrong just to the extent the exaggeration used to help us get what we were trying to say right turns out to have implications we had not anticipated. Which I think creates a problem for those that would try to understand me because if you are to understand me, it means you must read me. This is a daunting challenge haunted by the thought that the result may not be worth the effort.

I, of course, cannot guarantee a good result. Indeed one of the frustrations for anyone willing to undergo the regime of reading me is that when you are finished, you will not be able to neatly summarise what you have learned. If I cannot neatly summarise 'my position', why should anyone else be able to do so? Arne Rasmusson, Sam Wells, and Emmanuel Katongole have ably used what I have done to say better than I have said what needs to be said, but I think none of them (each of whom know my work better than I do) would claim they have provided a summary of what I have been about. I have, like Barth and Wittgenstein, tried to write in a manner that defies summary.

It is, of course, pretentious to suggest even superficially any comparison between my work and that of Barth and Wittgenstein. I have no illusions that what I have tried to do is in that league. However, I also recognise that I have to take responsibility for wanting to mess with lives like Wells' and Nation's. I confess I sometimes try to distance myself from what I have done by playing what we call in the South the 'Southern con'. The 'Southern con' is the pretension that we really are a dumb hick when in reality we have degrees from Harvard. It is a con because we want you to agree with us not because of our intellectual power but because underneath it all we are really just another 'good ol' boy'. That 'role' is always a temptation for me partly because of the history Mark recounts. It is very hard to take oneself seriously as an intellectual when you know what it means for some to work all their lives with their hands.

Which is why, I think, I have always tried to keep my work so to speak 'close to the ground', that is, to write for people who are not 'academics'. I suspect that accounts for some of the misunderstanding my work engenders, because my more serious readers quite understandably think they can skip my more 'popular' writing. Yet my more popular work I regard as the most serious theology I do exactly because I am able to write for and to people who at least claim they want to be Christians. Such folk are or should be, I assume, the primary audience of theologians. Indeed I assume one of our primary tasks today is to help the Christian people be confident speakers of the language of the Church. Of course, one of our difficulties is that too often Christians have lost the skills of Christian speech because theologians have argued they could not actually mean what they had been taught to say.

I am, of course, more a creature of the modern university than I am of the Church. Yet I regard the modern university – which has not only made me what I am but which I also deeply love – as an extremely doubtful institution. I think the university, having lost any sense of whom it serves, has become morally and intellectually unintelligible. Yet I owe the university everything so I continue to try to serve it faithfully by telling the truth about the problems facing us. So I have tried at once to write for others trained as I have been trained, that is, in the discourses of the university, but also for those who have not suffered the disadvantages of having acquired a PhD. This makes it difficult to know how to read my books since they usually are a strange mixture of academic and more 'popular' articles. That, of course, makes it hard to 'pin down' what I am about, because you will not get the 'real me' by reading my 'academic articles'. Indeed the latter are but the means to train myself to be able to write a book like *The Truth About God: The Ten Commandments in Christian Life.*

That I write so much as well as writing popularly are among the reasons I am not taken seriously as a theologian. But I am also aware it is hard to take me seriously because of who I am. I have not only written about the importance of 'having character', I also am 'a character'. The Texas accent is not 'a put on', but rather an indication of who I am. But it is hard to take someone seriously who talks the way I talk. And it is not just the accent. There is also my inability to resist wanting to be entertaining. Indeed one of my faults is I have no tolerance for the boring. The result is often my willingness to say bluntly what might have more persuasive power if I were willing to say what I had to say in a more qualified fashion befitting the mores of academia.

Epigrams like 'the Church's first task is not to make the world more just, but to make the world the world' are meant to invite thought. I realise they can equally lead to misunderstanding, but I think that a risk worth taking. At the very least such an epigram should make the reader ask twice, 'I wonder what he means by justice?', as well as recognise why Christian social theory cannot help but be a correlative of our eschatological views. At least involved in such a claim is the presumption that 'Church/world' maps how Christians should understand our ongoing witness to and in a world that does not recognise, except in fits and starts, that all that is is God's good creation.

The temptation for many is to try to understand me by focusing on this or that epigram. The oft-made claim that I am a sectarian, or that I am careless, or overstate my positions, is I think often the result of those that are content to make up their minds about what I am about by thinking or reading no further than such epigrams. Indeed I suspect that many who share such judgements about my work are people who have formed an impression about what I must think, given what they think I must think is the basis of what they think. It does not occur to them that I am trying to change the way they think – i.e., why it is a mistake to ask 'What is the relation between Christ and culture?'. As I noted above, if you want to understand me you have to read what I have written. What I write and how I write is, at least to the best of my abilities, of a piece with my theological convictions. I refuse to be a systematic theologian, but that does not mean what I write is not interconnected. The interconnections, moreover, are my attempt to change the questions rather than provide answers to previously-agreed questions.

To change the questions requires more than simply changing how we think. You have to change the habits of how we have learned to speak, read, and write. That is at least one of the reasons I write so much as well as the character the writing assumes. I am not only trying to force others into different verbal habits, I am trying to force myself to think more accurately. Writing (and reading) is one of the most basic forms of moral training we have. It therefore becomes crucial to force ourselves into new habits of theological expression if we are to recover the power of our language of and about God for the formation of our lives and, thus, recover how the world is unintelligible if the God of Jesus Christ does not exist.

That is one of the reasons I so admire Barth's work. He knew he had to forge a different theological imaginary. He rightly refused to accept his critics' questions on their own terms. Rather he repetitively displayed the implications that Jesus Christ is Lord until at least some of his critics rightly forgot their questions. Lacking Barth's extraordinary theological imagination, I have perhaps been far too ready to accept the presuppositions of the criticism directed at me. But Biggar is right to identify me as a follower of Barth. My understanding of the Church is no doubt more Catholic than Barth's more Reformed ecclesiology. But I think how I do theology avoids the self-enclosed appearance – and I genuinely believe it is more an appearance than a reality – of Barth's theology.

For example, the oft-made claim that I am sectarian, a claim that Nigel Biggar wonderfully counters in his essay, presupposes foundationalist epistemological presuppositions I have time and again questioned. You may well think that I am wrong about the neo-Kantian framework that shaped Troeltsch's account of sectarianism; but I am not particularly impressed by those who continue to call me sectarian without attending to the way I have tried to direct attention away from the epistemological assumptions necessary to make the charge of sectarianism intelligible. That is what I must do, namely, redirect attention. If you try to counter the epistemological starting point on its own terms then you will only reproduce the mistake you are trying to avoid: thus the necessity of changing the question.

The way I have tried to avoid being an epistemologist is by doing 'ethics'. This has led some to assume I do not need to be taken seriously as a theologian because I am really an 'ethicist'. Of course I no more believe in ethics than I believe in epistemology. My focus on ethics is not to promulgate some new theory of ethics, i.e., virtue ethics, but rather to focus on the way people actually conduct their lives and the way Christianity corrects errors or offers guidance of that conduct. Accordingly my work can be viewed as a series of case studies of what is actually going on in societies like America or Britain, rather than overly general debates about whether such societies are or have become secular. That is why I also resist requests that I systematise my work – 'When is Hauerwas finally going to write the "big book?"' The very notion of system associated with the 'big book' betrays the very orientation I am trying to correct. Rather than offering a system, I try to offer instead thick descriptions of strategies of argument and criticism that witness to the work theological discourse can and must do. (I am indebted to Peter Ochs for this way of putting what I have been trying to do.)

I suppose if I were forced to name any one motif to characterise my work, I would say I have been trying to show the connections, to take just one example, between our worship of Jesus Christ and why Christians have and should make space in our lives for welcoming the mentally handicapped. In other words, I think it has been impossible for us as Christians to understand why what we believe is true when our 'beliefs' about God have been abstracted from fundamental practices such as caring for the mentally handicapped or such practices as fidelity in marriage or nonviolence. For example, I think any consideration of why it is that what we believe is true best starts with why it is as Christians we do not think we can lie. All I have tried to do over the years I have been working is to make those kinds of connections.

As I noted above, this strategy has meant that many think of me primarily as an 'ethicist' rather than as a theologian. I have often complained about such an identi-fication, not only because I am not particularly attracted by what is usually identified as 'ethics' in distinction from theology, but primarily because the very distinction between theology and ethics distorts the argument I have tried to make about the character of theological language. For example, why is it assumed that 'justice' is about ethics and 'creation' is theology if, as I would maintain, any Christian understanding of justice requires display in terms of the eschatological virtue of charity? I am, therefore, particularly grateful to Colin Gunton for no other reason than his willingness to take me seriously as a theologian.

Yet as appreciative as I am of Gunton's essay, I do not think he is right to suggest that my understanding of the cross is in danger of an exemplarism, and that correlatively I may well be Pelagian. When I am accused of Pelagianism by American Protestants committed to accepting the 'other' irrespective of our characters, I often respond you cannot be Pelagian enough today. Of course Gunton is anything but that kind of Protestant, and I am certainly closer to him on most matters than to Protestant liberals. But I do wonder if Gunton and I do not have a funda-mental disagreement which, as he quite rightly suggests, is christological. I think that disagreement may simply mirror the classical differences between the Reformed and those whom we now call the Anabaptist. That difference being, as I learned from John Howard Yoder and tried to exhibit in *The Peaceable Kingdom*, that discipleship is not a subject to be treated after christological reflection but rather how we are called to follow Christ is inseparable from our knowing who Christ is. I mention this not to distinguish myself from Gunton, but rather to provide an example of how my understanding of the task of theology often requires me to reframe standard theological positions.

Which is but a way to indicate, as Nation rightly suggests, the profound influence of John Howard Yoder. In many ways I have been doing no more than trying to think through the implications of what I learned from Yoder. Yoder at once changes everything without changing any of the most basic convictions that have made Christians Christian across time and space. If I have any wish it is that if I am to be taken seriously (if I must take myself seriously), the result will be that others will learn that Yoder must be taken seriously. To take Yoder seriously may even be a more daunting task than taking me seriously. His work may seem even more scattered than mine, but I am convinced that no one has charted our way forward more helpfully than has John Howard Yoder. If my work has served to witness to Yoder's witness, I will think I have had a good run indeed.

Enough About Me

I hope the reader will forgive the self-indulgent venting represented by the readers' guide I have just tried to provide. But dammit, I suppose being sixty may give one certain privileges. Yet I fear nothing is quite as boring as the reflections of an academic reviewing their 'career' in the interest of 'setting the record straight'. Moreover, I have never wanted to foment or represent a 'movement'. The movement I want to represent I assume already exists. It is called Church and I seek to do no more than call it to be what it is. If that is being prophetic so be it. Of course it is a burden as well as a theological mistake to be identified as prophetic. How could anyone presume to play that role?

Moreover, Jesus is the end of prophecy which means only the Church can properly be prophetic.

I am, therefore, extremely grateful to the contributors to this volume that they have not so much focused on 'me', but rather on questions my work has raised for them. I cannot pretend to respond to the many interesting issues raised in the various essays. What follows is but some random responses that I hope will be of interest. For example, the kind of reflection on Christian spirituality and mental sickness offered by Stephen Sykes is the kind of work I think we so desperately need. There can be no question that the development of medical models for understanding mental sickness has been a great benefit for the care of those who so suffer. But for Christians to underwrite the mechanistic metaphysics that often shape the presuppositions of 'medicine' has surely been a mistake. I suspect Sykes is right that we may well have much to learn from our Muslim brothers and sisters on such matters.

The challenge Sykes puts before us concerning mental sickness means we cannot avoid the questions John Milbank raises concerning the relation of Christians to the modern university. The knowledges that have constructed our understanding of mental illness, knowledges that have reduced theology to 'spirituality', have been produced and reproduced by university curricula. The one factor that seems to best predict whether or not a person will no longer attend church in America is whether they have received a university education. In spite of my suspicion about such 'studies', I nonetheless think they at least suggest that whatever we do in the university, we make it hard for people to continue to think that Christian convictions have any claim to be considered true. The practical atheism that grips believer and non-believer alike in modernity no doubt has its source in economic relations more determinative than university curricula. Yet the significance of university curricula are not to be underestimated just to the extent the knowledge those curricula reflect and create are meant to underwrite the economic presumptions that make it reasonable to assume God does not matter.

So I cannot help but join Milbank in his call for theology to refuse to surrender its hegemony to secular inquiries into religion. I think, moreover, he is right to question the development of theology into sub-disciplines, which was a wonderful strategy if you want theology at best to support or at least not to inhibit the growth of the secular state. Milbank, I think rightly, is not suggesting that all that we know is dependent on our knowledge of God. Rather, like Aquinas, he is suggesting that theology must be ready to judge whether what we know is true, good, or beautiful. Such judgements require not only the account of truth as an adequation of knowledge with the real, but also some account of the ordering of what we know in terms of what we need to learn first in order to know better what we hope to know. That such questions cannot even be raised in most American universities is but a confirmation of Milbank's analysis.

I am aware many may well wonder, however, how I can at once seem to agree with Milbank on such matters while at least claiming to be primarily influenced by Barth and Yoder. 'Hegemony' is a Constantinian word. This is not the context for me to try to discover or explore the deep agreements or disagreements between what I have been trying to do and those identified with Milbank's extraordinary project. Suffice it to say I think what Milbank has been trying to do at the highest theoretical level I think must be done, so to speak, closer to the ground. How that difference may have to do with Milbank's Platonism in contrast with my Aristotelianism – or the difference between our Christologies, or my commitment to nonviolence which Milbank, I think, must think is immoral – would be fascinating to explore. What is clear, however, is I have learned much from Milbank and we have common enemies. Having the same enemies does not entail that theologically we be friends; but I suspect given the character of the challenges before us we will be, whether we like it or not, joined at the hip.

Yet I hope these comments at least indicate that Nigel Biggar is not mistaken when he suggests at the end of his essay that he senses a 'softening' in my position toward

'Christendom'. The word 'softening', however, suggests this is a new development. I have always thought it necessary for Christians to develop ways of life, cultural habits, to sustain our calling. I have also assumed that we would find such habits present in various ways among those who do not understand themselves to be Christian. What I have rejected is the presumption that Christians in the name of being players in so-called liberal or pluralist societies should downplay the way of life that makes us Christians.

Though I am not opposed to attempts to make common cause with some aspects of liberal practice, which is often richer than its theory can account for, I do think that Christians have no stake in Western civilisation nor should we try to rescue the epistemological or political forms of liberalism. The reasons are very simple – whatever we have been or are, Western civilisation is an insufficient description of the history we inherit or the world in which we now find ourselves. In other words, the very description, 'Western civilisation', makes Christianity part of a project that alienates us from the unity of the Church. The reason Christians should not underwrite the epistemology and politics of liberalism is very simple: they are not true. I do not think you need to be a Christian to share the latter judgement; but given the Christian commitment to truthfulness we ought not to perpetrate descriptions that distort our self-understanding as well as mislead those who do not share our convictions.

Let me put my views as succinctly as I can: I believe that Christians in America and Britain should be appropriately grateful to those who have sacrificed to make it possible for us to live in a relative peace that is at least partly the result of a legal system that aspires to be just. As Christians I think we should try to support as well as enhance societies so established. I do not think such support, however, requires grand justifications that suggest that 'democracy' or liberalism names social systems that are normative for Christians in a way that other forms of rule are not. The first political responsibility of Christians is to be people who can tell one another the truth, which at the very least means the ability to see through descriptions that fail to acknowledge the coercion we inflict on one another in the name of the good.

Duncan Forrester is, therefore, right to remind me that the epigram that the Church does not have a social ethic but is a social ethic does not name a status, but rather a task. I have from the very beginning of my work thought that the major challenge anyone that would pretend to do theology must face is this: how Christians at best failed to challenge and at worst co-operated in the destruction of European Jewry. But surely that co-operation was the result of the Christian identification with German state and society that Yoder has helped us name and criticise. No doubt many good Germans, who otherwise found Hitler abhorrent, fought in his armies and served in his bureaucracies because they were grateful and, thus, loyal to those whom they thought had made their way of life possible. How different is that from the many justifications given for why Christians should support liberal democratic societies? The assumption seems to be that liberal democratic societies would not be capable of such horrors. But I see no good reason why we should believe that to be the case. If a church does not exist capable of saying 'No' to the powers when they ask us to kill in the name of what we owe one another, then I think we are indeed in a night when all cats are grey.

To be able to say 'No' requires that we be able to see what is around us. To be able to see what is around us requires the kind of training Gerard Loughlin so wonderfully displays in his extraordinarily imaginative essay. The way Loughlin helps us see the films we have seen but not known how to narrate is the kind of ongoing work the Church must make possible. If a church does not exist that is, as he imaginatively puts it, Plato's cave turned inside-out, then we will not have the ability to distinguish the shadows from reality. Of course that process, at least in Loughlin's skilful hands, is a bit frightening. The only thing I can think of that would be more frightening is not to know as Christians that we live in a dangerous world.

About Women

I am never sure how to deal with the current politics of gender. For example, if I say that I am appreciative of Linda Woodhead's criticism of my failure to address gender issues, I cannot help but appear patronising. Yet I appreciate not only that she has called me to account, but how she has done so. For she has shown how my way of working should have led me to deal more directly with gender than I have done. I think she is right, but in my defence I can only say that time makes a difference. When the first feminist challenges began, it was not clear how any male could respond without appearing reactionary or patronising. I more or less assumed that would not be my battle.

I took that stance for several reasons. First, I thought the feminists often failed to appreciate the challenge before Christians in the world in which we found ourselves. The views of language often assumed by feminist theologians I found deeply problematic. In short I thought most of the theological proposals put forth on behalf of feminism were in one form or another what Lindbeck identified as experiential/expressivism. In other words, what bothered me was not the feminism, but the theory being used on behalf of feminist causes. I am, after all, a Methodist – which means I have little use for appeals to experience. Having been raised Methodist, by the time I was twelve I had had enough experience to last me a lifetime.

I also thought feminist identification of patriarchy as *the* enemy was a mistake. Such an identification not only seemed to 'essentialise' gender, but also failed to provide the kind of textured reading necessary to understand the complexity of male and female relations across time. Getting to know members of Catholic religious orders made me aware that women were anything but victims. Of course comments about Catholic religious orders will invite some to suggest I still do not 'get it'. Some read the very existence of such orders as but continued repression of women. I confess I have nothing to say to those who hold such views other than to say we have nothing to say to one another.

For me of course, the Pentagon, not patriarchy, was the enemy. At least some versions of feminism were just too bourgeois (which is another way to say politically liberal) for me. The egalitarian assumptions that often seemed to fuel feminist demands I simply did not share. Good communities have goods in common which produce hierarchies of service to one another for the achievement of those goods. Equality is not an end in itself, but a means to ensure that those with talent and aspiration toward particular goods are not excluded on arbitrary grounds from achieving those goods for the common good. The evil of capitalism is, at least, partly revealed by how capitalist modes of production institutionalise the egalitarian presumption that each person's worth is determined by their ability to make money. That women in capitalist societies demand to be treated 'equally' is surely right, but it is not clear to me that to be so treated is good for any of us.

That women have been excluded from modes of service in the Church because they are women is surely being rightly challenged. The discovery that women are priests, a discovery that is at least the result of liberal political developments for which we ought to be grateful, I regard as a great good. I think that discovery, however, still awaits fuller Christian narration in terms of how a community of the sanctified locate in the community those that are appropriately set aside for the task of presiding at the Eucharist. In other words, I think the discovery that women are called to the priesthood should force us to think harder about the priesthood as a servant role. Of course that task is a task for the whole Church, not for particular gendered roles.

I hope these remarks, insufficient though they may be, at least suggest why I find Woodhead's critique so appropriate. For she rightly challenges me to attend to the material practices of actual churches to discern how presumptions about gender, acquired from God knows where, prevent the full recognition of the gifts of the Spirit for the upbuilding of the community. However, before I appear too agreeable, I need to make clear a view that feminists may find abhorrent. At least one of the most determinative practices that I believe should characterise the Christian community is to welcome children into our lives. Only women are capable of having children. That does not mean that every woman will be called to having children, but no account of our life together as Christians can avoid the acknowledgement that women have a gift, which is also a power, that men do not. This means, I believe, that whatever Christian feminism entails, it surely involves an account of marriage in which a man and a woman can happily entertain the calling of being parents. The question, of course, is how that calling can at once be seen as a great good without becoming an excuse for 'keeping women in their place'.

This, of course, brings me to the question Ann Loades so forcefully raises, that is, the question of abortion. The reason Ann's paper is so challenging for me is because, as she knows, I am in complete agreement with most of what she has to say about abortion. We both think that abortion should not be an issue for Christians because we should be a community in which abortion just does not come up. Our lives should be appropriately ordered so that if a child is conceived, that child represents a gift to the community. That we have not thought through what this means is indicated, as Loades observes, by the lack of any account of the theological significance of mothering – a calling, perhaps, that in some aspects can be shared by men. I have tried to say something about such matters by arguing that every Christian is called to be a parent whether they have biological children or not. Indeed I have gone so far, and I believe this, as to say that adoption is the first mode of parenting among Christians.

The issue for Loades (and for me) is the so called 'hard cases'. The problem, at least in America, is that given the way abortion is discussed, the 'hard cases' are no longer even part of the agenda for most people. I argued many years ago (and I confess I remain unclear how the argument is best made) that women in life against life cases, cases of rape and incest, or abandonment, should not be compelled to carry through their pregnancies. That does not mean they should resort to abortion, but they may do so. A woman, however, who would risk her life to have her child is not doing wrong to make such a choice, tragic though it may be. Moreover, each of the cases I enumerated involve different sets of discriminations that are important for helping us discern how best to understand what is happening, without the account we give becoming a general justification for abortion.

I have nothing else to say than what I have said about these matters except I think they raise an issue that is as important as it is ignored. The issue is quite simply how to understand the kind of community the Church must be to envision actions in which some have to pay an undue cost for living faithfully. The willingness and obligation to tell the truth in a world of liars means some will lose their jobs. What kind of community should Church be to provide the support for truth-telling in a world of mendacity? What kind of community does the Church need to be that women can have children under less than ideal conditions? Avoiding such questions makes lesser of two evil arguments far too tempting. The way I think about these matters is, of course, shaped by my presumption that in a world of violence Christians are called to live nonviolently. For Christians to live nonviolently means that the innocent may have to pay for our convictions. Of course it is not clear that those that would use violence, even as disciplined by just-war practice, can avoid a similar challenge. What I refuse to do, however, is to privilege the presumption that such a result requires me to qualify my commitment to nonviolence, particularly if you remember nonviolence is but one name for discipleship.

Rather, what we must remember is that nonviolence is not a heroic ethic for individuals. Nonviolence only makes sense not as a exceptional mode of behaviour but as a characteristic of our everyday interactions. Nonviolence is as common as our desire to speak truthfully to one another or to be a community capable of having children joyfully. If such a community does not in fact exist, then the God we Christians worship does not exist. I know, however, such a community exists because how else can I explain that sisters and brothers exist that have made me more than I could imagine? Attempts to think about exceptions to nonviolence or abortion cannot help but go wrong if they are abstracted from these kinds of considerations.

Ending with Enda

I have, perhaps, not yet appropriately acknowledged that the contributors to this book are from the British Isles. In spite of my attempts to sustain my Texas and Southern upbringing, I am painfully aware that my work is parochially American. Unfortunately, in this time when 'American' names an ontological condition, this means I represent an imperialism that pretentiously claims to be 'global'. That at least some of what I have been about seems to raise questions worth pursuing for theologians in the British Isles, I hope suggests that the struggle to acquire a Christian voice even in America is of some help for their own work.

While I am grateful to all the contributors who took the time to write essays for this book, I am particularly grateful to Enda McDonagh, not just for his essay, but for being Enda McDonagh. As he indicates, we have been friends for many years. Our friendship began at Notre Dame and has continued through letters and occasional visits to Ireland. Our friendship is all the more important to me because we obviously do not think the same way. That does not mean we disagree, though we no doubt do about some matters, but that we just are different. Part of the difference that I so value is manifest in Enda's essay; for Enda is a 'global' presence that Catholicism, not capitalism, made possible.

I shall never forget a night in New York City in which Enda told a group of neo-conservatives he would rather live in Zimbabwe than America. He wonderfully defended his 'preference' in the face of their utter disbelief that any 'rational' person would actually make such a choice. How could you not want to live 'in the lead society' of the world? Enda pointed out he already lived in the 'lead society' of the world. It was called the Catholic Church. I think that's exactly right for no other reason than that a person like Enda McDonagh exists and that he exists must have something to do with his being Catholic. He is a person, that is, at once so particularly Irish, which admittedly is a tautology, yet also able to identify with the struggle of the poor in Latin America, with the challenge of establishing social and political institutions in Zimbabwe, and dealing with the challenge of HIV-Aids in Sub-Saharan Africa.

Toward the end of his theological autobiography, Enda observes that he is trying to visualise a catholic Church that names a worldwide network of local churches whose diversity will seek to promote the reign of God in ecumenical alliances. That is the vision of peace. For surely it would be unthinkable for people in such a network to kill one another for any loyalties that are not determined by the network itself. If what I have done in some way contributes to the growth of such a network, I will be extremely grateful. But I am aware that more important than my 'work' is that people like Enda McDonagh exist. As grateful as I am to those who have contributed to this book, it makes me even happier to express my indebtedness to Enda who is the imagination my work, however inadequately, has tried to describe.

Index